MENTAL WEALTH ECONOMIC

Prospering through Psychological Capital Investment

SAURABH BISHT

Mental Wealth Economics

Imagine a hidden treasure trove within every organization, a resource more valuable than gold and more powerful than the latest technology. This untapped wellspring of potential isn't found in balance sheets or cutting-edge equipment, but in the minds and hearts of employees. Welcome to the world of mental wealth – the new frontier of organizational success.

Just as financial capital and physical resources are important for businesses to thrive, the collective psychological well-being of a company's workforce represents an invaluable form of capital that drives innovation, productivity, and long-term prosperity. **"Mental Wealth Economics: Prospering through Psychological Capital Investment"** explores this critical concept, making a compelling case for why prioritizing employee mental health is not just a moral imperative, but an economic one.

Learning from the latest research, real-world case studies, and evidence-based best practices, it offers actionable insights into the tangible benefits of nurturing mental wealth - from boosting workforce engagement and retention, to enhancing creativity and decision-making, to mitigating costly losses from absenteeism and turnover.

Ultimately, " **Mental Wealth Economics: Prospering through Psychological Capital Investments** " makes a powerful argument that an organization's greatest competitive advantage lies in the psychological capital of its people.

Why I'm Writing This Book

I penned **"Mental Wealth Economics: Prospering through Psychological Capital Investments"** with a vision to bridge the gap between corporate management and employee mental health. The evolving landscape of workplaces demanded a comprehensive guide that not only dissects the intricacies of organizational psychology but also serves as a practical handbook for new managers navigating the complexities of team dynamics. The book unfolds in a structured journey, exploring the historical evolution of work environments, the science of happiness hormones, and the foundations of organizational psychology.

As the chapters progress, the narrative transitions seamlessly from understanding mental health challenges to implementing strategies for a mentally healthy workplace. Real-life case studies, practical applications, and a roadmap for cultivating a supportive corporate culture provide actionable insights. It aims not only to empower new managers with leadership practices that nurture a mentally healthy workforce but also serves as a valuable resource for anyone seeking to unravel the psychological nuances of the corporate world. This book, derived from the extensive table of contents, endeavours to transform workplaces into sanctuaries where mental health is not merely an afterthought but a guiding principle, shaping harmonious and thriving work cultures.

"Mental Wealth Economics: Prospering through Psychological Capital Investments" stems from a profound recognition of the critical intersection between management practices, organizational dynamics, and the mental well-being of employees. The genesis of this book lies in a commitment to provide a comprehensive resource for new managers, shedding light on the often-overlooked psychological aspects of corporate environments.

In Part 1, **"Setting the Stage,"** I'll take you through the historical evolution of work environments. Recognizing that the foundation of a mentally healthy workplace rests on understanding its evolution, this section sets the stage for an insightful exploration. The workplace has undergone significant transformations over the years, and comprehending this journey is fundamental for new managers seeking to navigate the contemporary corporate landscape.

The subsequent sections, especially Part 2 on **"Understanding Mental Health and Workplace Dynamics,"** break down the science behind happiness hormones and gets into the organizational psychology. These chapters offer new managers a solid grounding in the fundamental psychological elements that shape employee behavior and workplace culture. The exploration of leadership dynamics, communication strategies, and the cultivation of a psychologically flourishing environment equips managers with tools to foster positive workplace dynamics.

As the narrative unfolds in Part 3, **"Identifying and Addressing Mental Health Challenges,"** the book shifts focus to the silent struggles faced by employees. Realizing that mental health challenges are often hidden, this section aims to equip new managers with the knowledge to identify and address these issues effectively. By offering guidance and presenting real-life case studies, the book becomes a practical guide for new managers navigating the complexities of mental health in the workplace.

In Part 4, **"Implementing Strategies for a Mentally Healthy Workplace,"** the emphasis is on proactive measures. Strategies such as integrating happiness into corporate strategies, understanding the role of leadership in mental health, and empowering employees with self-care strategies provide actionable steps for new managers. These insights not only contribute to the immediate well-being of the team but also set the stage for long-term organizational success.

The subsequent sections, particularly Part 5 on **"Cultivating a Mentally Healthy Corporate Culture,"** underscore the importance of organizational culture in promoting mental health. Leadership practices, strategies for creating a supportive environment, and the role of culture in psychological well-being become critical pillars for new managers seeking to create a positive workplace culture.

This book doesn't just stop at providing insights; it takes a deep dive into **"Initiatives and Strategies for Mental Health"** in Part 6 of the book. Exploring different mental health programs, effective communication, stress management, and specialized areas like remote work are all explored. By presenting practical strategies and real-world case studies, the book becomes an essential toolkit for new managers navigating the nuances of mental health in various workplace scenarios.

In Part 7 named **"Specialized Areas and Challenges",** the focus extends to overcoming challenges, rethinking strategies, and embracing innovative approaches. Sections on remote work, overcoming stigma, and rethinking mental health strategies challenge new managers to adapt and evolve in response to the ever-changing landscape of the corporate world.

Finally, in Part 8, **"Conclusion and Final Thoughts,"** the book draws to a close by summarizing key takeaways and providing a roadmap for initiating change. It encourages readers, especially new managers, to become ambassadors for mental health in their workplaces and beyond.

"Mental Wealth Economics" isn't merely a book; it's a guide crafted with a vision to empower new managers and individuals interested in understanding the psychology of the corporate workforce wellbeing. It aims to transform workplaces into sanctuaries where mental health is not an afterthought but the guiding principle in shaping harmonious and thriving work cultures. Through this extensive exploration, the book becomes a companion for those committed to fostering well-being within the corporate sphere.

Feel free to join us in understanding the tricky world of corporate psychology, because when we understand it, we can change how companies work. "Mental Wealth Economics" invites you to be part of this change, going beyond just reading words on pages. Let's uncover what's really going on with mental health at work and together, make our workplaces a better and healthier space.

Contents

PART 3: IDENTIFYING AND ADDRESSING MENTAL HEALTH CHALLENGES

PART 4: IMPLEMENTING STRATEGIES FOR A MENTALLY HEALTHY WORKPLACE

PART 5: CULTIVATING A MENTALLY HEALTHY CORPORATE CULTURE

PART 7: SPECIALIZED AREAS AND CHALLENGES

PART 8: FINAL THOUGHTS

Part 1

Setting the Stage for Mental Health in this Corporate World

Introduction: The Crucial Intersection of Mental Health and the Corporate Landscape

Once upon a time, in the busy world of job interviews and work, people were often judged solely on their skills. However, something important was missing: an understanding of how they felt inside and their mental health. It was as if individuals were treated like machines, expected to start working immediately without any regard for their well-being.

Job changes occurred rapidly, often with no breaks in between. This created a never-ending cycle that reduced people to mere money-makers, causing them to forget that they had lives outside of their jobs. Family, hobbies, and contributions to society were pushed aside, leading to a situation where their entire identity was based solely on what they brought to the workplace.

In this rush to get things done, essential aspects of life—such as being a parent, a friend, or someone with hobbies—were overlooked. The result was a society where national progress was evident, yet individuals grew old alone, with little to leave behind after retirement.

Now, in the world of businesses and offices where everyone is busy with plans and money, there's something we often forget – the mental health of the people working there. It's like a building a strong base to stand tall and showing why it's so important and how it can make a big difference.

Corporate mental health is about how people in a company feel inside. It includes things companies do to support and improve their employees' mental health.

This has become more and more important in managing workplaces because we now know that mental health affects how much work gets done, how happy people are with their jobs, and how successful the whole company is.

You know, mental health is a crucial aspect of our overall well-being. It involves our emotional, psychological, and social health, influencing how we think, feel, and act. It also plays a significant role in how we handle stress, relate to others, and make choices in our daily lives. The World Health Organization defines mental health as not just the absence of mental illness but as a state of well-being where individuals can realize their potential, cope with the normal stresses of life, work productively, and contribute to their communities. Now, when we talk about corporate mental health, we're looking at how these principles apply specifically within the workplace. Corporate mental health focuses on the mental well-being of employees and how organizational structures and cultures impact that well-being. It's about understanding that the workplace environment can either support or hinder mental health. For example, high levels of stress, lack of support, or poor communication can lead to mental health challenges among employees. On the other hand, a supportive culture that promotes open communication and provides resources for mental well-being can enhance employee satisfaction and productivity. So how can you gauge the status of mental health in your organization? There are several effective methods to assess this:

1. **Surveys**: Conducting anonymous surveys can provide valuable insights into employees' perceptions of their mental health and the support available to them. You can ask questions about stress levels, job satisfaction, and overall well-being.

2. **Focus Groups**: Organizing focus groups allows for deeper discussions about mental health challenges employees face. This qualitative approach can uncover issues that surveys might miss.

3. **Performance Metrics**: Analyzing performance data such as absenteeism rates and turnover rates can help identify trends related to employee mental health.

4. **Feedback Mechanisms**: Establishing regular feedback channels encourages employees to share their thoughts on workplace mental health initiatives.

5. **Employee Assistance Program (EAP) Data**: If your organization has an EAP, reviewing data on employee usage patterns can highlight common mental health concerns.

Remember, fostering a culture that values mental health not only benefits individual employees but also enhances overall organizational performance.

Such corporate mental health initiatives as a superhero for your mind at work. It's like a guardian making sure your workplace is not just about getting things done but also about keeping everyone mentally well.

Tip: If anyone mentions that implementing mental health initiatives is too time-consuming and they can't maintain it regularly, at the very least, consider setting up a dedicated shelf stocked with self-help books. This would allow employees to read and reflect while enjoying their coffee. It's a simple yet effective way to promote mental wellness in the workplace without requiring extensive resources or time commitments.

Think of it as a mix of helpful strategies, strong support, and a culture that cares about how everyone is feeling. It's like having a friend watching out for your mental health in the workplace.

Individual mental health is like everyone having their unique way of feeling. Corporate mental health is like a special power that can spot if the workplace is making these feelings better or worse. It's like a guide steering everyone through the ups and downs of work stress.

Now, in the big picture of life, we're realizing that having a healthy mind isn't just important personally, but it can also make a big difference in your job. Mixing personal and work life is like a dance, and corporate mental health is the one making sure it's a good performance.

But here's a twist in our story — the manager. Instead of seeing them as a bad guy, think of them as a character trying to lead a team. Surprisingly, it's not their personality that bothers people. It's like they're playing a role but struggling to understand the human side of work. The tension comes when they miss seeing the people behind the work deadlines.

So, here's the key: managers aren't the villains. Sometimes, they're just playing a role that doesn't quite match up with the human side of work. In our ongoing story, the hero's mission is to recognize and fix these things for a team that's not just working but also happy and thriving.

When an employee is frustrated, it's not that they hate their manager. It's more like they're bothered by a version of the manager that tries to control everything to meet tight deadlines, causing stress for everyone involved. It's a bit like trying to juggle too many things at once.

Now, remember, mental well-being isn't just a small part of the story; it's the heart of a happy workplace. It's what keeps everyone feeling good and working well together. So, get ready for a journey – we're setting out to understand, appreciate, and support corporate mental health. It's about making the workplace a better, happier space for everyone. Let's dive into this adventure together!

1.1   The Cost of Neglecting Mental Health in the Workplace

Have you ever considered how mental health impacts not just individuals, but entire organizations? It's a crucial topic that often gets overlooked, yet it has significant implications for businesses. Mental health issues can lead to substantial financial losses, affecting productivity, employee engagement, and turnover rates. Let's explore some eye-opening statistics that highlight just how costly it can be when companies neglect mental health.

The Staggering Costs of Productivity Loss

First, let's talk about productivity. Mental health-related productivity losses are staggering—businesses can lose billions each year. According to the World Health Organization (WHO), depression and anxiety alone result in an estimated global loss of around $1 trillion in productivity annually. In the United States, unresolved depression leads to a 35% reduction in productivity, translating to about $210.5 billion lost each year due to absenteeism and decreased work performance. That's a massive hit!

Absenteeism and Presenteeism: A Double Whammy

Next, consider absenteeism and presenteeism. Employees struggling with mental health challenges often take more sick leave or come to work feeling unwell—a situation we refer to as presenteeism. In fact, in the U.S., the costs associated with mental health-related absenteeism and presenteeism are estimated at around **$225.8 billion** each year, according to the National Alliance on Mental Illness (NAMI). Those dealing with mental health issues can miss an average of 31.4 days per year, which only adds to productivity losses. Additionally, presenteeism can account for another 27.9 days lost annually because employees aren't functioning at their best. A recent report indicates that individuals diagnosed with depression lose about 58 working days a year, which is roughly a quarter of the typical work year defined as 240 days.

High Turnover Rates: A Costly Cycle

Then there's the issue of high turnover rates. A toxic work environment that fails to prioritize mental health can lead to employees leaving at alarming rates. The Center for Prevention and Health Services estimates that replacing an employee can cost anywhere from 50% to 200% of their annual salary when you factor in recruitment, training, and the inevitable dip in productivity during transitions. This high turnover doesn't just impact the budget; it disrupts team dynamics and overall morale.

Engagement Matters: The Link to Performance

Let's not forget about employee engagement. Poor mental health can significantly reduce engagement levels. According to Gallup's State of the Global Workplace report, only 15% of employees worldwide feel engaged in their jobs! This lack of engagement stifles innovation and creativity within organizations, leading to missed opportunities and lower performance overall. When mental health issues arise, they can hinder employees' ability to concentrate and perform effectively, further exacerbating the situation.

The Path Forward: Investing in Mental Health

When we look at all this data, it becomes clear that the financial implications of poor mental health in the workplace are extensive and far-reaching. Companies that ignore these critical issues risk facing significant economic losses while compromising their workforce's well-being and engagement. Investing in mental health support isn't merely a nice-to-have; it's essential for creating a productive and resilient workforce that thrives in today's competitive environment.Moreover, fostering a culture that prioritizes mental well-being benefits employees and enhances overall organizational performance. Companies that actively support mental health initiatives—such as providing access to counseling services or promoting work-life balance—create environments where employees feel valued and empowered. This supportive culture leads to increased loyalty, higher job satisfaction, and ultimately better business outcomes.

Calculating the Cost of Neglecting Mental Health

To quantify the cost of neglecting mental health within an organization, we can use a simple formula:

Total Cost = (Number of Employees × Average Salary × Turnover Rate) + (Number of Employees × Average Days Lost × Daily Wage) + (Number of Employees × Average Productivity Loss × Average Salary)

Where:

- Number of Employees is the total workforce.

- Average Salary is the mean annual salary per employee.

- Turnover Rate is expressed as a decimal (e.g., 0.50 for 50%).

- Average Days Lost is based on absenteeism due to mental health issues (e.g., 31 days).

- Daily Wage is calculated as Average Salary240240Average Salary (assuming 240 working days).

- Average Productivity Loss is expressed as a percentage (e.g., 35%).

This formula provides a comprehensive view by accounting for turnover costs, absenteeism losses, and productivity declines due to poor mental health. In summary, understanding and addressing mental health in the workplace is not just beneficial for employees; it's crucial for maintaining a healthy bottom line for organizations.

By investing in mental well-being initiatives and fostering supportive environments, companies can mitigate these costs while enhancing overall productivity and employee satisfaction

However this problem is worldwide and not just limited to one company and here is a brief snapshot of those data points from various sources offers a sobering insight into the scope of mental health issues in the workplace:

- **Global Impact:** The World Health Organization (WHO) estimates that over **264 million people** of all ages suffer from depression globally. In the corporate realm, these numbers translate into a significant portion of the workforce grappling with mental health challenges.

- **Anxiety's Grip:** Anxiety disorders, characterized by persistent worry and apprehension, affect approximately **284 million individuals** worldwide. The workplace, with its demanding nature and performance pressures, becomes a fertile ground for the development and exacerbation of anxiety-related issues.

- **Burnout is Real**: Burnout, often stemming from chronic workplace stress, is now recognized as an occupational phenomenon by the WHO. **The American Institute of Stress** reports that 83% of U.S. workers feel stressed about their jobs, and nearly 50% of them say they need help managing that stress.

- **Emergence of Millennials and Gen Z:** Younger generations entering the workforce, such as millennials and Generation Z, are experiencing mental health challenges at unprecedented rates. A report by Deloitte found that nearly 40% of millennials and 50% of Gen Z respondents had left a job due to mental health reasons.

- **Remote Work Amplification**: The shift to remote work brought about by the global pandemic has introduced new challenges. A study by FlexJobs and Mental Health America found that 75% of remote workers reported experiencing burnout, citing reasons like longer work hours, blurred work-life boundaries, and isolation.

- **Stigma and Unreported Cases:** Despite growing awareness, stigma surrounding mental health still hinders open discussions. Many employees hesitate to disclose their struggles due to fears of discrimination or reprisals, resulting in a substantial number of unreported cases.

These statistics highlight the alarming reality that mental health struggles aren't just happening to a few people here and there. they represent an epidemic that permeates workplaces across industries and geographies. Ignoring this problem doesn't just risk the well-being of employees, but it also puts in danger the foundations of getting work done, coming up with new ideas, and making the whole organization successful.

Facing this big challenge head-on can help organizations build a culture of caring, strength, and real concern – a culture that's good for both employees and the company's success.

To quantify the mental health of your organization, we can develop a formula that incorporates various measurable factors related to employee well-being. This formula can provide a numerical representation of the organization's mental health status, allowing leaders to track improvements or identify areas needing attention.

Formula for Measuring Organizational Mental Health

> **Mental Health Score (MHS) = (S + F + E + P + C) / 5**

Where:

- **S** = Survey Results Score (from regular mental health surveys)
- **F** = Feedback Mechanism Score (from employee feedback mechanisms)
- **E** = EAP Utilization Score (based on Employee Assistance Program usage)
- **P** = Performance Metrics Score (derived from performance data such as absenteeism and turnover rates)
- **C** = Communication Effectiveness Score (measured through leadership engagement and open communication initiatives)

Explanation of Each Component

1. **Survey Results Score (S)**: Conduct anonymous surveys to assess employees' perceptions of their mental well-being and the effectiveness of existing support systems. Each question can be rated on a scale (e.g., 1 to 5), and the average score can be calculated to represent overall sentiment regarding mental health in the organization.

2. **Feedback Mechanism Score (F)**: Establish channels for continuous feedback, such as suggestion boxes or pulse surveys. The effectiveness of these mechanisms can be evaluated based on participation rates and the quality of feedback received, contributing to the overall score.

3. **EAP Utilization Score (E)**: Analyze data from Employee Assistance Programs to understand how frequently employees seek help and for what issues. A higher utilization rate may indicate awareness and acceptance of mental health resources, while a low rate could suggest barriers to seeking help.

4. **Performance Metrics Score (P)**: Monitor performance indicators such as absenteeism rates, turnover rates, and productivity levels over time. These metrics can be converted into a score based on trends observed—improving metrics would yield a higher score.

5. **Communication Effectiveness Score (C)**: Evaluate how well leadership engages with employees regarding mental health topics. This can include assessing training programs for leaders on recognizing mental distress and fostering open conversations about mental health. Surveys can measure employees' perceptions of communication effectiveness.

Calculating the Mental Health Score

Once you have collected data for each component, you can plug the scores into the formula to calculate the Mental Health Score (MHS). This score will provide a numerical representation of the organization's mental health status, allowing for easy tracking over time.For example:

- If your scores are as follows:

- $S = 4.2$

- $F = 3.8$

- E = 4.0

- P = 3.5

- C = 4.1

Then the calculation would be:

$$MHS = \frac{(4.2+3.8+4.0+3.5+4.1)}{5} = \frac{19.6}{5} = 3.92$$

By implementing this formula, organizations can effectively quantify their mental health status, enabling leaders to make data-driven decisions regarding employee well-being initiatives. Regular assessments using this method will help create a culture that prioritizes mental health, ultimately leading to improved employee satisfaction and organizational performance.

But, here's the catch – companies, big or small, still find it hard to deal with mental health problems at work and there is no formula to convince a human being right on the top of the organisation.

There are lots of complicated reasons behind this. Let's dig deeper into these reasons to figure out why there's hesitation. So, here we go, exploring some common worries that organizations might have when it comes to dealing with mental health.

- **Lack of Awareness:** Some organizations and their leadership may lack a comprehensive understanding of the extent of mental health challenges within their workforce. They may underestimate the prevalence of these issues and their potential impact on employee well-being and overall productivity. Without this awareness, organizations may not perceive mental health as a priority area for intervention.

- **Cost Concerns:** Providing effective mental health support and accommodations can involve financial investments. This may encompass implementing programs like employee assistance programs (EAPs), offering counselling services, or making adjustments to workplace policies to accommodate individuals with mental health conditions. Organizations may be wary of these costs and the potential strain on their budgets.

- **Leadership Misunderstanding:** In some cases, organizational leaders and managers may not fully grasp the significance of mental health in the workplace. They may lack training or awareness in identifying and addressing mental health issues among their teams. Consequently, employees may feel unsupported, and management may inadvertently overlook the importance of mental health support.

- **Fear of Legal Issues:** Employers may harbour concerns about potential legal liabilities associated with mishandling mental health issues in the workplace. This apprehension can stem from a fear of discrimination claims, workplace harassment allegations, or other legal actions. As a result, organizations may adopt a cautious approach, potentially leading to avoidance rather than proactive support.

- **Stigma:** A prevailing issue in society, there is still a significant stigma surrounding mental health problems. In the workplace, this stigma can translate into a reluctance among employees to openly discuss their mental health concerns. They may fear discrimination or negative consequences, such as career setbacks or isolation, if they disclose their challenges. Employers, too, may hesitate to address mental health issues for fear of tarnishing the image of a high-performing, flawless work environment.

- **Productivity Concerns:** A prevalent misconception is that addressing mental health issues may adversely affect workplace productivity. However, research consistently demonstrates that when employees receive appropriate mental health support, it often leads to enhanced productivity and reduced absenteeism, countering this misconception.

- **Corporate Culture:** Organizational cultures that prioritize competitiveness and impose high-performance demands on employees may inadvertently discourage open discussions about mental health. Employees in such cultures may feel pressured to conceal their struggles, fearing that acknowledgment of mental health issues could jeopardize their standing or career prospects.

- **Resource Constraints:** Smaller organizations or those with limited resources may encounter practical challenges in implementing comprehensive mental health programs and support systems. Resource constraints, whether financial or related to staffing, can limit their ability to address mental health effectively.

Despite the many challenges they face, a growing number of organizations are realizing the significance of addressing mental health issues in the workplace. They're taking proactive measures to create an environment that encourages openness. This involves making mental health resources easily accessible and implementing policies and programs that prioritize the well-being of employees.

Initiatives such as Employee Assistance Programs (EAPs), campaigns to raise awareness about mental health, and leadership training are gaining popularity. These efforts aim to promote mental health support and reduce the stigma associated with it in the workplace.

However, even with these positive strides, there's still much work to be done to make a meaningful impact. Both organizations and employees need to continue evolving to better understand each other's challenges and create an environment that genuinely supports mental health. It's an ongoing process of learning and adapting as we strive for a workplace where everyone feels valued and supported in their mental well-being.

Chapter 2

The Evolution of Work Environments: From Past to Present

In the story of how workplaces have changed over time, we start with the problems people used to have at work. Work wasn't always like it is now. People faced challenges and worries when they went to work every day.

Then, we meet some clever thinkers who tried to make things better. One of them is Henry Ford, known for making peoples' cars. The assembly line innovations of Henry Ford, while revolutionary for manufacturing, brought monotonous and repetitive tasks to the forefront of corporate work, leading to growing disengagement and fatigue among today's employees. The relentless pace of production in these early factories left little room for the health and happiness of workers.

As we continue our journey, we find more smart folks like Chris Argyris and Carol Dweck. They wanted to make workplaces better by helping organizations learn and grow. But these guys were never popular as they didn't bring in massive revenues like Henry Ford. Specially Chirs taught us about the importance of having a "growth mindset," believing that we can get better at things if we try.

Before all these modern thinkers, there were other important people like Abraham Maslow and Frederick Herzberg. They helped us understand why we do our jobs and what makes us want to work.

And don't forget Elton Mayo, who realized that work isn't just about tasks; it's also about how we get along with our co-workers.

So, our journey takes us from the problems people faced at work in the past to how these clever thinkers like Chris, Carol, and others tried to make things better. It's a trip through time that shows how workplaces have changed into what they are today.

2.1 Maslow's Hierarchy of Needs: Laying the Foundation

Maslow's Hierarchy of Needs is a psychological theory proposed by Abraham Maslow in his 1943 paper "A Theory of Human Motivation." The theory suggests that human needs can be arranged in a hierarchical order, starting with basic physiological needs at the bottom and progressing to higher-level needs such as safety, love and belonging, esteem, and self-actualization. Maslow believed that individuals are motivated to fulfill these needs in a sequential manner, with lower-level needs taking precedence before higher-level needs come into focus. While the theory has faced criticism and debate, it remains influential in psychology and management studies.

Think of this theory as a plan, a step-by-step guide. Start by taking care of the essential needs – things like a fair salary, safe working conditions, and job security. These are the basics, the strong base for the mental well-being of employees. Once these needs are fulfilled, move on to the next levels – building connections, feeling a sense of belonging, earning respect, and achieving personal growth. This gradual progression creates an atmosphere that appreciates not just the work itself but the people doing it. It's like moving up a ladder, making sure each step is secure before reaching the next one.

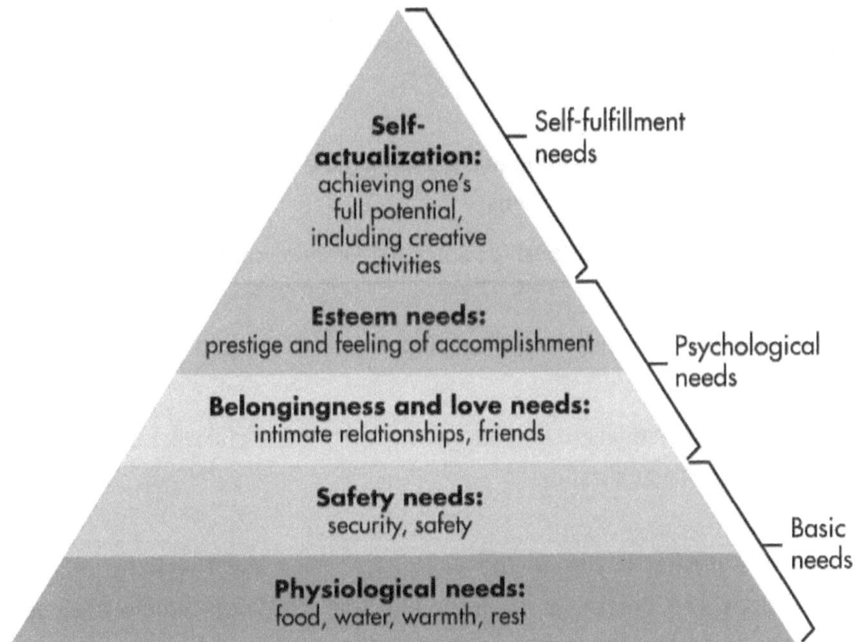

Detail:

Maslow's Hierarchy of Needs is often depicted as a pyramid with five levels:

1. **Physiological Needs:** These are the basic survival needs, such as food, water, shelter, and sleep.

2. **Safety Needs:** Once physiological needs are met, individuals seek safety, security, and stability in their environment.

3. **Love and Belonging:** The need for social connections, relationships, and a sense of belonging becomes important.

4. **Esteem Needs:** Individuals desire recognition, respect, and a positive self-image. This includes both self-esteem and the esteem of others.

5. **Self-Actualization:** At the top of the pyramid is the need for self-fulfilment, personal growth, and reaching one's full potential.

In the workplace, Maslow's theory suggests that employees' mental well-being can be enhanced by ensuring that their needs are met at various levels of the hierarchy. For instance:

- Providing fair compensation and a comfortable work environment addresses physiological and safety needs.
- Fostering positive relationships among colleagues satisfies the need for love and belonging.
- Offering opportunities for skill development and recognition caters to esteem needs.
- Supporting personal growth, autonomy, and meaningful work aligns with the need for self-actualization.

To improve mental health in the workplace using the Hierarchy of Needs, organizations can create an environment that considers employees' needs across the hierarchy. By addressing both basic needs and higher-order needs, organizations contribute to a sense of security, belonging, self-worth, and personal growth, all of which positively impact mental well-being.

Maslow's theory reminds us that meeting these needs is essential for creating a workplace where employees feel valued, supported, and motivated. When employees' needs are fulfilled, they experience improved job satisfaction, engagement, and mental health.

In summary, Abraham Maslow's Hierarchy of Needs theory emphasizes the importance of fulfilling various human needs to improve mental health in the workplace. By addressing physiological, safety, social, esteem, and self-actualization needs, organizations create an environment that supports employees' well-being and overall satisfaction.

2.2 Herzberg's Two-Factor Theory: Balancing Hygiene and Motivation

With the foundation in place, pivot to Herzberg's theory.

Herzberg's Two-Factor Theory identifies two sets of factors that influence employees' experiences in the workplace:

- **Hygiene Factors:** These are external factors that do not directly lead to job satisfaction but can prevent dissatisfaction. Examples include working conditions, job security, salary, and company policies. When these factors are lacking, employees may feel dissatisfied and demotivated.

- **Motivational Factors:** These are internal factors that directly contribute to job satisfaction and motivation. Examples include opportunities for growth, recognition, responsibility, and challenging work. When these factors are present, employees experience higher levels of job satisfaction and engagement.

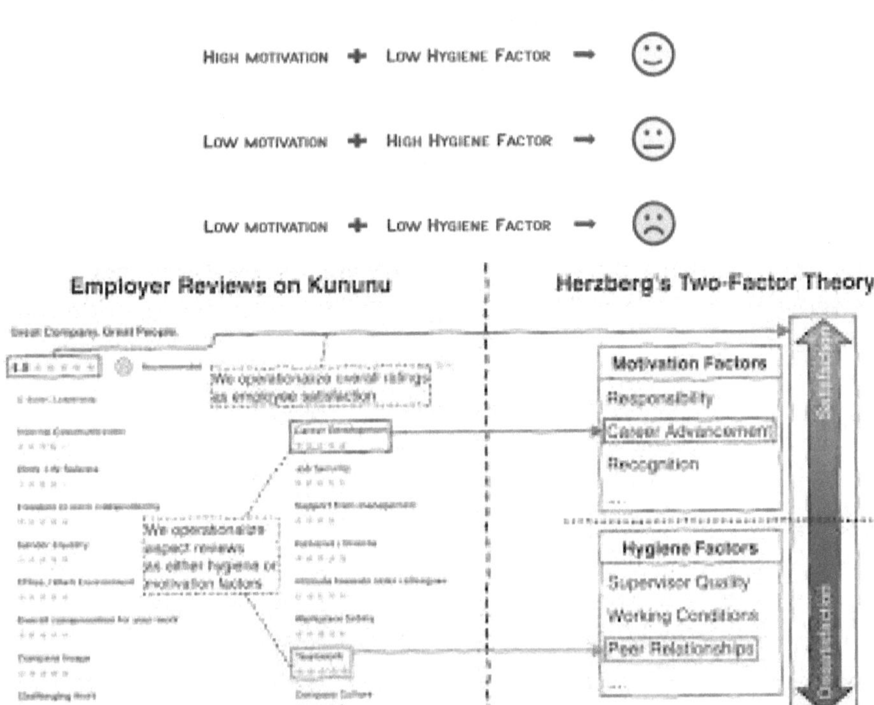

- Attend to **hygiene factors** – make sure employees have comfortable working conditions, clear expectations, and job stability. By removing dissatisfaction triggers, you set the stage for motivation to shine.

- Introduce **motivational factors** – offer opportunities for growth, autonomy, and recognition. This balanced approach creates a workplace where well-being thrives on a bed of satisfaction and achievement.

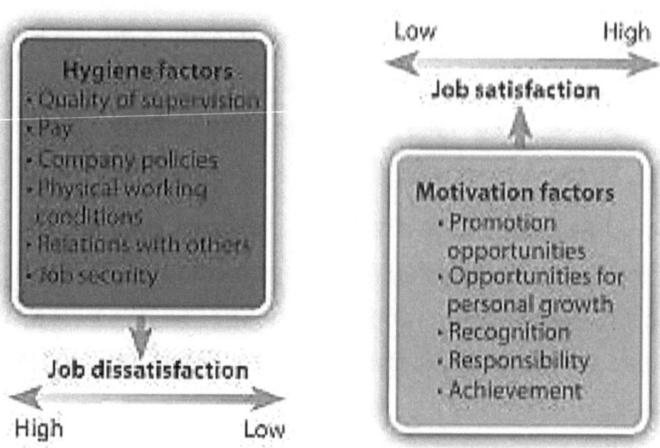

In the context of improving mental health in the workplace, Herzberg's theory suggests that organizations should focus on providing both hygiene factors and motivational factors to create an environment that promotes psychological well-being.

To enhance mental health in the workplace using the **Two-Factor Theory,** organizations can:

- Address **hygiene factors** to prevent dissatisfaction and **reduce stress**. This includes ensuring fair compensation, providing safe working conditions, and offering job security.

- Focus on **motivational factors** to promote job satisfaction and **psychological well-being**. Providing opportunities for growth, recognizing employees' contributions, and offering challenging tasks can positively impact mental health.

By attending to both hygiene and motivational factors, organizations create an environment that supports employees' overall well-being, job satisfaction, and mental health. Herzberg's theory reminds us that addressing the factors that lead to satisfaction and removing those that lead to dissatisfaction are essential for promoting a positive work experience.

In summary, *Frederick Herzberg's Two-Factor Theory* emphasizes the importance of addressing hygiene and motivational factors to enhance job satisfaction and mental health in the workplace. By providing a supportive and rewarding environment, organizations contribute to employees' psychological well-being and overall engagement.

2.3 Mayo's Human Relations Approach: Nurturing Interactions

As the foundation is laid and motivation fostered, shift focus to Mayo's approach.

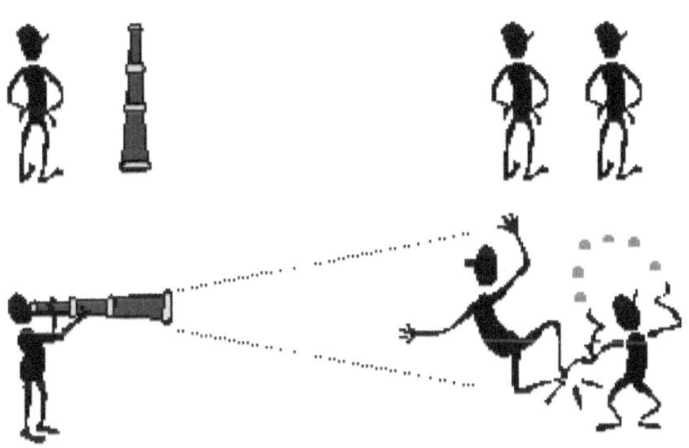

Mayo's research, conducted at the Western Electric Hawthorne Works in Chicago, initially aimed to understand the relationship between lighting conditions and productivity. However, the studies led to unexpected findings related to the influence of social factors on employee behavior and performance.

The **Hawthorne Effect** refers to the phenomenon where individuals modify their behavior in response to being observed or studied.

In the context of the workplace, *Mayo's research revealed that employees often improved their performance simply because they were aware they were being studied.* This emphasized the importance of attention and recognition in influencing behavior and motivation.

Mayo's research went beyond the Hawthorne Effect and introduced the concept of the **Human Relations Approach**. He emphasized that employees' social needs, interactions, and relationships with colleagues and supervisors significantly impact their job satisfaction, motivation, and mental well-being. The theory suggests that employees are not just motivated by monetary rewards or working conditions; they also thrive in environments that support positive relationships and teamwork.

To enhance mental health in the workplace through the Human Relations Approach, organizations can implement several straightforward strategies:

1. **Regular Check-Ins**

   - **Action:** Schedule brief, regular one-on-one meetings between managers and employees.

   - **Purpose:** This promotes open communication, allows employees to share concerns, and shows that management cares about their well-being.

2. **Team-Building Activities**

   - **Action:** Organize monthly team-building exercises or social gatherings (virtual or in-person).

   - **Purpose:** These activities foster camaraderie, improve relationships, and create a sense of belonging among team members.

3. **Recognition Programs**

   - **Action:** Implement a simple recognition program where employees can acknowledge each other's efforts (e.g., shout-outs in meetings or a dedicated board).

   - **Purpose:** Recognizing achievements boosts morale and reinforces positive behaviors.

4. **Open Communication Channels**

   - **Action:** Create anonymous feedback channels (like suggestion boxes or online surveys) to encourage employees to voice their opinions.

   - **Purpose:** This helps employees feel heard and valued, which can enhance their emotional well-being.

5. **Flexible Work Arrangements**

   - **Action:** Offer options for flexible working hours or remote work when possible.

   - **Purpose:** Flexibility can reduce stress and help employees balance their personal and professional lives better.

6. **Mental Health Resources**

   - **Action:** Provide access to mental health resources, such as counseling services or workshops on stress management.

   - **Purpose:** Ensuring employees know where to seek help contributes to a supportive work environment.

7. **Encourage Breaks**

   - **Action:** Promote regular breaks throughout the day, encouraging employees to step away from their desks.

   - **Purpose:** Short breaks can improve focus, reduce stress, and enhance overall productivity.

8. **Create a Positive Work Environment**

   - **Action:** Make small changes to the workspace, such as adding plants or comfortable seating areas.

   - **Purpose:** A pleasant environment can boost mood and well-being.

In summary, Elton Mayo's Hawthorne Effect and Human Relations Approach highlight the importance of social interactions and relationships in the workplace. By recognizing the significance of emotional well-being and fostering a supportive environment, organizations contribute to improved mental health and overall job satisfaction.

2.4 Argyris's Theory of Action: Aligning Values

With relationships flourishing, dive into Argyris's theory. Cultivate self-awareness and authenticity. Encourage employees to align their personal values with organizational goals. This step fosters a sense of purpose and meaning, creating a bridge between individual aspirations and collective endeavours. This alignment paves the way for mental well-being to be rooted in authenticity and a shared sense of direction.

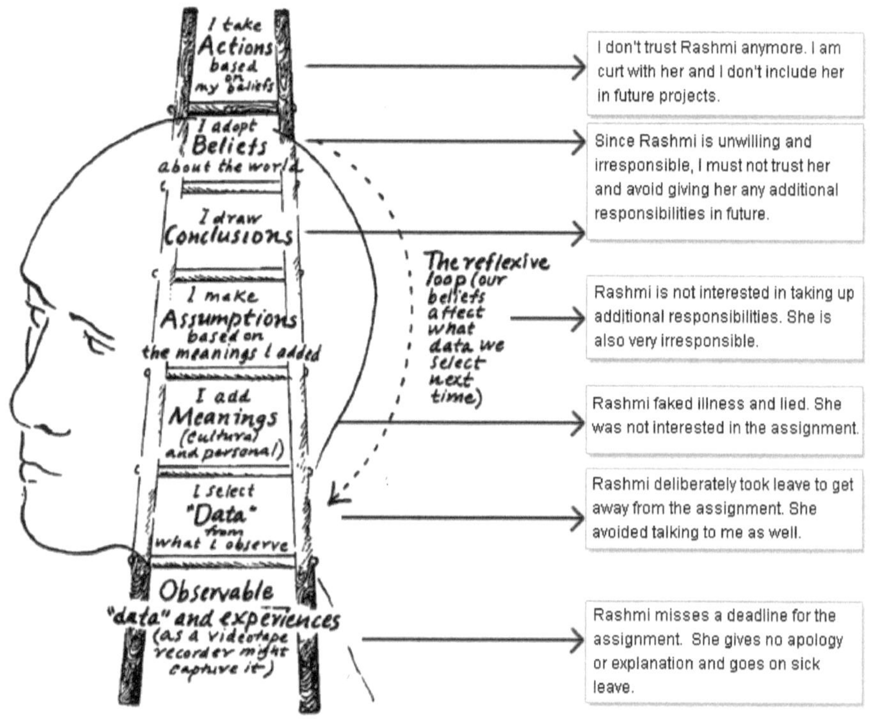

(Source: The Fifth Discipline By Peter Senge)

Argyris emphasized that individuals have a set of beliefs and assumptions about themselves which I call "self-image", others, and the world around them which I call "worldview" These beliefs shape their perceptions, decisions, and actions. The Theory of Action suggests that to understand human behavior, it's important to uncover the thought processes and beliefs that drive it.

In the context of the workplace, Argyris highlighted the significance of aligning employees' goals, values, and assumptions with those of the organization. When there is congruence between individual values and organizational goals, employees are more likely to be engaged, motivated, and satisfied in their work. This alignment contributes to psychological well-being and job satisfaction.

Argyris also introduced the concept of "double-loop learning," which encourages individuals and organizations to question their underlying assumptions and beliefs when faced with challenges or failures. This process of self-awareness and self-reflection allows for more adaptive and effective responses to problems.

Encouraging self-awareness, self-reflection, and authentic engagement helps individuals understand their own motivations and drives, leading to a more fulfilling work experience. When employees feel that their values and beliefs are acknowledged and integrated into their work, they experience a stronger sense of purpose and psychological well-being.

In summary, Chris Argyris's Theory of Action emphasizes the importance of aligning individual values and beliefs with organizational goals. Encouraging self-awareness, self-reflection, and authentic engagement contributes to employee satisfaction, psychological well-being, and a more harmonious relationship between individuals and their work environments.

2.5 Dweck's Growth Mindset: Cultivating Resilience

With values aligned, embrace Dweck's theory. Promote a growth mindset where effort, learning, and embracing challenges are celebrated. Cultivate resilience by encouraging employees to view setbacks as opportunities for growth. This mindset shift strengthens mental resilience, helping individuals navigate the complexities of the corporate world with a positive outlook.

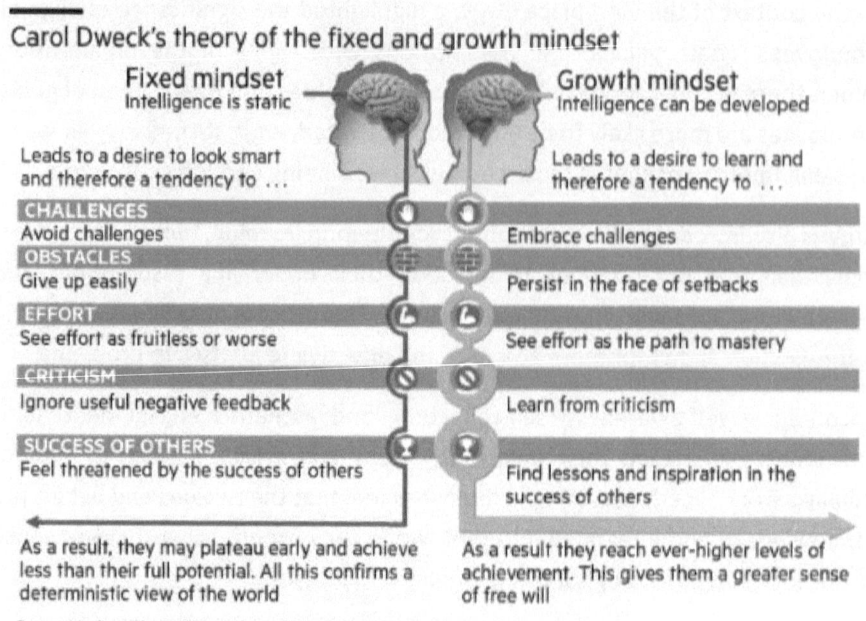

Dweck's Growth Mindset theory distinguishes between two mindsets: a fixed mindset and a growth mindset.

- ✓ **Fixed Mindset:** Individuals with a fixed mindset believe that their abilities and qualities are inherent and unchangeable. They tend to avoid challenges and setbacks to protect their self-perception.

- ✓ **Growth Mindset:** Individuals with a growth mindset believe that their abilities and qualities can be developed through effort, learning, and perseverance. They embrace challenges as opportunities to learn and grow.

In the workplace, fostering a growth mindset contributes to improved mental health by reducing fear of failure and encouraging resilience. Employees with a growth mindset are more likely to take on challenges, seek feedback, and view setbacks as learning experiences. This mindset promotes a positive relationship with mistakes and failures, reducing stress and anxiety.

To enhance mental health in the workplace using the Growth Mindset theory, organizations can promote a culture that values effort, learning, and development. Encouraging employees to embrace challenges, providing opportunities for skill-building, and offering constructive feedback helps them cultivate a growth mindset. This, in turn, contributes to increased job satisfaction and psychological well-being.

By shifting from a fixed mindset to a growth mindset, individuals can develop greater self-confidence, adaptability, and a healthier perspective on their work and abilities. This mindset shift supports mental well-being by reducing self-imposed pressure and creating a more positive work environment.

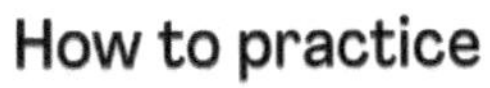

To determine if a candidate has a growth or fixed mindset during an interview, consider the following strategies:

1. **Behavioral Questions**: Ask about past challenges and responses to feedback. Look for indications of resilience and adaptability, such as how they handled setbacks or utilized constructive criticism.

2. **Self-Reflection**: Inquire about mistakes and lessons learned. Candidates with a growth mindset will demonstrate self-awareness and articulate their growth from experiences.

3. **Future Orientation**: Assess their views on personal development by asking about skills they wish to improve or how they plan to grow professionally. A growth mindset will be reflected in enthusiasm for learning.

4. **Language Cues**: Pay attention to the language used. Phrases indicating learning and improvement suggest a growth mindset, while statements about fixed abilities may indicate a fixed mindset.

5. **Enthusiasm for Learning**: Ask about recent resources that inspired them or how they stay current in their field. Candidates with a growth mindset will actively seek knowledge and express excitement about opportunities for improvement.

By employing these strategies, you can effectively assess whether a candidate embodies a growth or fixed mindset, which is important for their potential success within your organization.

In summary, Carol Dweck's Growth Mindset theory emphasizes the importance of cultivating a belief in the potential for growth and development. Fostering a growth mindset in the workplace contributes to improved mental health, increased engagement, and a culture of continuous learning and improvement.

2.6 Edmondson's Psychological Safety: Fostering Openness

As resilience takes root, transition to Edmondson's theory. Create an environment of psychological safety where employees feel comfortable sharing ideas, taking risks, and expressing concerns. This safe haven nurtures innovation and reduces stress, allowing mental well-being to flourish amidst open communication and collaboration.

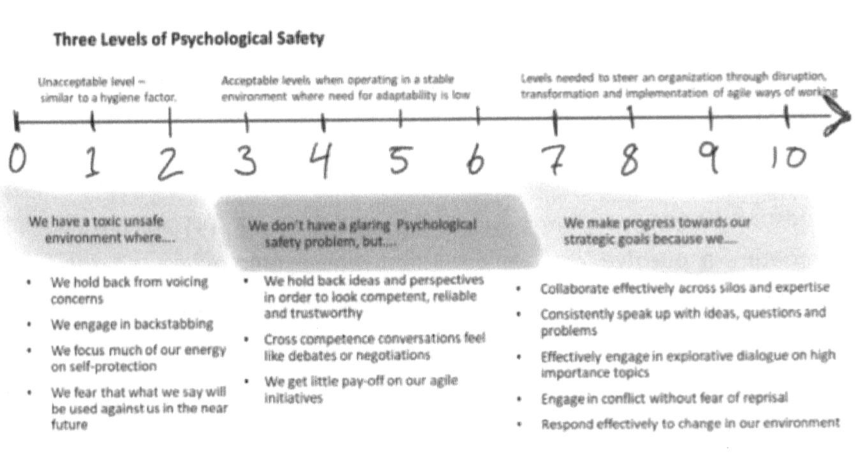

Psychological safety refers to a shared belief that the team and organization will not punish or humiliate individuals for speaking up, sharing opinions, or making mistakes. This concept is crucial for promoting mental well-being and fostering open communication.

Key aspects of Psychological Safety that contribute to workplace mental health include:

- ✔ **Open Communication:** Employees feel comfortable sharing their thoughts, concerns, and ideas without fear of retribution or judgment. This contributes to reduced stress and improved mental well-being.

- ✓ **Risk-Taking:** Psychological safety encourages employees to take calculated risks, which can lead to innovation, creativity, and a sense of accomplishment.

- ✓ **Learning Culture**: An environment that supports psychological safety promotes a culture of learning from failures and mistakes. This reduces anxiety related to making errors and promotes a growth mindset.

To improve mental health in the workplace using Psychological Safety, organizations can focus on creating a culture that values open communication, welcomes diverse perspectives, and treats mistakes as opportunities for growth. When employees feel safe to express themselves, they experience reduced stress, improved job satisfaction, and enhanced psychological well-being.

Edmondson's theory acknowledges the importance of psychological safety in promoting a positive work environment where employees can thrive. By fostering an atmosphere of trust and open dialogue, organizations contribute to employees' mental health, engagement, and overall satisfaction.

In summary, Amy Edmondson's theory of Psychological Safety highlights the significance of creating an environment where employees feel safe to voice their opinions and take risks. This practice contributes to improved mental health, reduced stress, and a culture of collaboration and learning in the workplace.

2.7 Seligman's Positive Psychology: Nurturing Positivity and Well-Being

As the stage of openness is set, embrace Seligman's tenets, including the profound concept of learned helplessness and his PERMA happiness theory. By delving into his insights, a transformative journey unfolds. Through learned helplessness, Seligman unearths the impact of uncontrollable negative experiences on individuals' agency and mental wellness.

The PERMA Model In A Nutshell

The PERMA model was created by American psychologist and educator Martin Seligman. The PERMA model is a framework for happiness and wellbeing based on positive psychology through five elements: positive emotion, engagement, positive relationships, meaning, and accomplishment.

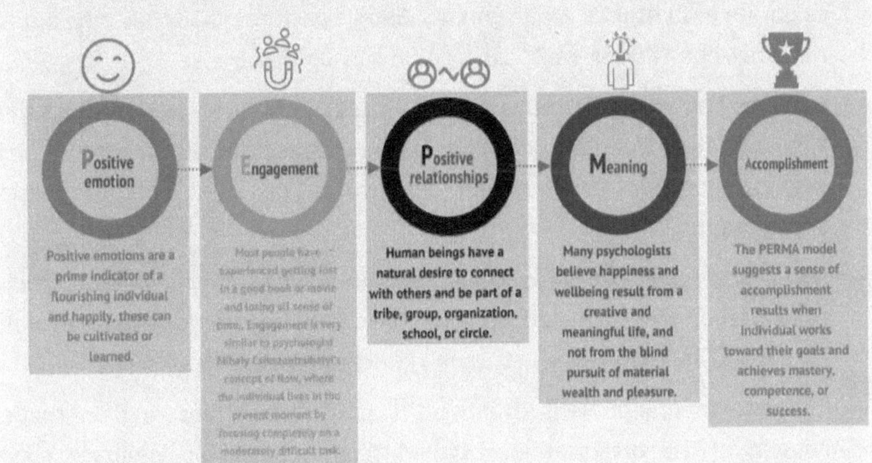

At the heart of Seligman's Positive Psychology is the PERMA model, which consists of five essential components that contribute to psychological well-being:

- P - Positive Emotions: Encourage a culture that promotes positive emotions and an optimistic outlook on life.

- E - Engagement: Foster an environment where employees can experience deep engagement or flow in activities that challenge and captivate them.

- R - Relationships: Build and nurture positive relationships and connections among team members.

- M - Meaning: Help employees find purpose in their work through activities that align with their values and beliefs.

- A - Accomplishments: Support employees in setting and achieving goals, allowing them to experience a sense of accomplishment and success.

To effectively implement Seligman's Positive Psychology principles and improve mental health within the organization, consider the following actionable steps:

- ✓ **Promote Positive Emotions**: Create a recognition program where employees celebrate each other's achievements. Simple gestures like shout-outs during meetings or a **"Kudos Wall"** can significantly uplift morale.

- ✓ **Enhance Engagement:** Encourage employees to participate in projects that align with their interests and skills. Offering **opportunities for professional development** or **skill-building** workshops can also foster deeper engagement.

- ✓ **Foster Strong Relationships**: Organize team-building activities that promote collaboration and connection among colleagues. **Regular social events**, both virtual and in-person, can strengthen interpersonal bonds.

- ✓ **Cultivate Meaning:** Help employees connect their roles to the broader mission of the organization. Regularly communicate or **feedback every quarter** around how individual contribution impact overall goals, fostering a sense of purpose.

- ✓ **Support Accomplishments:** Set clear, achievable goals for employees and celebrate milestones along the way. Providing encouragement like bonuses or awards or recognition around any progress reinforces a sense of accomplishment and motivates further success.

- ✓ **Encourage Open Communication:** Establish channels for open dialogue where employees feel safe sharing their thoughts and concerns. Regular check-ins can help identify issues before they escalate.

- ✓ **Implement Well-Being Surveys:** Use tools like the Workplace PERMA Profiler to assess employee well-being regularly. This allows organizations to understand areas needing improvement and tailor interventions accordingly.

- ✓ **Create a Supportive Environment:** Ensure that the workplace is physically comfortable, with access to natural light, quiet spaces for focus, and areas for relaxation. A positive physical environment contributes significantly to mental well-being.

In a nutshell, Martin Seligman's Positive Psychology theory unfurls the banner of fostering strengths, gratitude, mindfulness, and positive relationships to kindle improved mental health. By embracing these principles within the workplace, organizations sow the seeds for a well-being culture, cultivating an ecosystem attuned to the psychological and emotional needs of their employees.

2.8 Csikszentmihalyi's Flow Theory: Nurturing Engagement

Now let us finally, wrap up this symphony with Csikszentmihalyi's theory. Mihaly Csikszentmihalyi's Flow Theory is a psychological concept that explores the state of optimal human experience and performance. Developed by Csikszentmihalyi in the 1970s, the theory suggests that individuals can achieve a state of flow when they are fully immersed in an activity, experiencing deep concentration and enjoyment. Flow is characterized by a sense of complete absorption, a loss of self-consciousness, and a feeling of being in control of one's actions.

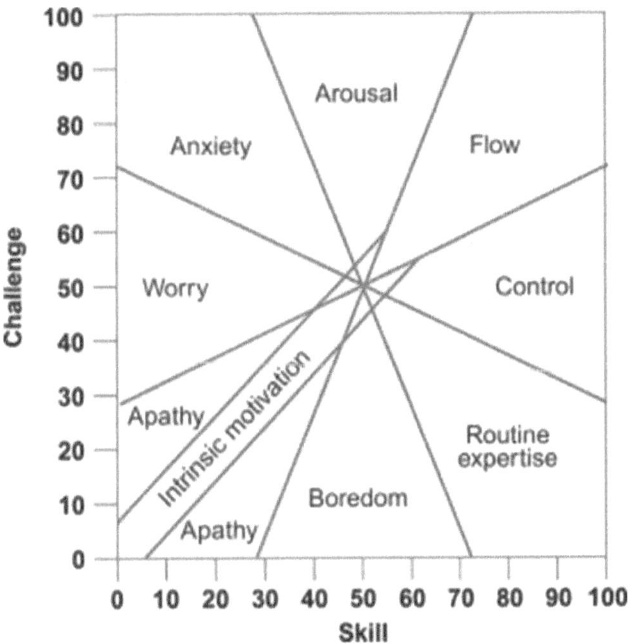

In Csikszentmihalyi's Flow Theory, the key challenge is to find the right balance between the perceived challenge of an activity and the individual's skill level. When these factors are appropriately matched, individuals are more likely to experience the state of flow.

Here's a breakdown of challenges and skills within the context of the theory:

Challenge:

- **Underwhelming Challenge:** If the challenge of an activity is too low compared to an individual's skill level, they may experience boredom. The lack of stimulation and novelty can prevent the emergence of flow.

- **Overwhelming Challenge**: On the other hand, if the challenge is too high relative to the individual's skill level, it may lead to anxiety and frustration. The person may feel overwhelmed and unable to cope with the demands of the task.

Skills:

- **Developing Skills:** To increase the likelihood of experiencing flow, individuals can work on enhancing their skills in a particular activity. Continuous learning and improvement contribute to a sense of mastery, making the activity more engaging.

- **Setting Clear Goals:** Clearly defined goals provide a sense of direction and purpose. Individuals can break down larger tasks into smaller, manageable goals, creating a structured path to progress.

- **Adapting to Challenges:** Developing the ability to adapt to increasing challenges is crucial. It involves pushing oneself to take on tasks that are slightly beyond one's current skill level, promoting growth and skill acquisition.

- **Finding Intrinsic Motivation:** Intrinsic motivation, or engaging in an activity for the inherent satisfaction it brings, can contribute to the enjoyment of the process. This internal drive can sustain interest and focus during challenging tasks.

Csikszentmihalyi's Flow Theory emphasizes the conditions that lead to the experience of flow:

- **Clear Goals:** Individuals have clear goals and objectives for their tasks, providing a sense of purpose and direction.

- **Concentration:** The activity is challenging enough to require full concentration, preventing boredom and distractions.

- ✔ **Feedback:** Immediate and clear feedback is available, allowing individuals to adjust their actions and maintain focus.

- ✔ **Skill-Balance:** The level of skill required for the task matches the individual's abilities, leading to a sense of accomplishment and confidence.

In summary, ***the challenge is to find the sweet spot where the difficulty of the task matches an individual's skill level.*** Developing skills, setting clear goals, adapting to challenges, and fostering intrinsic motivation are key elements that can help individuals navigate and optimize their experiences in the state of flow.

There are countless theories on employee well-being and organizational psychology, but the real value lies in applying these insights from such theories at different phases of an employee's journey—from recruitment to engagement and even during their exit.

Part 2

Understanding Mental Health and Workplace Dynamics

Chapter 3

The Science of Happiness Hormones and Employee Behavior

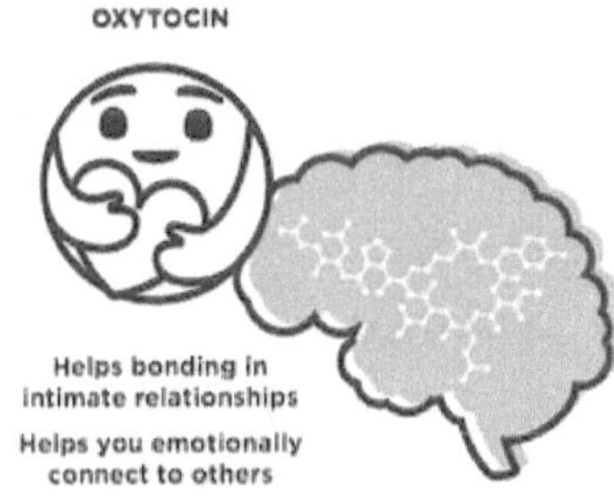

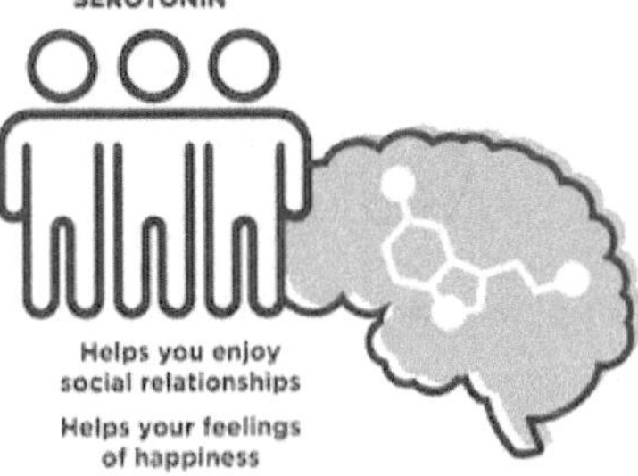

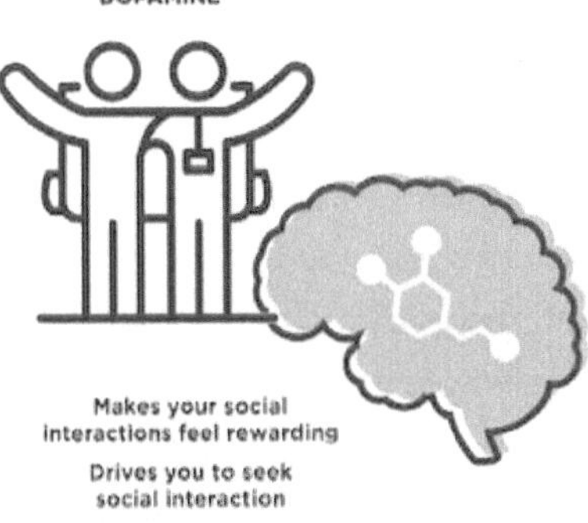

Have you ever considered how hormones influence our daily lives, especially in the workplace? Hormones are powerful chemical messengers produced by our endocrine glands that travel through the bloodstream, affecting everything from mood and energy levels to overall health. In a work environment, hormonal balance—or imbalance—can significantly impact employee performance, productivity, and mental health.For instance, hormones like cortisol, often referred to as the stress hormone, can affect our ability to concentrate and manage stress. Fluctuations in hormones such as estrogen and testosterone can lead to mood swings, fatigue, and cognitive difficulties, which can hinder job satisfaction and productivity. This is particularly relevant for women experiencing hormonal changes during significant life stages like pregnancy or menopause, as they may face unique challenges that affect their work life.

Creating a supportive workplace culture that acknowledges these hormonal influences is essential. Organizations that implement wellness programs focused on hormonal health can foster an inclusive environment where employees feel valued and understood. This not only enhances trust among team members but also improves overall morale.

Let's deep dive into the impact of hormones on workplace dynamics and explore practical strategies that employers can adopt to support their employees' hormonal health.

By prioritizing this aspect of well-being, we can cultivate a more productive and engaged workforce. Here's how this can be applied across different life stages to create a thriving, holistic work environment.

Childhood: Nurturing Endorphin Euphoria

Think of the carefree days of childhood, filled with laughter and play. Those moments of joy come from endorphins—nature's feel-good chemicals released during physical activity. Organizations that incorporate movement into the workday can bring a similar sense of joy to employees. Simple practices like physical breaks or playful spaces can uplift moods and enhance creativity.

- **Hormones Involved**: Endorphins, dopamine, and growth hormones.

- **Effects:** High levels of physical activity and play are associated with the release of endorphins, which improve mood and energy. During adolescence, dopamine levels are also significant as they contribute to motivation, learning, and reward-seeking behavior.

- **Impact on Mental Health:** A strong release of these hormones supports emotional resilience, positive self-esteem, and social engagement

- **Example**: Google's offices include game rooms and playful elements that encourage employees to take active breaks. This helps rejuvenate their minds and boost endorphin levels.

Practical Tips for Organizations:

- **Physical Activity Breaks**: Introduce short, energizing breaks with stretching or mini dance sessions.

- **Outdoor Team-Building**: Schedule activities in outdoor settings to combine exercise and team spirit.

- **Exercise Challenges**: Create fun challenges with rewards to motivate physical activity.

Young Adulthood: Chasing Dopamine Dreams

In young adulthood, people are driven by career aspirations and personal goals. Dopamine, the neurotransmitter responsible for motivation and reward, plays a central role during this phase. Workplaces that celebrate achievements and create opportunities for growth can harness this natural source of drive.

- **Hormones Involved:** Dopamine, cortisol (stress hormone), and sex hormones (testosterone and estrogen).

- **Effects:** Dopamine drives motivation, reward-seeking, and goal achievement. Elevated stress from work and personal life can increase cortisol levels, which, if unmanaged, negatively affects mental health.

- **Impact on Work and Personal Life:** Balanced dopamine levels enhance productivity and a sense of accomplishment, while chronic high cortisol can lead to burnout, anxiety, and reduced cognitive performance.

- **Example**: Microsoft's goal-setting workshops help employees break down their objectives and track progress. This practice taps into dopamine's power to boost motivation.

Practical Tips for Organizations:

- **Recognition Programs**: Create platforms for employees to celebrate each other's achievements.

- **Goal Workshops**: Host workshops that guide employees in setting and achieving clear objectives.

- **Innovation Contests**: Encourage idea submissions with the incentive of recognition and rewards.

Midlife: Cultivating Oxytocin Bonds

As employees reach midlife, their focus shifts from personal achievements to building relationships and contributing to the community. Oxytocin, known as the "connection molecule," promotes trust and social bonding. Workplaces that foster a collaborative and supportive culture can help strengthen these bonds.

- **Hormones Involved**: Oxytocin and cortisol.

- **Effects:** In midlife, relationships and social bonds become more important, driven by the release of oxytocin, which fosters trust and social cohesion. However, life stressors such as career challenges or family responsibilities can trigger higher cortisol levels.

- **Impact on Mental Health:** Healthy oxytocin levels promote strong interpersonal relationships and emotional well-being. High cortisol levels, if sustained, can contribute to anxiety, depression, and stress-related disorders.

- **Example**: LinkedIn's mentorship programs pair seasoned professionals with newer employees, enhancing knowledge-sharing and building strong relationships.

Practical Tips for Organizations:

- **Mentorship Initiatives**: Develop programs connecting experienced employees with newcomers.

- **Team Volunteering**: Organize volunteer activities that foster teamwork and a sense of purpose.

- **Social Gatherings**: Hold regular events to encourage employees to form connections.

Old Age: Basking in Serotonin's Glow

In the later years of an employee's career, serotonin—the hormone linked to contentment and well-being—becomes more significant. Workplaces that honor their senior employees and give them opportunities to share their experience can promote a peaceful, fulfilling environment.

- **Hormones Involved**: Serotonin and melatonin.

- **Effects**: Serotonin plays a critical role in mood regulation and a sense of contentment. Lower levels are associated with depression and anxiety, while melatonin affects sleep patterns, which are essential for mental and physical health.

- **Impact on Mental Health**: High serotonin levels contribute to feelings of peace and satisfaction, aiding mental health and reducing stress. Proper sleep, supported by melatonin, is key for cognitive health and overall well-being.

- **Example**: Intel's legacy projects enable retirees to contribute their expertise, fostering a sense of purpose and satisfaction.

Practical Tips for Organizations:

- **Advisory Roles**: Create positions where senior employees can mentor and advise.

- **Family Days**: Organize events where employees can bring their families, strengthening bonds.

- **Celebratory Events**: Recognize and celebrate the achievements of senior staff.

The Case for Applying This Theory in the Workplace

By incorporating strategies that align with each life stage, organizations can nurture employees' mental health and well-being. When employees feel valued and supported, productivity, creativity, and retention rates soar. Companies like Google, Microsoft, LinkedIn, and Intel have shown that investing in employees' emotional well-being fosters a happier, more engaged workforce.

To summarize it we can say that leveraging the power of endorphins, dopamine, oxytocin, and serotonin ensures not just individual satisfaction but a thriving organizational culture.

- ✔ **Endorphin-focused Initiatives for younger employees:** Introduce programs that integrate physical activity into the workday, such as scheduled exercise breaks, group fitness challenges, or outdoor team events. These activities help release endorphins, boosting mood and enhancing creative thinking.

- ✔ **Dopamine-enhancing Strategies for young aged employees**: Implement goal-setting workshops where employees can plan and track their professional objectives. Establish systems for regular recognition and rewards to celebrate achievements and maintain high levels of motivation and engagement

- ✔ **Oxytocin-supportive Environments for middle aged employees**: Develop mentorship programs that pair experienced employees with newcomers to build strong bonds and facilitate knowledge sharing. Organize team-building events that promote trust, empathy, and social connection within the workplace.

- ✔ **Serotonin-promoting Approaches for matured employees**: Provide senior employees with opportunities to take on advisory roles, participate in legacy projects, or mentor younger staff. Arrange events where experienced employees can share their insights, fostering a culture of appreciation and community while enhancing their sense of fulfillment and well-being.

A well-rounded approach that respects these life stages enhances both individual and collective well-being, driving productivity and innovation. It underlines that, beyond mere productivity metrics, understanding human behavior and the interplay of hormones can significantly improve workplace culture, ensuring employees feel valued at every stage of life.

Understanding and supporting hormonal health can lead to significant gains in productivity, employee satisfaction, and financial performance. Let's break down how this works and explore practical strategies to integrate into your workplace.

1. Boosting Productivity and Efficiency

Hormonal balance, particularly involving **cortisol**, the stress hormone, plays a vital role in maintaining focus and efficiency. When employees face chronic stress, cortisol levels spike, leading to reduced concentration and productivity. By implementing wellness programs that include stress management techniques like meditation, guided breathing exercises, or designated quiet zones, companies can help maintain healthier cortisol levels.

Practical Steps:

- **Scheduled Mindfulness Breaks**: Integrate short guided meditation or stretching sessions during the workday.

- **Designated Relaxation Areas**: Create quiet spaces where employees can unwind and reset their focus.

Economic Impact: Companies that promote wellness programs often see productivity gains of **10-15%**. For an organization of 500 employees, even a 10% productivity boost can translate into substantial revenue increases, potentially adding hundreds of thousands of dollars to the bottom line.

2. Reducing Absenteeism and Healthcare Costs

Hormonal imbalances contribute to physical and mental health issues, which can lead to higher absenteeism. By educating employees on hormonal health and offering flexible working policies, companies can support preventive care and reduce sick days.

Practical Steps:

- **Workshops on Hormonal Health**: Partner with healthcare professionals to provide educational sessions on managing stress and hormonal changes.

- **Flexible Scheduling**: Allow employees to adjust their work hours for health appointments or self-care activities.

Economic Impact: The **World Health Organization (WHO)** estimates that every dollar invested in mental health and wellness initiatives yields a **$4 return** in improved health and productivity. Reducing absenteeism by even **5%** can mean significant cost savings in healthcare expenses and lost productivity.

3. Enhancing Employee Retention and Reducing Turnover Costs

High employee turnover is expensive, often costing **50-200%** of an individual's annual salary to replace them. Hormonal health, particularly during life changes such as pregnancy or menopause, can influence job satisfaction and emotional well-being. Creating supportive policies can help retain employees during these critical periods.

Practical Steps:

- **Mentorship Programs**: Connect employees experiencing significant life transitions with mentors who can provide support and guidance.

- **Training for Managers**: Offer training sessions that teach managers how to recognize and respond compassionately to hormonal health-related issues.

Economic Impact: Reducing turnover rates by even **10-15%** can save companies hundreds of thousands in recruitment and training costs annually. IBM, for instance, saw a **44% reduction** in turnover after implementing comprehensive wellness and support programs.

4. Stimulating Creativity and Innovation

Dopamine, the neurotransmitter associated with motivation and reward, fuels creative thinking and problem-solving. Workplaces that encourage activities stimulating dopamine release—such as idea-sharing sessions or playful, interactive spaces—can foster an environment of innovation.

Practical Steps:

- **Innovation Labs**: Set up spaces dedicated to brainstorming and creative activities.

- **Active Breaks**: Implement short, energizing physical activities that boost dopamine levels and enhance creativity.

Economic Impact: Companies like Google and Microsoft have reaped the benefits of fostering creativity, driving innovation that keeps them industry leaders. A workforce that feels motivated and engaged is more likely to produce breakthrough ideas, enhancing the company's competitive edge.

5. Building Long-Term Sustainability and Reputation

As employees reach later stages in their careers, hormones like **serotonin** become essential for mood regulation and overall well-being. Companies that honor senior employees with opportunities to mentor or advise can tap into their wealth of knowledge while supporting their emotional health.

Practical Steps:

- **Advisory Roles**: Create part-time positions for senior employees to share their expertise.

- **Recognition Programs**: Host events that celebrate the achievements and contributions of long-serving employees.

Economic Impact: Companies with strong reputations for valuing employees' well-being attract and retain top talent, reducing recruitment costs by up to **50%**. A respected workplace culture also fosters loyalty and improves customer relationships.

Understanding the economic implications of supporting hormonal health in the workplace can transform the way businesses operate. Practical initiatives—from wellness programs and educational workshops to flexible policies and mentorship opportunities—lead to a more productive, engaged, and satisfied workforce. The result is not only improved employee well-being but also tangible business gains through higher productivity, reduced absenteeism, better retention, and enhanced innovation. Investing in hormonal health is investing in the long-term success of both your employees and your organization.

Chapter 4

The Corporate Brain: Understanding Organizational Psychology

Every business has something called a "corporate brain." This is like the mind of the company, made up of all the people who work there. It decides how the company acts and reacts to different situations. Think of it as the neural network that dictates the rhythm of operations and responses to challenges, encapsulating a fusion of organizational culture, shared values, operational norms, and employee interactions.

Now picture the corporate brain as a bustling marketplace of ideas, fueled by collective decision-making, shared values and norms, hierarchical structures, organizational goals, and adaptation to change.

Unlike the individual silos of other job settings, the corporate brain thrives as a vibrant ecosystem—a network of diverse individuals uniting under common goals. While individual roles possess their unique cognitive processes, the corporate brain emerges from the collective musings, behaviors, and interplay of the workforce.

Imagine the corporate brain as the central hub where all the ideas, decisions, and actions of the company come together. It's like the engine that drives the business forward, guiding its direction and responses to various challenges and opportunities.

Within this corporate brain, there's a dynamic interplay of various elements:

- **Collective Decision-Making:** Instead of decisions being made by one person, they're often the result of input from multiple people across different levels and departments of the company. This collective decision-making process ensures that diverse perspectives are considered, leading to more well-rounded outcomes. For example, when launching a new product, the marketing, design, and finance teams might all be involved in the decision-making process to ensure that the product meets customer needs, is financially viable, and is marketable. This collective approach encourages diverse perspectives, leading to more well-rounded and effective decisions. By involving different departments, the organization benefits from a broader range of expertise and reduces the likelihood of overlooking critical factors.

- **Shared Values and Norms:** Every business has its own set of values and norms that guide how employees behave and interact with each other. These shared values create a sense of unity and purpose within the organization, fostering a cohesive corporate culture. For instance, a company might prioritize innovation, customer satisfaction, and teamwork, which would shape how employees approach their work. These shared values not only help maintain a positive corporate culture but also create a sense of unity and purpose. In companies that emphasize collaboration, such as Google, employees are encouraged to share ideas openly, fostering an environment of mutual respect and creativity, ultimately driving success.

- **Hierarchical Structures:** While the corporate brain thrives on collaboration and teamwork, it also operates within a hierarchical structure. This structure defines the chain of command and decision-making authority within the company, ensuring that tasks are delegated efficiently and responsibilities are clear. For example, in a company with a traditional hierarchy, the CEO sets the overarching vision, while department heads manage the day-to-day operations and allocate tasks to their teams. This hierarchy ensures that tasks are delegated efficiently and that employees understand their roles and responsibilities. A clear structure prevents confusion and helps in the smooth execution of company operations, as seen in organizations like Apple, where the leadership clearly defines roles from the executive team down to department heads.

- **Organizational Goals:** At the heart of the corporate brain are the company's overarching goals and objectives. These goals provide a sense of direction and purpose, guiding the actions of employees and aligning their efforts towards achieving common targets. For example, if a company's primary goal is to increase market share in a competitive industry, every department—from R&D to sales—will align their strategies to support this objective. These goals provide employees with a sense of direction and a framework within which they can make decisions. Companies like Tesla, for instance, have ambitious goals like accelerating the world's transition to sustainable energy, guiding all teams to innovate and execute with this overarching purpose in mind.

- **Adaptation to Change:** The corporate brain is not static; it's constantly evolving and adapting to changes in the business environment. Whether it's technological advancements, market trends, or shifts in consumer preferences, the corporate brain must be flexible and agile in responding to these changes. For example, during the rise of e-commerce, traditional brick-and-mortar retail companies had to quickly adapt by developing online platforms and digital sales channels. Another example can be, with the rise of remote work, HR departments have had to quickly adapt by implementing flexible work policies, leveraging technology for virtual communication, and rethinking performance management systems.

Overall, the corporate brain is a dynamic and multifaceted entity that encompasses the collective intelligence, culture, and behavior of the company. By understanding how it operates and leveraging its strengths, businesses can navigate challenges more effectively and drive sustainable growth and success.

4.1 Unlocking the Power of the Corporate Brain: Enhancing Mental Health and Economic Success

Understanding the concept of "The Corporate Brain" provides valuable insights into how organizations function and adapt to various challenges. By connecting this idea to mental health and economics, we can gain a deeper understanding of how organizational dynamics impact employee well-being and financial outcomes, both for individuals and the company as a whole.

Mental Health Implications:

1. **Collective Decision-Making and Employee Well-being:** In a corporate brain, decision-making is often a collective process. This approach, involving input from various departments and levels within the organization, can have a positive impact on mental health. When employees feel their voices are heard, their stress levels may decrease, and job satisfaction improves. In contrast, top-down decision-making can lead to feelings of powerlessness, increasing stress and burnout. By embracing collective decision-making, companies can foster a culture of inclusion, which positively influences mental health by empowering employees.

2. **Shared Values and Norms:** The shared values and norms within a company shape its corporate culture and directly impact employee mental health. A workplace that values collaboration, respect, and transparency can promote psychological safety. Employees in such environments feel comfortable expressing themselves, which reduces anxiety and increases job satisfaction. On the other hand, a toxic culture with unclear values or competitive norms can lead to stress, anxiety, and even depression. Understanding the role of corporate culture in mental health can guide companies to create environments that nurture well-being, which, in turn, leads to higher employee engagement and productivity.

3. **Adaptation to Change and Mental Health:** The corporate brain's ability to adapt to changes is crucial not just for business success, but also for mental health. For example, when companies swiftly adjust to remote work or technological shifts, they can reduce the stress that comes with uncertainty. However, when change is poorly managed or employees are not supported through transitions, mental health issues such as anxiety and burnout can emerge. Providing employees with the tools and support they need during periods of change is key to maintaining mental health in the workplace.

Economic Implications:

1. **Hierarchical Structures and Economic Efficiency:** A clear hierarchical structure helps ensure economic efficiency by defining roles and responsibilities. When employees understand their place within the organization and know what is expected of them, they are more productive, which drives business success.

However, a rigid hierarchy can also create bottlenecks or communication breakdowns. Flexible, well-structured teams that balance hierarchy with autonomy can improve both economic performance and employee morale.

2. **Organizational Goals and Economic Alignment:** The corporate brain's focus on organizational goals ensures that all efforts are aligned toward achieving the company's economic objectives. Whether it's increasing market share or launching a new product, clear goals guide departments and employees, making their actions purposeful and aligned with the company's financial success. When employees see how their work contributes to broader organizational goals, it can lead to higher motivation, better performance, and, ultimately, increased profitability.

3. **Economic Impact of a Healthy Corporate Brain:** A company that invests in maintaining a healthy corporate brain—by fostering collaboration, clear communication, and mental well-being—tends to be more economically successful. For instance, companies that prioritize work-life balance, employee engagement, and mental health resources see lower turnover rates and reduced absenteeism, leading to cost savings and higher productivity. This demonstrates that the well-being of employees is directly linked to a company's financial performance.

Practical Takeaways for Our Audience:

1. **Embrace Collective Decision-Making:** Encourage participation from all levels of the company in decision-making processes. This leads to better decisions, increased employee engagement, and a healthier work environment, which can reduce burnout and stress.

2. **Cultivate a Positive Corporate Culture:** Ensure your company's values and norms align with respect, inclusivity, and transparency. This can reduce workplace anxiety and foster a supportive environment where employees feel valued and motivated.

3. **Support Adaptation to Change:** As businesses face new challenges, such as technological advancements or remote work, offer resources and support systems that help employees navigate these changes. This helps reduce stress and supports long-term mental and financial success.

4. **Invest in Clear Organizational Structures:** Create a structure that balances hierarchy with flexibility, ensuring clarity in roles while fostering collaboration and autonomy. This promotes both efficient operations and employee satisfaction.

5. **Align Organizational Goals with Employee Purpose:** Make sure that employees understand how their individual contributions align with the company's broader economic goals. This creates a sense of purpose and motivates employees to work towards shared success, driving profitability.

By understanding the corporate brain, companies can optimize their organizational structure and culture to benefit both the mental health of employees and the economic success of the company

4.2 Leadership Dynamics: Sculpting the Corporate Mindset and Employee Well-being

Leadership within an organization is akin to the conductor of an orchestra, orchestrating the workplace's tone, tempo, and harmony. Understanding the pivotal role of leadership dynamics in shaping the corporate mindset and employee well-being unveils a critical facet of organizational psychology.

Take, for example, let see **Travis Kalanick,** the co-founder and former CEO of Uber, faced criticism for his aggressive management style and toxic workplace culture. Kalanick's combative leadership approach, coupled with allegations of workplace harassment and discrimination, contributed to a series of scandals that tarnished Uber's reputation and led to his resignation as CEO.

The episode underscores the importance of prioritizing mental health and fostering a positive work environment in corporate leadership.

Different leadership styles have a profound influence on employee mental health. Whether visionary and empathetic or autocratic and laissez-faire, each style leaves a distinct mark on the organizational psyche.

Another example is of **Steve Jobs,** the co-founder and former CEO of Apple Inc., is another notable example of a leader who faced challenges related to mental health. While Jobs was widely admired for his visionary leadership and innovative contributions to technology, he also struggled with mental health issues throughout his life.

Jobs' intense perfectionism, demanding leadership style, and relentless pursuit of excellence often strained his relationships with colleagues and employees. He was known for his volatile temper and uncompromising standards, which could create a high-pressure work environment.

Additionally, Jobs faced personal challenges, including bouts of depression and health issues. His battle with pancreatic cancer, which ultimately led to his passing in 2011, undoubtedly took a toll on his mental and emotional well-being.

While Jobs' leadership style and approach contributed to Apple's success in revolutionizing industries like personal computing, music, and smartphones, his struggles with mental health underscore the complexities of leadership and the importance of addressing mental well-being in high-pressure environments.

When it comes to leadership roles, it's essential that individuals are not only qualified but also accepted by their peers and the corporate brain before they officially step into those positions. Ideally, a candidate should already be demonstrating the behaviors and competencies required for the role within the organization. Alternatively, they should have experience in a similar leadership position at another company before being integrated into a new environment.

To ensure a smooth transition and foster acceptance, organizations should implement a behavioral interview or team assessment as a mandatory part of the hiring process. This approach allows current team members to evaluate the candidate's fit within the existing culture and dynamics of the organization.

By prioritizing these practices, companies can cultivate a leadership team that is not only skilled but also well-integrated into the corporate brain. This leads to improved collaboration, reduced friction, and ultimately, a healthier organizational culture where everyone feels empowered to contribute to shared goals. In this way, effective leadership becomes a key driver of both employee satisfaction and organizational success

Overall, Steve Jobs serves as a compelling example of a leader who achieved remarkable success despite grappling with mental health challenges, highlighting the need for organizations to support and prioritize the well-being of their leaders.

Empathetic and supportive leadership fosters environments where employees feel heard, valued, and understood, promoting robust mental health and well-being.

In fact, many leaders like **Satya Nadella**, the CEO of Microsoft, has been a vocal advocate for mental health awareness and support. Under his leadership, Microsoft has implemented various programs aimed at promoting employee well-being, including mental health resources, counseling services, and flexible work arrangements. Nadella has openly discussed his own experiences with empathy and vulnerability, helping to reduce stigma surrounding mental health in the workplace.

So, I always say that any kind of Leadership also role always includes and establishes the groundwork for trust and psychological safety within teams. When leaders foster open communication, encourage risk-taking, and embrace failure as opportunities for growth, they create safe spaces for employees to express themselves, leading to heightened mental health and creativity in problem-solving.

Now let's look at leadership not in corporate level but at country level looking at the 37th President of the United States, Richard Nixon, faced immense stress and pressure during the Watergate scandal. The relentless scrutiny and mounting legal troubles took a toll on his mental health, leading to anxiety and paranoia. Eventually, Nixon resigned from office in 1974, becoming the only U.S. president to do so, largely due to the mental strain of the scandal.

During times of change and adversity, effective leadership is paramount. Leaders play a vital role in reassuring employees, providing clarity, and offering support amidst upheavals such as mergers or industry shifts. Their guidance significantly impacts employee resilience and adaptability

Leadership is not just a title but a mantle of responsibility entwined with the mental health of an organization. Effective leaders shape cultures, inspire teams, and create environments where employees flourish. Recognizing and nurturing these leadership dynamics is not only imperative but transformative for building mentally healthy workplaces.

A critical yet often overlooked aspect of leadership is the transition from a functional role to leadership positions. A person who excels in product development or engineering possesses specialized skills that contribute to creating high-quality products or innovative solutions. However, when such individuals are promoted to positions like Head of Engineering or Head of Product, they face an entirely different set of challenges that require distinct leadership skills. Unfortunately, many companies lack structured programs to develop these essential leadership capabilities. Promotions are frequently based on loyalty or personal relationships rather than on demonstrated leadership potential. This gap can lead to significant issues within teams, as technically skilled individuals may struggle with people management, conflict resolution, and strategic decision-making—skills that are crucial for effective leadership.

Understanding the impact of leadership on mental health should be a central agenda item for any leadership discussion. After all, all leadership is about people management, and people management is deeply connected with mental health. Thus, prioritizing the psychological well-being of employees becomes fundamental to effective leadership and organizational success.

Different leadership styles profoundly influence the corporate brain's functionality by shaping decision-making processes, organizational culture, employee engagement, and adaptability to change. Effective leadership that encourages collaboration (democratic), inspires innovation (transformational), or prioritizes employee well-being (servant) tends to create a healthier corporate brain that drives organizational success. Conversely, autocratic or laissez-faire styles may lead to disengagement or fragmentation within the corporate brain.

Here's a detailed examination of how various leadership styles impact the corporate brain:

1. Autocratic Leadership

Characteristics: In this style, leaders make decisions unilaterally, with little input from team members.

Effects on Corporate Brain:

- **Decision-Making**: This approach can stifle collective decision-making, as employees may feel their opinions are undervalued. This can lead to a lack of engagement and creativity.

- **Culture**: An autocratic environment often fosters a culture of fear rather than collaboration, which can diminish psychological safety and increase stress levels among employees.

- **Example**: Companies led by autocratic leaders may struggle with innovation since employees might hesitate to share ideas or take risks.

2. Democratic Leadership

Characteristics: Democratic leaders encourage participation and input from team members in the decision-making process.

Effects on Corporate Brain:

- **Collective Decision-Making**: This style enhances collective decision-making, leading to more well-rounded outcomes as diverse perspectives are considered. Employees feel valued and engaged.

- **Culture**: A democratic approach fosters a positive corporate culture characterized by collaboration and mutual respect, which can enhance employee morale and reduce stress.

- **Example**: Organizations like **Google**, which emphasize open communication and collaborative brainstorming sessions, often see higher levels of innovation and employee satisfaction.

3. Transformational Leadership

Characteristics: Transformational leaders inspire and motivate employees to exceed their own self-interests for the sake of the organization.

Effects on Corporate Brain:

- **Vision and Goals**: This style helps align individual goals with organizational objectives, fostering a sense of purpose among employees. When leaders articulate a compelling vision, it energizes the workforce.

- **Adaptation to Change**: Transformational leaders are typically adept at guiding organizations through change, encouraging adaptability and resilience within the corporate brain.

- **Example**: Leaders like **Satya Nadella** at Microsoft have transformed company culture by promoting innovation and inclusivity, leading to improved employee engagement and performance.

4. Laissez-Faire Leadership

Characteristics: Laissez-faire leaders provide minimal direction and allow employees considerable autonomy in how they work.

Effects on Corporate Brain:

- **Employee Empowerment**: While this style can empower skilled employees to take ownership of their work, it may also lead to confusion if roles and expectations are not clearly defined.

- **Culture of Independence vs. Isolation**: A lack of guidance can create a fragmented corporate brain where teams work in silos rather than collaboratively, potentially hindering overall organizational effectiveness.

- **Example**: In creative industries where independence is valued, such as design firms, laissez-faire leadership can foster innovation; however, it may also lead to misalignment with organizational goals if not managed properly.

5. Servant Leadership

Characteristics: Servant leaders prioritize the needs of their team members and focus on their development and well-being.

Effects on Corporate Brain:

- **Employee Well-Being**: This style promotes a culture of support and care, enhancing psychological safety and reducing workplace anxiety. Employees feel valued as individuals, which boosts morale.

- **Collective Success**: By fostering an environment where employees can thrive, servant leadership enhances collaboration and commitment to shared goals within the corporate brain.

- **Example**: Companies like **Starbucks**, which emphasize employee development and community engagement through servant leadership principles, often see high levels of employee satisfaction and loyalty.

Understanding these dynamics allows organizations to adopt leadership practices that enhance their corporate brain's effectiveness while promoting mental health economics—ultimately leading to improved productivity, employee retention, and financial performance.

4.3 Cultivating a Culture of Communication: Foundations for Psychological Wellness

Communication, the lifeblood of organizational interactions, holds the key to unlocking mental wellness within workplaces. Cultivating a culture of effective and empathetic communication forms the bedrock upon which psychological wellness thrives.

Open, transparent communication breeds trust among employees and their leaders. When communication channels are clear, honest, and receptive, it establishes a foundation of trust crucial for psychological safety, enabling individuals to express concerns, share ideas, and seek support without fear of judgment or reprisal.

For instance, consider the case of Buffer, a company known for its transparent communication practices. Buffer openly shares financial information, employee salaries, and even the minutes of their executive meetings with all employees. This transparency fosters trust and psychological safety, contributing to a positive work environment and strong employee engagement.

Effective communication acts as a salve for conflicts and stress. When communication lines are robust, misunderstandings diminish, and conflicts are addressed promptly. This proactive approach reduces workplace stress, enhancing mental well-being and promoting a harmonious work environment.

Conversely, the lack of effective communication can lead to detrimental outcomes. Take the example of Volkswagen's emissions scandal, where poor internal communication and lack of transparency led to a major crisis. The company's failure to communicate honestly about the issue eroded trust among employees and the public, resulting in severe damage to its reputation and financial losses.

A culture of communication empowers employees to have a voice. When individuals feel heard, acknowledged, and valued for their contributions, it elevates their sense of belonging and self-worth. This empowerment significantly impacts mental health, fostering a sense of purpose and commitment.

One positive example is Starbucks' **"My Starbucks Idea"** platform, which allows employees to submit suggestions for improving the company. This initiative not only encourages open communication but also empowers employees to contribute to the company's growth and success, enhancing their sense of fulfilment and well-being.

Communication isn't merely the transmission of words; it's the catalyst for fostering a psychologically healthy workplace. Recognizing its transformative power is imperative for organizations aiming to prioritize mental health.

Here are 10 ways employees, bosses, or company leadership can communicate to reduce mental health issues, along with real-world examples:

- ✓ **Encourage Open Dialogue:** Create an environment where everyone feels comfortable talking about their feelings, thoughts, and concerns without worrying about being judged. For example, companies like Google and Salesforce have implemented "open-door" policies, encouraging employees to speak openly about their mental health.

- ✓ **Active Listening:** When someone is talking to you, give them your full attention. Listen carefully to what they're saying and show that you understand and care about how they feel. An example of active listening in action is demonstrated by the CEO of Starbucks, Howard Schultz, who often engages in listening tours to hear directly from employees about their experiences and concerns.

- ✓ **Regular Check-ins:** Schedule regular meetings between managers and employees to talk about how things are going, what challenges they're facing, and how they're feeling. At Microsoft, managers conduct monthly "stay interviews" to check in with employees and address any issues or concerns they may have.

- ✓ **Provide Resources:** Make sure everyone knows about the support available for mental health, like counseling services, employee assistance programs, and helplines. Companies like Facebook offer mental health resources through their Employee Assistance Program, providing confidential counseling and support to employees.

- ✓ **Normalize Conversations About Mental Health:** Talk openly about mental health in meetings and company communications to help reduce stigma and raise awareness. Bell Canada launched the "Bell Let's Talk" campaign, which encourages open conversations about mental health in the workplace and has sparked similar initiatives in other companies.

- ✔ **Flexibility:** Offer flexible work options, like working from home or flexible hours, so people can manage their work alongside their personal responsibilities and take care of their mental health. Buffer, a fully remote company, gives employees the flexibility to work from anywhere in the world, allowing them to create a work-life balance that suits their needs.

- ✔ **Lead by Example**: Show healthy work habits as a leader by taking breaks, looking after yourself, and setting realistic expectations for work. Arianna Huffington, founder of Thrive Global, advocates for prioritizing self-care and unplugging from work to avoid burnout, leading by example in promoting work-life balance.

- ✔ **Training and Education:** Provide training sessions on mental health awareness, stress management, and resilience-building for everyone in the company. Lloyds Banking Group offers mental health awareness training to all employees, equipping them with the knowledge and skills to support themselves and their colleagues.

- ✔ **Promote Social Connections:** Arrange opportunities for people to socialize and get to know each other, like team-building activities, to help them feel connected and supported. Zappos organizes regular team-building events and social gatherings to foster a sense of community and belonging among employees.

- ✔ **Follow Up and Support:** Check in with people regularly after you've talked about mental health, and offer ongoing support and resources to help them deal with any issues they're facing. At Apple, managers follow up with employees after discussions about mental health to ensure they have access to the support they need through the company's Employee Assistance Program.

By implementing both long-term and short-term strategies, HR heads can create a holistic approach to improving the mental health of employees throughout their tenure in the organization. This proactive approach not only supports employees' well-being but also contributes to a positive and productive work environment

And they can encourage and leader to support hem in fostering transparent, open channels of communication, companies pave the way for psychological wellness, creating environments where employees feel respected, supported, and empowered. This recognition of communication's significance serves as a clarion call for organizations to build cultures where communication is not just a tool but a cornerstone for mental health and organizational success.

4.4 Crafting Strategies for a Mentally Flourishing Workplace Environment

Crafting a workplace environment conducive to mental flourishing isn't an abstract goal but an achievable endeavor rooted in strategic planning and proactive measures. These strategies serve as a roadmap for organizations to foster a culture where mental health thrives.

Prioritizing work-life balance initiatives is paramount for mental well-being. Encouraging flexible schedules, offering remote work options, and promoting breaks rejuvenates employees, reducing burnout and enhancing overall mental wellness. For instance, companies like Google and Microsoft have implemented policies that allow employees to set their own schedules and work from home, contributing to improved work-life balance and employee satisfaction.

Raising awareness through educational programs and workshops destigmatizes mental health discussions. When employees are equipped with knowledge and resources to address mental health concerns, it fosters a supportive atmosphere for seeking help and support. For example, Deloitte offers mental health training sessions and resources to its employees, empowering them to prioritize their well-being and seek assistance when needed.

Offering accessible mental health resources and counseling services communicates a genuine commitment to employee well-being. Access to confidential counseling sessions or mental health hotlines provides avenues for seeking professional help when needed. Companies like Facebook and Salesforce provide comprehensive mental health support, including counseling services and employee assistance programs, to ensure their employees have access to the resources they need to maintain their mental wellness.

Creating a culture of feedback and recognition strengthens employee morale. Regular feedback sessions and acknowledging achievements cultivate a positive atmosphere, enhancing self-worth and mental resilience. Companies like Amazon and Apple prioritize feedback and recognition as part of their performance management processes, fostering a culture of appreciation and support among their employees.

Equipping managers and leaders with training in mental health awareness and empathetic leadership fosters environments where supportive and understanding leadership thrives. Leaders who prioritize mental health set the tone for a psychologically healthy workplace. For example, IBM offers leadership training programs that include modules on mental health awareness and empathetic communication, empowering its managers to support their teams' mental well-being effectively.

Crafting a mentally flourishing workplace necessitates deliberate actions and thoughtful strategies. These interventions, when implemented cohesively, lay the foundation for a workplace culture where mental health isn't just acknowledged but actively nurtured. By prioritizing work-life balance, implementing mental health awareness programs, providing supportive resources and counseling, encouraging regular feedback and recognition, and prioritizing training for managers and leaders, organizations can create environments where employees thrive both personally and professionally.

Establishing comprehensive mental health policies is crucial for addressing employee well-being throughout their tenure in the organization. These policies should cover recruitment, onboarding, training, career development, and offboarding processes, ensuring that mental wellness is prioritized at every stage of the employee lifecycle. Here are some of the long and short term strategies

Some of the Long-term strategies are:

- ✓ **Integrated Mental Health Policies:** Develop comprehensive mental health policies that encompass recruitment, onboarding, training, career development, and offboarding processes. These policies should prioritize mental well-being at every stage of the employee lifecycle.

- ✓ **Stress Management Workshops:** Conduct regular stress management workshops to equip employees with coping mechanisms and resilience-building skills. These workshops can help employees navigate work-related stressors effectively.

- ✔ **Employee Assistance Programs (EAPs):** Implement long-term EAPs that provide confidential counseling, therapy sessions, and mental health resources to employees. EAPs should be easily accessible and well-publicized within the organization.

- ✔ **Leadership Training:** Provide ongoing leadership training for managers and supervisors to cultivate empathetic leadership skills and create psychologically safe work environments. Training should focus on effective communication, conflict resolution, and recognizing signs of mental distress in team members.

- ✔ **Career Development Opportunities:** Offer career development opportunities that prioritize employee growth and well-being. This could include mentorship programs, skills training, and career counseling to help employees progress in their careers while maintaining mental wellness.

Some of the Short-term strategies that can looked upon depending on the company culture;

- ✔ **Mental Health Screenings:** Conduct mental health screenings during the recruitment process to identify any potential issues early on. This can help ensure that candidates are adequately supported from the outset.

- ✔ **Flexible Work Arrangements:** Implement short-term flexible work arrangements, such as remote work options or flexible hours, to accommodate employees' individual needs. This can help alleviate immediate stressors and improve work-life balance.

- ✔ **Wellness Initiatives:** Launch short-term wellness initiatives, such as mindfulness sessions, yoga classes, or meditation workshops, to provide employees with immediate relief from stress and anxiety.

- ✔ **Peer Support Groups:** Facilitate short-term peer support groups where employees can connect with others facing similar challenges. Peer support can provide validation, empathy, and practical advice for coping with mental health issues.

- ✔ **Regular Check-ins:** Schedule short-term check-in meetings between managers and employees to discuss workload, stressors, and overall well-being. These check-ins can help managers identify any immediate concerns and provide support where needed.

By implementing both long-term and short-term strategies, HR heads can create a holistic approach to improving the mental health of employees throughout their tenure in the organization. This proactive approach not only supports employees' well-being but also contributes to a positive and productive work environment.

However, the ultimate question is what can a Leader or a CEO do to see immediate result? Here are several actionable suggestions from a leader's perspective to enhance mental health and reduce stress in the workplace, focusing on initiatives that can be implemented without overwhelming leadership responsibilities:

1. **Mental Health Resource Shelf**

   o   Create a dedicated shelf in the office with books on mental health and well-being for employees to borrow and read.

2. **Recorded Mental Health Training**

   o   Develop and provide access to recorded training sessions on mental health awareness and stress management that employees can watch at their convenience.

3. **Work-Life Balance Workshops**

   o   Organize workshops focused on work-life balance strategies, offering practical tips and tools for employees to manage their time effectively.

4. **Celebration Events**

   o   Host regular events to celebrate achievements, milestones, and mental health awareness days, fostering a positive workplace culture.

5. **"Best Place to Work" Criteria**

   o   Establish criteria for internal awards recognizing departments or teams that excel in promoting a healthy work environment.

6. **24/7 Helpline**

   o   Provide a confidential 24/7 helpline for employees to access support for mental health issues whenever they need it.

7. **On-Site Psychologist**
   - Consider having a psychologist available on-site or through telehealth services to provide counseling and support for employees.

8. **New Manager Training**
   - Implement training programs for new managers focused on recognizing signs of stress in their teams and effective communication strategies.

9. **360-Degree Reviews for Middle Management**
   - Conduct regular 360-degree feedback reviews for middle management to assess their impact on employee well-being and identify areas for improvement.

10. **Mental Health Goals in Annual Reports**
    - Include specific mental health goals in the company's annual report, such as reducing employee stress levels by a certain percentage or increasing participation in wellness programs.

11. **Conduct Mental Health Audits**
    - Regularly assess the workplace environment through mental health audits to identify potential stressors and areas needing improvement.

12. **Limit After-Hours Work**
    - Implement policies that restrict work-related communications outside of office hours to encourage employees to disconnect and recharge.

13. **Overtime Compensation**
    - Ensure fair compensation for overtime work, which can help alleviate stress related to workload and financial pressures.

14. **Mindfulness and Relaxation Spaces**
    - Create designated quiet areas or relaxation rooms where employees can take breaks, practice mindfulness, or engage in stress-relief activities.

15. **Encourage Peer Support Networks**

   o   Facilitate the formation of peer support groups where employees can share experiences and coping strategies related to stress and mental health challenges.

List of suggestion is endless but real value lies in implementation of all these ideas and allocation a budget or time around it or by identifying a stakeholder whose hard or soft KRAs (key responsibility) can be to manage mental health index or create a process around it.

4.5   The Impact of Leadership Bias on the Corporate Brain: Shaping Decision-Making and Innovation

Have you ever considered how your biases might shape the decisions you make as a leader? This is an important question, especially since leadership bias can significantly impact your organization's effectiveness and culture. Leadership bias plays a significant role in shaping the corporate brain, which is the collective mindset and decision-making framework of an organization. When leaders allow their biases—whether conscious or unconscious—to influence their decisions, it can lead to distorted perceptions and flawed judgments that ripple throughout the corporate brain.

For instance, biases such as confirmation bias can cause leaders to favor information that aligns with their existing beliefs while ignoring contradictory evidence. This selective attention can result in poor strategic choices that do not reflect the true needs or potential of the organization.

Leadership bias can have a profound impact on a leader's mental health, creating a cycle of stress and anxiety that is difficult to break. When leaders allow their biases to influence their decisions, they may experience guilt and inadequacy, especially if they recognize that their favoritism is harming team morale and productivity. This internal conflict can lead to heightened stress levels and feelings of isolation, as leaders grapple with the repercussions of their biased actions.

Additionally, the pressure to project confidence and competence can exacerbate mental health issues; when biases result in poor decision-making or a lack of trust within the team, leaders may feel they are failing in their roles, further deteriorating their well-being.

The fear of losing power or control can also drive leaders to cling to outdated practices or resist necessary changes, leading to increased frustration and burnout. Ultimately, unchecked leadership biases not only create an unhealthy work environment for employees but also take a toll on leaders themselves. By actively recognizing and addressing these biases, leaders can alleviate some of the mental strain associated with their roles and foster a healthier workplace culture that benefits everyone involved.

Let us, now explore the effects of leadership bias, how leaders can recognize and mitigate it, and the challenges leaders face in letting go of control to allow others to thrive.

The Impact of Leadership Bias

Leadership bias can have profound consequences for an organization:

- **Reduced Employee Morale:** When team members perceive favoritism or bias in decision-making, it can lead to disengagement and lower motivation. Employees may feel undervalued, which can decrease productivity and increase turnover rates.

- **Limited Diversity and Innovation:** Biases can hinder efforts to hire and promote diverse talent. When leaders favor individuals who mirror their own backgrounds or ideas, they miss out on a wealth of perspectives that drive innovation and creativity.

- **Poor Decision-Making:** Leadership biases can lead to decisions that do not reflect the best interests of the organization or its employees. For instance, a leader might prioritize personal connections over qualifications when selecting team members, resulting in less effective teams.

How Leaders Can Recognize and Mitigate Bias

Leaders can take immediate steps to recognize and mitigate their biases, such as seeking feedback from team members, participating in unconscious bias training, and implementing structured decision-making processes that prioritize diverse input. However, leaders often face the challenge of relinquishing control and allowing others to take the lead.

Many leaders may unconsciously choose to promote individuals who align with their vision or who they perceive as "safe" choices—often their "chosen ones"—rather than selecting the most qualified candidates for critical roles. This reluctance to let go of power not only perpetuates bias but also prevents the corporate brain from evolving and benefiting from fresh ideas and talents.

So, how can you start addressing your biases right now? Here are some practical steps:

1. Conduct a Self-Assessment

Reflect on your decision-making patterns. Ask yourself:

- Do I tend to favor certain types of employees?
- Am I making assumptions based on stereotypes?

Example: If you notice that you often promote individuals who share your background based on language or religion or gender, commit to actively seeking out diverse perspectives in future promotions.

2. Seek Feedback from Your Team

Create a culture where team members feel comfortable sharing their thoughts on your leadership style. Encourage honest feedback about any perceived biases.

Example: Implement anonymous surveys that ask team members how they feel about fairness in decision-making processes. Use this feedback to identify areas for improvement.

3. Participate in Unconscious Bias Training

Engage in training focused on unconscious bias to help identify your biases and understand their impact on your leadership.

Example: Attend workshops that include activities designed to reveal common biases, such as group discussions that challenge stereotypes.

4. Implement Structured Decision-Making Processes

Establish clear criteria for hiring, promotions, and evaluations to minimize subjectivity.

Example: Use standardized interview questions for all candidates rather than relying solely on gut feelings. This ensures every candidate is evaluated fairly.

5. Encourage Diverse Perspectives in Meetings

Make it a priority to invite input from all team members, especially those who may not typically speak up.

Example: At the start of each meeting, remind everyone that all opinions are valued and encourage quieter team members to share their thoughts first.

The Challenge of Letting Go

One significant challenge leaders face is the reluctance to relinquish control over ideas and decisions. Many leaders fear that by allowing others to take the lead or contribute equally, they might lose their power or influence within the organization. This fear can result in leaders favoring those who align with their vision—often their "chosen ones"—over more qualified candidates who could bring fresh perspectives and innovative solutions.

This tendency not only stifles creativity but also perpetuates a culture where only a select few feel empowered to contribute meaningfully. Leaders must recognize that true strength lies in empowering others and allowing diverse ideas to flourish beyond their own vision.

Recognizing and overcoming leadership bias is essential for fostering an inclusive environment where every employee feels valued. By taking immediate actions—like conducting self-assessments, seeking feedback, participating in training, implementing structured processes, and encouraging diverse input—you can begin to mitigate the effects of bias in your leadership style.

As we work together toward creating a thriving organizational culture, let's commit ourselves to recognizing our biases and ensuring that our decisions reflect the diverse perspectives within our teams. By embracing inclusivity and empowering others, we enhance not only our effectiveness as leaders but also the overall health of our organizations. Thank you for joining me in this important conversation!

Chapter 5

The Corporate Conscience: Confronting Vices, Cultivating Virtues

Have you ever felt torn between wanting to achieve your goals independently and collaborating with others to achieve a common objective? Or perhaps you've grappled with the dilemma of pursuing personal gain versus considering the welfare of those around you? In the fast-paced and competitive world of business, these internal conflicts often manifest themselves as battles between our desires for individual success and our obligations to the greater good.

Consider, for instance, the challenge of balancing pride in one's accomplishments with the humility to acknowledge the contributions of others. In a corporate setting, this struggle can play out in team dynamics, where individual recognition competes with the collective effort required to achieve organizational goals.

Similarly, the tension between greed, driven by the pursuit of wealth and material gain, and charity, rooted in compassion and generosity, shapes decisions regarding resource allocation, corporate social responsibility, and ethical conduct. Businesses must grapple with these competing priorities, weighing financial interests against social and environmental concerns.

These conflicts extend beyond individual behavior to influence organizational culture and industry practices. For example, the clash between wrath, characterized by impatience and impulsiveness, and patience, marked by calmness and restraint, can impact decision-making processes, employee relations, and customer interactions.

In exploring these battles between virtues and vices, we aim to shed light on their profound impact on the corporate landscape. By understanding the motivations behind our actions and the consequences of our choices, we can cultivate a more ethical and sustainable approach to business leadership and decision-making:

5.1 Battle of Pride Vs Humility

Pride is an inflated sense of one's own importance, leading to an unwillingness to acknowledge shortcomings or accept help. Pride is an exaggerated sense of self-worth or importance, often leading to arrogance and a disregard for others. Pride stems from a desire to feel superior or validated, often fueled by insecurity or a need for recognition.

For instance, a manager might refuse constructive feedback from subordinates due to an excessive belief in their own capabilities.

"Pride is the mother of arrogance." - Toba Beta

However, at the crux of it pride is just another a complex emotion that serves various psychological and social functions, often rooted in individual and societal dynamics. Here are some reasons why people experience pride:

- **Self-Identity:** Pride can stem from a sense of self-identity and self-worth. When individuals achieve success or accomplishments aligned with their values and goals, they may experience pride as a positive affirmation of their abilities and efforts.

- **Validation:** Pride can serve as a form of validation or recognition from others. When individuals receive praise, admiration, or approval from peers, family, or society for their achievements or attributes, they may feel a sense of pride in their accomplishments.

- **Competitive Instincts:** In competitive environments, such as sports, academia, or the workplace, pride can arise from a desire to outperform others and assert one's superiority or competence. Competitive instincts drive individuals to strive for excellence and take pride in their achievements relative to others.

- **Social Comparison**: People often engage in social comparison, evaluating themselves against others to assess their status, abilities, or accomplishments. When individuals perceive themselves as superior or more successful than others in certain aspects, they may experience pride as a result of favorable comparisons.

- **Group Identity:** Pride can also be associated with group identity and affiliation. When individuals belong to a particular community, organization, or cultural group, they may take pride in shared values, traditions, or achievements that contribute to a sense of belonging and identity.

- **Defense Mechanism**: In some cases, pride may serve as a defense mechanism to protect individuals from feelings of inadequacy, vulnerability, or insecurity. By emphasizing their strengths, achievements, or social status, people may bolster their self-esteem and shield themselves from negative self-perceptions or external criticisms.

- **Cultural Influences:** Cultural norms and expectations play a significant role in shaping individuals' experiences and expressions of pride. In cultures that value individualism, autonomy, and success, pride may be encouraged as a marker of personal achievement and social status.

- **Evolutionary Perspective:** From an evolutionary perspective, pride may have adaptive functions related to social status, mate selection, and group cohesion. Demonstrating competence, success, or leadership can enhance individuals' reproductive fitness and social standing within their communities.

While pride can be a positive and motivating force, it can also lead to negative consequences when it becomes excessive or arrogant.

During interviews, questions such as *"Can you tell me about a project where you faced criticism or feedback from colleagues or supervisors? How did you handle it?"* Look for signs of defensiveness or an unwillingness to acknowledge areas for improvement. Candidates who consistently attribute success solely to their own efforts without recognizing the contributions of others may also display excessive pride.

Balancing pride with humility, empathy, and ethical considerations is essential for maintaining healthy relationships and personal well-being. To achieve this balance, here are some control strategies:

- **Practice humility:** Acknowledge one's limitations and recognize the contributions of others. This fosters a sense of humility and prevents arrogance from overshadowing interactions.

- **Cultivate gratitude:** Focus on the collective achievements of the team rather than solely individual successes. Expressing gratitude fosters a sense of appreciation and unity among team members.

- **Seek feedback and constructive criticism**: Actively listen to feedback from others to maintain a realistic self-image. Embrace opportunities for growth and improvement rather than viewing feedback as a threat to one's ego.

- **Foster empathy:** Consider others' perspectives and experiences, fostering understanding and compassion in interactions. Empathy strengthens connections with others and promotes mutual respect.

- **Embrace vulnerability as a strength:** Rather than seeing vulnerability as a weakness, view it as an opportunity for growth and connection with others. Embracing vulnerability fosters authenticity and trust in relationships.

- **Surround yourself with diverse perspectives:** Engage with individuals from diverse backgrounds and viewpoints to broaden your understanding and stay grounded. Exposure to diverse perspectives enhances creativity and innovation.

- **Practice mindfulness:** Stay present in the moment and avoid getting lost in ego-driven thoughts. Mindfulness cultivates self-awareness and helps in managing reactions to challenging situations.

In addition to individual efforts, it's important to manage the broader context by fostering a culture of collaboration and teamwork. Creating an environment where collaboration is valued and teamwork is encouraged promotes mutual support and shared success. By managing both individual behaviors and the organizational culture, a balance between pride and humility can be achieved, leading to healthier relationships and greater personal well-being.

Humility as a Counter to Pride: Humility encourages individuals to recognize their limitations, acknowledge the contributions of others, and approach life with modesty and openness. By cultivating humility, individuals can overcome the arrogance and self-centeredness associated with pride, fostering a sense of interconnectedness and mutual respect.

Humility is the quality of being modest and respectful, acknowledging one's limitations and recognizing the value of others.

Example: A CEO who actively seeks input from all levels of the organization and attributes the company's success to the collective efforts of the team rather than personal achievements.

> *"Humility is not thinking less of yourself, it's thinking of yourself less."*
> - C.S. Lewis (Author)

Balancing pride with humility, empathy, and ethical considerations is vital for nurturing healthy relationships and personal well-being. This equilibrium can be achieved through a series of control strategies that not only shape individual behavior but also cultivate a supportive organizational culture.

Firstly, **practicing humility** is key. By acknowledging one's limitations and recognizing the contributions of others, individuals can foster a sense of humility that prevents arrogance from overshadowing interactions. This humility is complemented by the cultivation of gratitude, where the focus shifts from individual achievements to the collective successes of the team. Expressing appreciation fosters unity and reinforces the importance of collaboration.

Seeking feedback and constructive criticism is another essential aspect of maintaining this balance. Actively listening to feedback allows individuals to maintain a realistic self-image and embrace opportunities for growth. Moreover, fostering empathy by considering others' perspectives and experiences strengthens connections and promotes mutual respect within relationships.

Embracing vulnerability as a strength is a transformative mindset shift. Rather than viewing vulnerability as a weakness, it is seen as an opportunity for growth and authentic connection with others. This authenticity nurtures trust and strengthens interpersonal bonds.

So to stay grounded amidst the complexities of interpersonal dynamics, surrounding oneself with diverse perspectives is invaluable. Engaging with individuals from various backgrounds broadens understanding and fosters creativity and innovation. Additionally, practicing mindfulness cultivates self-awareness and helps manage reactions to challenging situations, ensuring that ego-driven thoughts do not cloud judgment.

At the heart of effective leadership and collaboration lies humility—the recognition of one's limitations and the value of others. In interviews, candidates who acknowledge their mistakes, celebrate team achievements, and display a modest demeanor exemplify this virtue. By fostering humility, organizations encourage a culture of openness, learning, and mutual respect.

During interviews, questions such as ***"Can you share a time when you acknowledged your mistakes or sought feedback from others to improve?"*** can provide insights into a candidate's humility. Positive indicators include a willingness to admit shortcomings, humility in recognizing the contributions of others, and a modest demeanor. This approach not only helps in selecting candidates who align with the organization's values but also contributes to building a culture of humility and mutual respect.

So, in conclusion, achieving a balance between pride and humility is essential for fostering healthy relationships, driving personal growth, and promoting success within organizations. By practicing humility, individuals can acknowledge their limitations, recognize the contributions of others, and cultivate a mindset of continuous learning and improvement. This humility not only strengthens interpersonal connections but also fosters a culture of openness, collaboration, and mutual respect within teams and organizations.

Ratan Tata: Humility and Resilience in the Face of Criticism

A compelling story that showcases how Ratan Tata overcame pride with humility involves his interactions with Ford Motor Company during the late 1990s and early 2000s. In 1999, Tata Motors was struggling with the launch of its first passenger car, the Tata Indica. Despite the ambitious vision behind the vehicle, sales were disappointing, leading Tata to consider selling the company. During a meeting with Ford executives, Ratan Tata and his team faced humiliation when Bill Ford arrogantly told them, "You do not know anything; why did you start the passenger car division at all? We are doing you a big favor by buying your car division."

Rather than responding with anger or pride, Tata chose humility. He left the meeting feeling dejected but resolute. Instead of giving in to defeat, he committed himself to improving Tata Motors and the Indica. This determination paid off; over time, the Indica became a popular choice among Indian families and a staple in the taxi industry.

Fast forward to 2008, when Ford found itself in financial trouble during the global recession and needed to sell its luxury brands, Jaguar and Land Rover (JLR). Ratan Tata saw an opportunity and made a bold move by acquiring JLR for $2.3 billion. At this point, Bill Ford acknowledged Tata's role in saving Ford from further losses, saying, "You are doing us a big favor by buying JLR."

This story is a powerful testament to how Ratan Tata's humility allowed him to rise above pride and criticism. Instead of seeking revenge or harboring resentment after being belittled by Ford, he focused on hard work and perseverance. His actions ultimately turned a moment of humiliation into one of triumph, demonstrating that true strength lies in humility and resilience.

5.2 Battle of Greed Vs Charity

Greed: The insatiable desire for more, often at the expense of others. This could manifest as manipulating financial data to boost personal wealth, disregarding the well-being of stakeholders.

Greed is an insatiable desire for material wealth or possessions, often leading to selfishness and exploitation. Greed arises from a fear of scarcity or a belief that one's worth is tied to external possessions or status symbols.

Greed, like many human emotions, has roots in psychology, biology, and societal influences. Here are several reasons why people may experience greed:

- **Evolutionary Legacy:** From an evolutionary perspective, the drive for acquiring resources, such as food, shelter, and mates, was essential for survival and reproductive success. Greed may be a modern manifestation of this primal instinct, where individuals seek to accumulate wealth and resources to ensure their well-being and that of their offspring.

- **Scarcity Mentality:** In environments where resources are limited or perceived to be scarce, people may develop a mindset of scarcity, fearing deprivation or lack. This scarcity mentality can fuel greed as individuals hoard resources to protect themselves against future uncertainties or competition from others.

- **Social Comparison:** People often engage in social comparison, evaluating their status, wealth, and possessions relative to others. In a culture that values material wealth and social status, individuals may experience pressure to acquire more than others to maintain or improve their perceived standing in society.

- **Consumer Culture**: Modern consumer culture, fueled by advertising, media, and societal norms, promotes the idea that happiness and success are linked to material possessions and wealth. This constant bombardment of messages can reinforce greed by encouraging excessive consumption and the pursuit of luxury goods.

- **Psychological Factors**: Greed can also be driven by psychological factors such as insecurity, low self-esteem, or a need for external validation. Acquiring wealth or possessions may serve as a way for individuals to bolster their self-worth or compensate for perceived deficiencies in other areas of their lives.

- **Socialization and Upbringing**: Family upbringing, cultural values, and peer influences play a significant role in shaping individuals' attitudes towards wealth and material possessions. Children who grow up in families or communities that prioritize material success and accumulation may internalize these values and exhibit greedy tendencies in adulthood.

- **Reward Circuitry in the Brain**: Neuroscientific research suggests that the brain's reward circuitry, particularly the mesolimbic dopamine system, plays a role in motivating behaviors associated with seeking rewards, including money and material possessions. Greed may be partly driven by the brain's response to the anticipation and acquisition of these rewards.

- **Economic Systems**: Economic structures and incentives within societies can contribute to the prevalence of greed. In capitalist economies, where profit maximization and competition are central, individuals and corporations may prioritize financial gain over ethical considerations, leading to behaviors driven by greed.

While greed can be a natural human inclination, it can also have negative consequences for individuals and society, such as inequality, exploitation, and environmental degradation. Recognizing the underlying factors contributing to greed and promoting values of moderation, generosity, and social responsibility can help mitigate its harmful effects and foster a more equitable and sustainable world.

"Greed is a bottomless pit which exhausts the person in an endless effort to satisfy the need without ever reaching satisfaction." - Erich Fromm

- Avoid: Focus on creating value rather than accumulating wealth.

- Realize: Understand that true fulfillment comes from meaningful connections and experiences, not material possessions.

- Control: Set ethical boundaries and prioritize the well-being of stakeholders.

Control Strategies:

- Cultivate gratitude by appreciating what you have rather than focusing on what you lack.

- Practice generosity by giving back to others and supporting charitable causes.

- Set clear financial goals and budget responsibly to avoid excessive consumption.

- Foster contentment by finding fulfillment in experiences and relationships rather than material possessions.

- Challenge consumerist culture and prioritize sustainable living practices.

- Develop empathy by considering the needs and well-being of others before your own desires.

- Reflect on the true sources of happiness and fulfillment beyond material wealth.

- Manage: Implement transparency and accountability measures in financial dealings.

Now how to find this greed during an interview?

- Question: "How do you prioritize your work when faced with limited resources or competing demands?"

- Red Flag: Beware of candidates who prioritize personal gain or advancement over the well-being of the team or organization. Signs of greed may include a focus on financial compensation or a lack of concern for ethical considerations in decision-making.

Charity as a Counter to Greed: Charity involves selfless giving, generosity, and compassion towards those in need. By practicing charity, individuals can overcome selfishness and materialism, cultivating a spirit of abundance and sharing that transcends the desire for wealth and possessions associated with greed.

Charity: Charity encompasses selfless love and generosity towards others, both in giving material resources and offering compassion and kindness.

Now how to find this quality during an interview?

Beyond profit margins and market share, true success is measured by the impact we have on others. Candidates who prioritize giving back, volunteer their time, and demonstrate compassion embody the virtue of charity. By embracing charity, organizations cultivate a sense of purpose and social responsibility, driving positive change within and beyond their walls.

Question: "How have you contributed to your community or supported others in need, either personally or professionally?"

Positive Indicator: Candidates who prioritize giving back to others, volunteer their time or resources, and demonstrate compassion and generosity in their actions are likely to embody the virtue of charity

- Example: A company that allocates a percentage of its profits to charitable causes and encourages employees to volunteer their time for community service projects.

  "The simplest acts of kindness are by far more powerful than a thousand heads bowing in prayer." - Mahatma Gandhi (Leader)

- Bringing the Quality: Cultivate empathy and compassion, actively seek opportunities to help those in need, and prioritize the well-being of others.

- Practice: Volunteer for philanthropic initiatives, donate to charitable organizations, and offer support and encouragement to colleagues facing challenges.

- Grow: Expand your understanding of social issues and explore ways to address them, advocate for causes you believe in, and inspire others to join you in acts of kindness.

- Daily Practice: Perform random acts of kindness, practice active listening and empathy in interactions with others, and look for opportunities to make a positive impact in your community.

For those of you who still do not believe in above I'll request to read the story below;

A Victory of Charity Over Greed: Sachin Tendulkar's Ethical Stand

Sachin Tendulkar's unwavering refusal to endorse alcohol and tobacco products throughout his illustrious cricket career is a powerful testament to his commitment to ethical values and social responsibility. In a landscape where many athletes readily accepted lucrative endorsement deals, Tendulkar stood apart by prioritizing integrity over financial gain.

One notable instance occurred during the 1996 Cricket World Cup, where the title sponsor was Wills, a tobacco brand. While many of his teammates displayed the brand's logo on their gear, Tendulkar chose to play without any branding on his bat. This decision underscored his dedication to maintaining a positive image and serving as a role model for millions of young fans who looked up to him.

In 2010, the UB Group approached Tendulkar with an offer of ₹20 crore to endorse their liquor products. Despite the substantial financial incentive, he declined the offer, adhering to the principles instilled in him by his father: "Never accept endorsements for alcohol or cigarettes, no matter what they offer." His choice was widely praised, with Maharashtra's Minister of Social Justice, Shivajirao Moghe, commending Tendulkar for setting a commendable example in society and contributing to de-addiction campaigns.

Even as other cricketers participated in campaigns for alcohol brands during the Indian Premier League (IPL), Tendulkar consistently opted out of advertising that promoted such products. His decisions reflect a profound understanding of his influence as a public figure and the responsibility that comes with it.

Tendulkar's actions resonate deeply with fans and the public alike, reinforcing the notion that true greatness lies not only in athletic achievement but also in moral integrity. By rejecting opportunities that could have compromised his values, he has established himself as a role model who champions charity and social responsibility over greed. His legacy serves as an inspiring reminder that ethical choices can lead to lasting respect and admiration, showcasing a victory of charity over greed in the world of sports.

5.3 Battle of Wrath Vs Patience

Wrath: Intense anger that leads to impulsive or harmful behavior towards colleagues or employees. An example would be a supervisor berating team members publicly for minor mistakes. For example, imagine a supervisor publicly berating team members for minor mistakes; this not only damages morale but also fosters a toxic work environment. Wrath arises from feelings of powerlessness, injustice, or unmet expectations, triggering a primal fight-or-flight response.

Mark Twain insightfully remarked, "Anger is an acid that can do more harm to the vessel in which it is stored than to anything on which it is poured." This highlights the internal damage that unchecked anger can inflict on individuals, often leading to regret and further complications.

The Roots of Wrath

The emotion of wrath can stem from various psychological, social, and biological factors. Here are several reasons why individuals may experience this intense emotion:

- **Threat Response:** Anger is a natural response to perceived threats or injustices. When individuals feel threatened, whether physically, emotionally, or psychologically, their body's stress response system activates, triggering the emotion of anger as a way to prepare for self-defense or confrontation.

- **Violation of Expectations:** Anger can also stem from the violation of expectations or boundaries. When individuals experience disappointment, betrayal, or frustration due to unmet expectations, they may react with anger as a way to express their displeasure and assert their needs or rights.

- **Injustice**: Witnessing or experiencing injustice, discrimination, or unfair treatment can evoke feelings of anger and indignation. When individuals perceive that their or others' rights have been violated, they may respond with anger as a way to challenge or protest against the perceived injustice.

- **Power Dynamics:** Anger can be a response to power imbalances or perceived threats to one's autonomy or control. When individuals feel powerless, marginalized, or oppressed, they may use anger as a means of asserting themselves and reclaiming their sense of agency or dignity.

- **Pain or Hurt:** Anger can mask underlying feelings of pain, hurt, or vulnerability. When individuals experience emotional wounds or rejection, they may suppress feelings of sadness or fear and instead express their distress through anger as a way to protect themselves from further harm.

- **Cultural and Social Norms:** Cultural and social norms shape how anger is expressed and perceived within different societies. In some cultures, expressing anger openly may be acceptable or even encouraged as a way to assert dominance or defend one's honor. In others, anger may be stigmatized or seen as a sign of weakness.

- **Personality Traits:** Individual differences in temperament and personality can influence how people experience and express anger. Some individuals may have a predisposition towards irritability, impulsivity, or hostility, making them more prone to experiencing wrath in response to various triggers.

- **Biological Factors:** Biological factors, such as genetics, brain chemistry, and hormonal fluctuations, play a role in regulating emotions, including anger. Imbalances in neurotransmitters or hormones, such as serotonin or testosterone, can affect individuals' susceptibility to anger and their ability to regulate it effectively.

Strategies for Managing Wrath

To navigate the complexities of wrath effectively, consider implementing the following strategies:

- **Avoid:** Practice empathy and perspective-taking to understand others' viewpoints.

- **Realize:** Acknowledge that underlying insecurities or unmet needs often fuel anger.

- **Control:** Develop healthy coping mechanisms such as mindfulness practices or physical exercise.

Control Strategies:

- Utilize emotional regulation techniques like deep breathing and mindfulness to manage feelings of anger.

- Identify underlying triggers contributing to feelings of wrath and address them proactively.

- Communicate assertively rather than aggressively when addressing conflicts.

- Take a moment before reacting impulsively; this pause allows for reflection and perspective.

- Seek support from trusted friends, mentors, or professionals to process emotions effectively.

- Practice empathy by considering the perspectives and emotions of others involved in conflicts.

- Channel negative emotions into constructive outlets such as exercise or creative expression.

Cultivating Patience as an Antidote

Patience emerges as a powerful counterbalance to wrath—the ability to endure difficulties calmly while maintaining composure in challenging situations is invaluable in both personal and professional contexts. By cultivating patience, individuals can transform their responses to frustration and conflict into opportunities for growth and understanding.

Finding Patience in Interviews: In today's fast-paced business environment, patience enables individuals to navigate challenges with grace and resilience. Candidates who demonstrate composure under pressure exemplify this virtue.

- **Question**: "Describe a situation where you faced delays or obstacles in achieving your goals. How did you handle it?"

- **Positive Indicator**: Look for candidates who remain calm during adversity and display resilience when facing setbacks. For example, a manager who reassures team members during crises showcases patience and leadership.

Joyce Meyer aptly states, *"Patience is not the ability to wait but the ability to keep a good attitude while waiting."* This perspective underscores the importance of maintaining a positive mindset even amidst challenges.

Bringing Patience into Practice

To cultivate patience effectively:

- **Practice Mindfulness**: Engage in mindfulness exercises that enhance emotional resilience.

- **Set Realistic Expectations**: Establish achievable timelines and prioritize tasks effectively.

- **Embrace Growth Opportunities**: Learn from setbacks by developing long-term perspectives and seeking feedback for improvement.

- **Daily Practice**: Take breaks to recharge your mind, practice gratitude for progress made, and remind yourself of the bigger picture during challenging times.

Understanding wrath involves recognizing its roots and consequences while actively working towards managing it constructively through patience and emotional intelligence. By fostering these qualities within ourselves and our organizations, we can create healthier environments conducive to collaboration and growth. The battle between wrath and patience is not just about managing emotions; it's about cultivating resilience that leads to personal development and harmonious relationships in both professional settings and everyday life.

The Power of Patience: How Nelson Mandela Overcame Anger to Become an Ideal Leader

Nelson Mandela's life exemplifies how patience can triumph over anger, leading to personal growth and societal transformation. Imprisoned for 27 years for his fight against apartheid, Mandela faced unimaginable hardships but chose to respond with patience rather than anger. This decision shaped his character and had a lasting impact on South Africa and the world.

Arrested in 1962 and sentenced to life imprisonment in 1964, Mandela endured harsh conditions at Robben Island. Many would have understood if he had reacted with anger towards his captors or the oppressive regime. However, Mandela recognized that allowing anger to consume him would hinder his goal of freedom and equality for his people.

Instead of succumbing to bitterness, Mandela focused on self-improvement during his imprisonment. He read extensively, studied law, and engaged in discussions about politics and philosophy. This commitment to personal growth helped him maintain mental fortitude and prepared him for future leadership. He famously stated, ***"Hating clouds the mind. It gets in the way of strategy. Leaders cannot afford to hate,"*** emphasizing how anger can obstruct effective decision-making.

Mandela's patience paid off when he was released from prison in 1990. Rather than seeking revenge against those who had wronged him, he advocated for reconciliation and forgiveness, playing a crucial role in transitioning South Africa from apartheid to democracy. In 1994, he became the first Black president of South Africa, promoting empathy and understanding to foster peace.

One notable example of Mandela's patience occurred during his presidency when he faced violent conflict between the African National Congress (ANC) and the Inkatha Freedom Party led by Mangosuthu Buthelezi. Instead of demonizing Buthelezi, Mandela welcomed him into his government, demonstrating that patience and dialogue could bridge divides.

Mandela's legacy is a powerful reminder that while anger is a natural response to injustice, it is through patience that individuals can cultivate understanding and achieve lasting change. His famous quote, "I learned that courage was not the absence of fear, but the triumph over it," encapsulates this philosophy.

In contrast, anger often leads to destructive outcomes—impulsive decisions that damage relationships and create long-lasting scars. Mandela's journey teaches us that embracing patience is essential for becoming an ideal person who contributes positively to society. By practicing patience, we can navigate conflicts more effectively and create a more harmonious world.

5.4 Battle of Envy Vs Kindness

Envy is a powerful emotion characterized by feelings of resentment towards others' success, often leading to destructive actions. For instance, a coworker might spread rumors to undermine a peer who received a promotion they desired.

This feeling of envy can arise from a comparison mindset, where individuals believe that others' achievements diminish their own worth or opportunities. Ralph Waldo Emerson aptly stated, ***"Envy is ignorance; imitation is suicide."***

This highlights how envy can cloud judgment and lead to negative outcomes. Envy often stems from various psychological, social, and cultural factors.

Social comparison plays a significant role; individuals assess their own worth relative to others, leading to feelings of inadequacy when they perceive others as more successful or fortunate.

Additionally, the **desire for status or recognition** can fuel envy, as people crave attention and approval from others.

Those with **insecurity and low self-esteem** may be more susceptible to envy, resenting those who appear more confident or accomplished.

Unmet needs or desires also contribute to feelings of envy. When individuals perceive that others possess something they lack—be it material possessions, talents, or opportunities—they may experience discontent.

Furthermore, **cultural and societal norms** shape perceptions of success; in cultures that prioritize material wealth or achievement, individuals may internalize these values and feel envious of those who conform to societal ideals. Competitive environments, such as workplaces or schools, can exacerbate these feelings as individuals vie for limited resources and recognition.

While envy is a common emotion, it can have detrimental effects on well-being and relationships if not managed effectively. Cultivating gratitude, self-awareness, and a sense of self-worth can help mitigate feelings of envy. Fostering empathy and compassion towards others' experiences allows individuals to shift their focus from comparison to connection.

Strategies for Managing Envy

To combat envy effectively, individuals can take several proactive steps. First, it's essential to cultivate self-awareness by recognizing feelings of envy without judgment. Practicing gratitude for one's strengths and accomplishments can also help shift the focus away from comparison. Celebrating the successes of others and using them as inspiration rather than sources of jealousy fosters a supportive environment.

Limiting exposure to social media and other sources that fuel comparison is crucial. Developing a network of friends and mentors who encourage and uplift rather than provoke envy can create a positive atmosphere. Organizations should foster a culture of support and mentorship where kindness prevails over competition.

Identifying Envy in Interviews

In an interview setting, one way to gauge a candidate's relationship with envy is by asking: *"How do you react when a colleague receives recognition or praise for their work, especially if you contributed to the project?"* Look for signs of resentment or jealousy in their response. Candidates who downplay the achievements of others may struggle with envy.

Kindness as a Counter to Envy

Kindness involves showing compassion, empathy, and goodwill towards others regardless of their circumstances or achievements. By practicing kindness, individuals can overcome feelings of resentment and comparison, fostering a sense of generosity towards the happiness and success of others. For example, a manager who cultivates a culture of appreciation in the workplace recognizes each team member's contributions.

Mark Twain famously said, *"Kindness is the language which the deaf can hear and the blind can see."* In organizational culture, kindness binds individuals together in empathy and support. Candidates who demonstrate empathy towards others exemplify this virtue.

Discovering Kindness in Interviews

To find candidates who embody kindness during interviews, ask: "How do you support and uplift your colleagues or team members in the workplace?" Look for responses that indicate empathy and compassion towards others, along with actions that foster a positive environment.

Triumph of Kindness Over Envy: The Inspiring Journey of Mahatma Gandhi

Mahatma Gandhi's life provides an inspiring illustration of how kindness can triumph over envy in the face of adversity. Born in 1869 in India, Gandhi faced significant discrimination during his time in South Africa. Upon arriving there in 1893 as a young lawyer, he was subjected to racial prejudice that included being forcibly removed from a first-class train compartment simply because he was Indian.

Instead of succumbing to anger or allowing envy towards the British colonialists who held power over him to take root, Gandhi chose to respond with compassion and action.

He founded the **Natal Indian Congress** in 1894 to advocate for Indian rights rather than harboring resentment against those who oppressed him.

Gandhi developed the philosophy of **Satyagraha**, emphasizing nonviolent resistance as a means to confront injustice. His commitment to kindness was evident during his leadership in various campaigns against discriminatory laws.

For instance, during the **Salt March** in 1930—a pivotal act of civil disobedience— he invited people from all walks of life to join him in producing salt from seawater as an act of defiance against British rule.

Throughout his life, Gandhi emphasized unity over division and compassion over hatred. Even during times when he faced criticism from various factions within India—especially during communal riots following partition—he advocated for peace between Hindus and Muslims through acts of fasting for harmony.

Mahatma Gandhi's story serves as a powerful reminder that while envy can lead to division and negativity, choosing kindness fosters connection and uplifts those around us. His journey illustrates that embracing kindness not only enhances personal relationships but also contributes positively to social change. Both Gandhi's life lessons and strategies for managing envy emphasize that prioritizing compassion over resentment creates an environment where everyone thrives.

By fostering kindness within ourselves and our communities, we can overcome feelings of inadequacy and build supportive relationships that benefit all.

5.5 Battle of Lust Vs Chastity

Lust: Unrestrained desire, particularly in the context of workplace relationships. This might involve using one's position of authority to coerce or manipulate others into engaging in inappropriate relationships. Lust is an intense desire for physical pleasure or gratification, often leading to objectification and exploitation of others. Lust arises from primal instincts and biological drives, as well as societal influences that prioritize sexual gratification.

"Desire is the kindling of lust." - Lailah Gifty Akita

Lust, a strong desire or craving for sexual gratification, is a complex emotion influenced by various psychological, biological, and social factors. Here are several reasons why people may experience lust:

- **Biological Instincts**: From an evolutionary perspective, sexual desire is a natural and essential aspect of human biology. The drive for reproduction and genetic propagation is hardwired into the brain's reward circuitry, motivating individuals to seek sexual encounters and opportunities for procreation.

- **Hormonal Influences**: Hormones such as testosterone play a significant role in regulating sexual desire and arousal in both men and women. Fluctuations in hormone levels, particularly during puberty, menstrual cycles, and periods of sexual arousal, can intensify feelings of lust and libido.

- **Psychological Factors**: Lust can be influenced by psychological factors such as fantasy, imagination, and arousal templates. People may experience lust in response to erotic stimuli, fantasies, or mental images that trigger sexual desire and arousal.

- **Social and Cultural Norms:** Cultural attitudes, values, and norms surrounding sexuality can shape individuals' experiences and expressions of lust. In societies where sexuality is taboo or stigmatized, people may suppress or repress feelings of lust, while in cultures that embrace sexual openness or freedom, expressions of lust may be more accepted or encouraged.

- **Media and Advertising**: Mass media, advertising, and popular culture often depict sexuality in glamorous or idealized ways, promoting unrealistic standards of beauty, desirability, and sexual performance. Exposure to sexualized imagery and messages in media can influence individuals' perceptions of sexuality and contribute to feelings of lust.

- **Desire for Intimacy and Connection**: Lust is not solely driven by physical attraction but can also stem from a desire for intimacy, connection, and emotional fulfillment. People may experience feelings of lust towards individuals with whom they feel a deep emotional or romantic connection, seeking physical intimacy as a way to bond and strengthen their relationship.

- **Stress and Escapism**: In times of stress, anxiety, or emotional distress, some individuals may turn to sexual activity or fantasies as a form of escapism or stress relief. Engaging in sexual behavior can temporarily alleviate negative emotions and provide a sense of pleasure and distraction from life's challenges.

- **Past Experiences and Conditioning**: Early experiences, upbringing, and past relationships can shape individuals' attitudes and behaviors related to sexuality. Positive or negative experiences with sex, intimacy, or relationships may influence how people experience and express feelings of lust in adulthood.

While lust is a natural and normal aspect of human sexuality, it's essential to recognize and understand its influences and effects on individuals' well-being and relationships. Practicing mindfulness, communication, and ethical conduct in sexual interactions can help ensure that feelings of lust are expressed and experienced in healthy, consensual, and respectful ways.

- Avoid: Establish clear boundaries in professional relationships.

- Realize: Acknowledge the potential consequences of inappropriate behavior on both personal and professional fronts.

- Control: Practice professionalism and refrain from engaging in behavior that could be construed as harassment.

Control Strategies:

- Practice mindfulness and self-awareness to recognize and understand triggers of lustful thoughts or behaviors.

- Cultivate respect and empathy for others as individuals with their own desires, boundaries, and autonomy.

- Develop healthy boundaries in relationships and avoid objectifying others for personal gratification.

- Engage in open and honest communication with partners about desires, boundaries, and consent.

- Redirect energy and focus towards meaningful activities and pursuits that align with personal values and goals.

- Challenge societal norms and media portrayals that objectify or exploit individuals for sexual gratification.

- Manage: Implement and enforce policies that prohibit harassment and discrimination.

- Seek support from therapists or support groups if struggling with compulsive or harmful behaviors related to lust.

The Impact of Lust on Mental Health

The consequences of unmanaged lust can significantly affect an employee's mental health. Prolonged feelings of sexual frustration—stemming from unmet desires—can lead to increased stress and anxiety levels. The persistent longing for physical gratification may erode self-esteem and foster negative self-perceptions. Symptoms such as irritability, difficulty concentrating, and sleep disturbances can arise from unresolved sexual desires.

Moreover, unresolved lust can strain interpersonal relationships both personally and professionally. When individuals engage in inappropriate behaviors or fail to establish healthy boundaries due to their desires, it can lead to conflicts and feelings of disconnection from colleagues or loved ones. This emotional turmoil not only affects individual well-being but also disrupts workplace harmony.

Strategies for Managing Lust

To navigate the complexities of lust effectively and mitigate its impact on mental health, individuals should adopt several proactive strategies:

- ***Practice Self-Discipline and Moderation:*** Establish clear boundaries in relationships to maintain professionalism and respect for oneself and others.

- ***Avoid Gossip:*** Engaging in gossip or spreading rumors undermines trust within any relationship. Prioritizing ethical behavior fosters a healthier environment.

- ***Self-Reflection:*** Regularly practicing self-reflection allows individuals to align their actions with their values, ensuring that their behavior remains consistent with personal ethics.

- ***Grow Personally:*** Develop a deeper understanding of personal values and boundaries. Seeking support from trusted mentors or counselors can provide guidance on navigating complex emotions related to lust.

- ***Daily Practice:*** Set intentions for ethical behavior each day to reinforce commitment to integrity. Practicing mindfulness and self-awareness in interactions helps individuals remain conscious of their actions and motivations.

- ***Celebrate Self-Control:*** Acknowledge moments of self-control and moderation to reinforce positive behavior changes and encourage continued growth.

Chastity as a Counter to Lust

Chastity involves purity of thought, word, and deed regarding sexuality and relationships. By practicing chastity, individuals cultivate self-control and respect for the sacredness of intimacy while emphasizing moderation in all aspects of life.

To promote chastity within professional environments, organizations should encourage open discussions about maintaining professionalism and boundaries in interactions with colleagues or clients. Candidates who prioritize integrity and ethical conduct while demonstrating respect for themselves and others are likely to embody this virtue.

Understanding lust's complexities while cultivating chastity allows individuals to navigate their desires healthily and ethically. By fostering kindness within ourselves and our communities—we can overcome feelings driven by base instincts while promoting an environment where everyone thrives based on mutual respect and understanding.

Additionally, recognizing how unrestrained desires can affect mental health is crucial; unhealthy expressions of lust can lead to emotional distress or relational conflicts. By practicing mindfulness and ethical conduct regarding our desires—we create healthier environments that support both individual well-being and collective harmony. Through self-discipline, moderation, and a commitment to personal growth, we can effectively manage feelings of lust while fostering respectful relationships built on trust and integrity.

Mother Teresa serves as an inspiring example of how kindness can triumph over desires like lust while navigating complex social dynamics. Born on August 26, 1910, in Albania as Agnes Gonxha Bojaxhiu, she felt a calling to serve others from a young age. After moving to India in 1929 to teach at a Catholic school in Calcutta, she was profoundly affected by the extreme poverty surrounding her.

In 1948, Mother Teresa decided to dedicate her life to helping the poorest of the poor after experiencing what she described as a "call within a call." She left her convent school to live among those suffering from poverty and disease in Calcutta's slums. Instead of allowing any desires for personal comfort or recognition to deter her from her mission—temptations that could easily arise from her position—she chose to fully immerse herself in service.

Mother Teresa founded the Missionaries of Charity in 1950 to provide love and care for those most in need. Her organization grew rapidly under her leadership, establishing homes for the dying, orphanages, schools for the poor, and leper colonies across India and beyond. She dedicated her life to serving others without seeking recognition or reward; her focus remained firmly on compassion rather than personal gain.

Throughout her life, Mother Teresa emphasized the importance of love and kindness over all else. Her famous quote—"Not all of us can do great things. But we can do small things with great love"—captures her philosophy perfectly. She believed that every act of kindness mattered immensely when directed towards those suffering from neglect or despair.

In recognition of her humanitarian work, Mother Teresa received numerous awards throughout her lifetime—including the Nobel Peace Prize in 1979—but she always redirected attention back to the people she served rather than herself. Her commitment to chastity was evident not only in her vows but also through her actions; she maintained purity in her mission by focusing solely on helping others without allowing personal desires to interfere.

Mother Teresa's story illustrates how choosing kindness over primal desires like lust can lead to profound social change. Her dedication to nonviolence and compassion demonstrates that prioritizing chastity not only enhances personal integrity but also contributes positively to society as a whole.

Understanding lust's complexities while cultivating chastity allows individuals to navigate their desires healthily and ethically. By fostering kindness within ourselves and our communities—much like Mother Teresa did—we can overcome feelings driven by base instincts while promoting an environment where everyone thrives based on mutual respect and understanding.

5.6 Battle of Gluttony Vs Temperance

Gluttony is characterized by excessive indulgence, often at the expense of resources or responsibilities. For example, an employee might exploit company funds for lavish personal expenses, ignoring financial constraints. This behavior can lead to significant negative consequences for both individuals and organizations.

"When eating, eat. When listening, listen. When resting, rest." - Zen Proverb

Gluttony, defined as the excessive consumption of food or drink beyond what is necessary for sustenance, can stem from various psychological, social, and cultural factors. Here are several reasons why people may experience gluttony:

Factors Contributing to Gluttony

- **Biological Instincts**: Humans have evolved with an inherent drive to seek out and consume food as a means of survival. This biological instinct can lead individuals to prioritize food acquisition and consumption, sometimes to excess.

- **Reward System Activation:** Consuming palatable foods triggers the brain's reward system, releasing neurotransmitters such as dopamine that induce feelings of pleasure and satisfaction. This neurological response can reinforce overeating behaviors, creating a cycle driven by the pursuit of pleasure.

- **Emotional Eating:** Food often serves as a source of comfort, stress relief, or distraction from negative emotions. People may turn to overeating as a coping mechanism to soothe emotional distress or alleviate boredom.

- **Cultural and Social Influences**: Cultural norms and traditions surrounding food can shape individuals' attitudes and behaviors related to eating. In societies where food abundance is celebrated and social gatherings revolve around feasting, overindulgence may be normalized.

- **Marketing and Food Industry Tactics:** The food industry employs various marketing strategies to promote overconsumption, such as large portion sizes and advertising that emphasizes indulgence. These tactics can influence perceptions and consumption patterns.

- **Availability and Accessibility:** The widespread availability of cheap, high-calorie, and heavily processed foods contributes to the prevalence of gluttony. Convenience foods make it easy for people to overeat without considering nutritional value.

- **Socioeconomic Factors:** Socioeconomic disparities can influence access to healthy foods. In low-income communities where fresh produce is scarce, individuals may rely on calorie-dense options that contribute to overeating.

- **Psychological Factors**: Impulsivity, lack of self-control, or disordered eating behaviors can lead to gluttonous behavior. Individuals may struggle with food addiction or binge eating disorder, impacting their ability to regulate intake.

- **Social Norms and Peer Pressure:** Social gatherings often involve abundant food offerings and pressure to partake in eating rituals. People may feel obligated to overeat in social settings to conform to expectations.

- **Lack of Mindful Eating Practices**: In today's fast-paced world, many engage in mindless eating habits, consuming food quickly without awareness of hunger cues or satiety signals.

The Impact of Gluttony on Mental Health

Excessive indulgence driven by gluttony can have profound implications for an employee's mental health. Overeating often leads to feelings of guilt and shame, which can exacerbate anxiety and depression. The cycle of emotional eating—using food as a coping mechanism—can create a reliance on unhealthy behaviors that further deteriorate mental well-being.

Moreover, the physical consequences of gluttony—such as weight gain and related health issues—can lead to decreased self-esteem and body image concerns. Employees struggling with these issues may experience difficulties in their professional lives, including reduced productivity and increased absenteeism due to health-related problems.

Strategies for Managing Gluttony

To effectively combat gluttony and promote healthier relationships with food, individuals should adopt several proactive strategies:

- **Practice Self-Discipline and Moderation**: Establish clear boundaries around consumption to maintain balance in both personal and professional life.
- **Avoid Gossip:** Engaging in gossip undermines trust within relationships; instead, prioritize ethical behavior in all interactions.
- **Self-Reflection:** Regularly reflect on personal values related to food consumption and align actions with these values.
- **Grow Personally:** Develop a deeper understanding of personal boundaries regarding food choices; seek support from mentors or counselors if needed.
- **Daily Practice:** Set intentions for ethical behavior each day; practice mindfulness in eating habits by paying attention to hunger cues.
- **Celebrate Self-Control:** Acknowledge moments of moderation as positive reinforcement for healthier choices.

Temperance as a Counter to Gluttony

Temperance involves moderation and self-restraint in all areas of life, particularly regarding indulgence in food or drink. By practicing temperance, individuals can exercise self-control while balancing desires with prudence.

To assess candidates' temperance during interviews, consider asking questions like: "How do you approach decision-making when it comes to resource allocation or budget management?" Be cautious of candidates who demonstrate excessive consumption or wastefulness; signs may include a lack of consideration for cost-effectiveness or extravagant spending without regard for the organization's financial health.

Additionally, ask candidates how they balance work demands with personal well-being: "Can you discuss how you balance work demands with personal well-being and self-care?" Look for those who demonstrate moderation in their behaviors and decisions while prioritizing balance over excess.

Understanding gluttony's complexities while cultivating temperance allows individuals to navigate their desires healthily and ethically. By fostering mindfulness within ourselves and our communities—we can overcome tendencies toward excessive indulgence while promoting an environment where everyone thrives based on mutual respect.

Recognizing how unrestrained desires affect mental health is crucial; managing gluttony through temperance supports individual well-being while fostering a culture of sustainability within organizations. Through self-discipline, moderation, and a commitment to personal growth, we can effectively address gluttonous tendencies while building respectful relationships grounded in integrity and responsibility.

Virat Kohli: Triumphing Over Gluttony with Temperance

Virat Kohli, the captain of the Indian cricket team and one of the most followed athletes globally, has an inspiring story of transformation that highlights his battle against gluttony through temperance. Early in his career, Kohli struggled with weight, reaching around 90 kilograms (198 pounds) and facing criticism for his physique. After a disappointing tour of England in 2014, he realized that his lifestyle was unsustainable and decided to take control of his health.

Kohli adopted a disciplined approach to nutrition, eliminating junk food, processed sugars, and alcohol while focusing on wholesome foods like lean proteins and vegetables. He famously stated, ***"Fitness is not about being better than someone else; it's about being better than you used to be."*** He learned to enjoy food in moderation, allowing himself occasional cheat meals while emphasizing balance: ***"You can't deprive yourself completely; that's not sustainable."***

As he transformed his eating habits, Kohli also recognized the importance of exercise. He worked with trainers to develop a rigorous workout routine that included strength training and cardio. His commitment to fitness not only improved his performance on the field but also enhanced his mental well-being.

In 2015, Kohli launched Chisel, a chain of gyms promoting fitness across India, followed by VAULT, a premium fitness chain aimed at providing comprehensive wellness solutions. He expressed his desire to inspire others by saying, ***"I want to inspire people to take their health seriously."***

Kohli's journey illustrates that overcoming gluttony is possible through self-awareness, discipline, and balance. By embracing temperance in all aspects of life—nutrition, exercise, and mental well-being—he demonstrates how dedication can lead to greatness both on and off the field.

5.7   Battle of Sloth Vs Diligence

Sloth is characterized by apathy or laziness, resulting in the neglect of duties and responsibilities. This often manifests as procrastination or consistently underperforming due to a lack of motivation. Sloth arises from feelings of overwhelm, apathy, or a lack of purpose in life. **As Edward Young wisely noted, "Procrastination is the thief of time."**

Factors Contributing to Sloth

Sloth can stem from various psychological, social, and environmental factors:

1. **Lack of Motivation**: A primary cause of sloth is the absence of intrinsic motivation or a sense of purpose. When individuals lack clear goals or direction, they may struggle to engage in productive activities.

2. **Fear of Failure or Perfectionism**: Individuals may avoid taking action due to a fear of failure or the desire to meet unrealistic standards. This fear can paralyze them, preventing risk-taking and initiative.

3. **Depression and Apathy**: Sloth can be symptomatic of underlying mental health issues such as depression, which manifests as persistent sadness and lethargy. Those experiencing depression often find it challenging to engage in daily activities.

4. **Burnout and Exhaustion**: Chronic stress and overwork can lead to physical and emotional exhaustion, causing individuals to withdraw from responsibilities as a coping mechanism.

5. **Lack of Self-Discipline**: Poor time management skills and a lack of self-discipline can contribute to slothful behavior. Individuals may procrastinate or avoid tasks altogether when they struggle to regulate their actions.

6. **Environmental Influences**: A sedentary lifestyle and social norms that devalue hard work can foster complacency. In environments lacking opportunities for growth, individuals may become resigned to their circumstances.

7. **Addictive Behaviors**: Addiction to technology or social media can exacerbate sloth-like tendencies, distracting individuals from meaningful activities and contributing to disengagement.

8. **Social Isolation**: Loneliness can fuel slothful behavior, as individuals may lack social support and accountability to stay active and engaged.

9. **Physical Health Issues**: Chronic health conditions or disabilities can limit energy levels, making it difficult for individuals to engage in activities requiring effort.

10. **Cultural Attitudes**: Cultural perceptions regarding work and productivity can influence behaviors related to sloth. In cultures that equate busyness with value, individuals may experience burnout and avoidance.

The Impact of Sloth on Mental Health

Slothful tendencies can significantly impact an employee's mental health. Procrastination and neglecting responsibilities often lead to increased stress levels, anxiety about unmet deadlines, and feelings of guilt or shame. This cycle can exacerbate existing mental health issues, creating a detrimental feedback loop that further diminishes motivation.

Additionally, employees who struggle with sloth may experience decreased job satisfaction and lower self-esteem due to perceived underperformance. The lack of accomplishment can contribute to feelings of hopelessness and disengagement from both work and personal life.

Strategies for Overcoming Sloth

Addressing slothful tendencies requires a combination of self-awareness, self-care, and behavioral change strategies:

1. **Set Clear Goals**: Establish realistic goals that provide direction and purpose, helping individuals prioritize tasks effectively.

2. **Recognize Opportunities**: Understand the importance of taking action; seizing opportunities fosters a proactive mindset.

3. **Break Tasks into Manageable Steps**: Dividing larger tasks into smaller, achievable steps can help overcome feelings of overwhelm.

4. **Develop Routines**: Establishing daily routines promotes productivity and accountability in everyday life.

5. **Prioritize Self-Care**: Engage in self-care activities such as exercise and relaxation to maintain energy levels and focus.

6. **Cultivate a Growth Mindset**: Embrace challenges as opportunities for learning rather than obstacles; this perspective encourages resilience.

7. **Surround Yourself with Supportive Individuals**: Building relationships with motivated peers can inspire action and accountability.

8. **Seek Professional Guidance**: If feelings of sloth persistently impact daily functioning, consider seeking support from mental health professionals.

Diligence as a Counter to Sloth

Diligence refers to perseverance, hard work, and conscientious effort in pursuing goals and responsibilities. By practicing diligence, individuals can overcome laziness and apathy while embracing a sense of purpose that energizes them toward fulfilling their potential.

To assess candidates' diligence during interviews, consider asking questions like: "Describe a time when you had multiple tasks or projects to complete within a tight deadline. How did you prioritize and manage your time?" Look for indications that demonstrate initiative rather than signs of procrastination or neglecting responsibilities.

Another insightful question could be: "Describe a time when you went above and beyond to achieve a goal or deliver exceptional results." Candidates who exhibit persistence in pursuing their goals are likely embodying the virtue of diligence.

Understanding the complexities surrounding sloth while cultivating diligence allows individuals to navigate their responsibilities effectively. By fostering self-awareness within ourselves—we can combat tendencies toward laziness while promoting an environment where everyone thrives based on mutual respect for hard work.

Recognizing how sloth affects mental health is crucial; overcoming these tendencies supports individual well-being while fostering a culture of productivity within organizations. Through setting clear goals, developing routines, practicing self-discipline, and committing to personal growth, we can effectively address slothful behaviors while building respectful relationships grounded in integrity and responsibility.

The Transformation of Dwayne "The Rock" Johnson: Overcoming Sloth with Diligence

Dwayne Johnson, popularly known as "The Rock," is not only a celebrated actor and former professional wrestler but also an inspiring example of overcoming sloth through diligence. His journey from a struggling athlete to one of the highest-paid actors in Hollywood showcases the power of hard work, discipline, and perseverance.

The Early Years: A Battle with Sloth

In his early life, Johnson faced numerous challenges. Growing up in a family of wrestlers, he initially struggled to find his footing in sports. After a brief stint playing college football at the University of Miami, he went undrafted in the NFL. With limited opportunities and feeling lost, he found himself at a crossroads, battling feelings of sloth and uncertainty about his future.

During this period, Johnson faced financial difficulties and was living in his car after being cut from the Canadian Football League. He could have easily succumbed to despair and lethargy, but instead, he made a conscious decision to embrace diligence. *"I found myself at rock bottom,"* he later reflected. "I had to make a choice: either stay down or get up and fight."

Embracing Diligence

Determined to change his circumstances, Johnson committed himself to hard work. He began training rigorously, not just for wrestling but also for life. He adopted a disciplined workout regimen that included weightlifting and cardiovascular exercises. He famously stated, *"Success isn't always about greatness. It's about consistency. Consistent hard work gains success."*

Johnson also focused on improving his skills in wrestling. He trained under the guidance of his father and became known for his dedication and work ethic. His diligence paid off when he made his debut in the WWE (World Wrestling Entertainment) in 1996 as Rocky Maivia, quickly rising to fame.

As he transitioned from wrestling to acting, Johnson continued to embody diligence. He took on various roles and worked tirelessly to hone his craft. He often shares motivational content on social media, encouraging others to pursue their dreams with hard work and determination.

The Impact of His Transformation

Johnson's commitment to diligence transformed not only his career but also his personal life. He became known for his incredible physique and work ethic, often sharing workout routines and healthy eating habits with his fans. *"I don't believe in shortcuts,"* he emphasizes. *"I believe in hard work."*

In addition to his fitness journey, Johnson launched the Project Rock brand in partnership with Under Armour, which focuses on athletic gear and fitness motivation. Through this venture, he aims to inspire others to adopt active lifestyles and prioritize their health.

Dwayne Johnson's story is a powerful testament to overcoming sloth through diligence. By recognizing the need for change and committing himself to hard work, he transformed his life from one of uncertainty into a successful career filled with achievements.

His journey illustrates that overcoming sloth is possible through self-awareness, discipline, and perseverance. Johnson's dedication serves as an inspiration for millions around the world, reminding us that with diligence and determination, we can achieve our goals and live fulfilling lives.

Let us remember that the battles we face are not just individual struggles but collective opportunities for growth and transformation. Together, let us build a corporate culture grounded in compassion, integrity, and resilience, where virtues triumph over vices, and the pursuit of excellence is guided by a commitment to the greater good.

5.8 The Power of Balance: Embracing Virtues for Ethical Leadership

As we explore the ideas in this book, I want to emphasize something really important: the need for balance in our journey toward ethical leadership and sustainable success. Each of the seven heavenly virtues serves as a counter to a deadly sin, but it's crucial to remember that even good qualities can lead to problems if taken too far.

Humility

Let's start with **humility**, which helps us fight against **pride**. Humility teaches us to value collaboration and recognize the contributions of others. However, if we're too humble, we might overlook our own needs or hesitate to speak up when it matters. Think about a leader who always downplays their achievements; they could miss out on chances for growth or fail to advocate for their team.

Charity

Next is **charity**, which stands against **greed**. Charity encourages us to support our communities and care for the planet. But if we give too much without considering our own financial situation, we can end up in trouble. Imagine a philanthropist who donates more than they earn; they might find themselves struggling financially, which would limit their ability to help others in the future.

Chastity

Now let's talk about **chastity**, which counters **lust** by promoting purity and moral integrity. However, focusing too much on chastity can lead to repression or an unhealthy view of natural desires. For example, someone who avoids all intimate relationships out of fear of lust may miss out on meaningful connections and emotional fulfillment.

Temperance

Moving on to **temperance**, which opposes **gluttony** by encouraging moderation. Yet, if we become overly focused on temperance, we might end up avoiding pleasure altogether. Think about someone who strictly restricts their diet; they could develop an unhealthy relationship with food, leading to binge eating or other issues.

Patience

Let's not forget about **patience**, which helps us manage **wrath** and promotes thoughtful decision-making. However, being too patient can lead us to be passive when action is needed. Consider a manager who tolerates poor performance for too long; they risk demoralizing their team and allowing problems to grow.

Kindness

Then there's **kindness**, which embodies compassion and empathy while countering **envy**. But being overly kind can lead us to neglect our own needs while prioritizing others'. A caregiver who ignores their own self-care while helping others may eventually face burnout and resentment.

Diligence

Finally, there's **diligence**, which stands against **sloth** by promoting hard work and commitment. However, working too hard without taking breaks can lead to burnout and decreased productivity. An employee who pushes themselves too much without rest may find their effectiveness slipping as fatigue sets in.

In closing, as we embrace virtues like kindness, generosity, and diligence in our workplaces, let's keep balance in mind. The path toward ethical leadership requires self-awareness and a commitment not just to our own growth but also to the well-being of our communities.

As we conclude our exploration of the battles between virtues and vices in the corporate world, it becomes clear that these conflicts are not mere abstractions but profound forces that shape the character and conduct of individuals and organizations alike. By acknowledging the complexities of human emotions and ethical dilemmas, we empower ourselves to navigate these challenges with wisdom and integrity.

In the face of pride, humility reminds us of the importance of collaboration and recognition of others' contributions. Charity counters greed, urging us to consider the well-being of our communities and the planet. Patience tempers wrath, fostering thoughtful decision-making and constructive dialogue.

Ultimately, the journey towards ethical leadership and sustainable success in business requires an ongoing commitment to self-awareness, empathy, and moral courage. By embracing the virtues of kindness, generosity, and diligence, we can strive to create workplaces that foster innovation, collaboration, and shared prosperity.

So as we continue through this book together, let's aim to create environments where both individuals and organizations can thrive—where virtues win over vices, and our pursuit of excellence is guided by a commitment to the greater good.

Thank you for being part of this journey!

Part 3

Identifying and Addressing Mental Health Challenges

Chapter 6

The Silent Struggle: Identifying and Addressing Mental Health Issues

Let's kick things off with a powerful reminder from Dwayne "The Rock" Johnson: *'Depression never discriminates. Took me a long time to realize it but the key is to not be afraid to open up. Especially us dudes have a tendency to keep it in. You're not alone.'*

This quote hits home the reality that mental health struggles don't discriminate based on gender, status, or background. It's a reminder that even the strongest among us can face battles with our mental well-being, and the key to overcoming them lies in breaking the silence and seeking support.

Approximately 1 in 4 individuals worldwide will traverse the terrain of mental health struggles at some point. Age, gender, race—these are mere boundaries unable to shield anyone from the touch of mental health challenges. Yet, why does this silent struggle persist?

This problem doesn't care about where you're from, how old you are, or what you look like. But even though so many people go through it, mental health isn't always taken seriously. Many times, it's brushed aside or not given the attention it needs.

This neglect is a big problem. When mental health issues are ignored, it can lead to a lot of suffering. People who are struggling with mental health feel alone and misunderstood. Relationships suffer, dreams go unfulfilled, and lives can fall apart. All of this happens because society doesn't always see mental health as important as physical health.

But we can change this. The first step is recognizing how serious mental health problems are. We need to talk openly about them, challenge the wrong ideas people have, and make sure everyone gets the help and support they need. It's time to break the silence, correct the misunderstandings, and create a world where mental health is treated just as seriously as physical health.

Addressing mental health issues requires an understanding of their prevalence, their impact, and the various strategies available for identification and support. Imagine a world where understanding and support flourish, where conversations flow without fear or judgment, and where seeking help for mental well-being is as natural as seeking a remedy for a physical ailment.

Come closer, and you'll see a pattern made of bad ideas and misunderstandings. People don't always understand mental health, and that can make it hard for those who are struggling. They might feel scared of being judged or misunderstood, so they keep quiet about how they feel. It's like they're hiding behind a pretend smile, even when they're hurting inside.

Despite growing awareness, stigma surrounding mental health remains a significant barrier to seeking help. Individuals often fear discrimination or judgment if they disclose their mental health struggles, leading to silence and avoidance of seeking support.

Misconceptions about mental health conditions persist, leading to a lack of understanding among the general population. This lack of awareness contributes to the perpetuation of stigma and inhibits open conversations about mental well-being.

In her memoir *"The Center Cannot Hold: My Journey Through Madness,"* Elyn Saks, a distinguished legal scholar, mental health advocate, and author, delivers a poignant reflection on the pervasive misunderstandings surrounding mental illness.

One quote from her book resonates deeply: ***"Perhaps the biggest misconception is that mental illness is something that happens to other people."***

Saks' words challenge the prevailing notion that mental health issues are distant concerns, affecting only a select few. Through her own courageous journey living with schizophrenia, she dismantles this misconception, shedding light on the universal nature of mental health challenges.

Her memoir serves as a powerful testament to the fact that mental illness knows no boundaries—it does not discriminate based on age, gender, race, or socioeconomic status. Instead, it touches the lives of individuals across all walks of life, often with profound and far-reaching effects.

Saks' quote encapsulates the urgent need for greater awareness and understanding of mental health issues. It calls upon society to recognize that mental illness is not an isolated phenomenon but an integral part of the human experience. By acknowledging the universality of mental health challenges, we can foster empathy, compassion, and support for those who are struggling.

In embracing Saks' message, we embark on a collective journey toward destigmatization and empowerment. We recognize that mental health is not a distant concern but a shared reality, deserving of attention, care, and advocacy.

But recognition begins with understanding. Mental health conditions often reveal themselves through subtle cues—an unexpected shift in behavior, a lingering sadness veiled behind a smile, or an anxious heart silently yearning for solace. The first step in this odyssey is recognizing these signs, acknowledging their existence, and lending an ear to those whispers seeking validation.

Recognizing Symptoms: Mental health conditions manifest in various ways, including changes in behavior, mood swings, persistent feelings of sadness or anxiety, withdrawal from social activities, and difficulty concentrating. Recognizing these symptoms is crucial in identifying potential issues.

Seeking Professional Help: Consulting mental health professionals, such as therapists, psychologists, or psychiatrists, can aid in accurately diagnosing and addressing mental health concerns. These professionals employ various therapeutic approaches tailored to individual needs.

Like a beacon cutting through the mist, professional help stands ready—a guide through the labyrinth of emotions. Therapists, psychologists, and psychiatrists hold lanterns of understanding, illuminating the path towards a clearer understanding of one's mental landscape. With personalized strategies and therapeutic approaches, they navigate these uncharted waters alongside those seeking solace.

Promoting Open Dialogue: Encouraging open conversations about mental health helps break down stigma and creates a supportive environment for individuals to seek help without fear of judgment.

"The more we talk about mental health, the more we can break down the stigma surrounding it. When we normalize these conversations, we create space for healing and support." - Prince Harry, Duke of Sussex

This quote from Prince Harry emphasizes the importance of promoting open dialogue about mental health. By acknowledging the significance of conversations, we pave the way for understanding and support within our communities. Research supports the idea that open dialogue contributes to decreased stigma and increased help-seeking behaviors. When individuals feel safe to share their experiences openly, it fosters empathy, acceptance, and validation. Encouraging open conversations about mental health creates a supportive environment where individuals can seek help without fear of judgment. By breaking down barriers and fostering understanding, we create opportunities for healing and growth, empowering individuals to address their mental health concerns proactively.

Emphasis on Self-Care: Encouraging self-care practices, including mindfulness, physical exercise, adequate sleep, and healthy coping mechanisms, can contribute significantly to overall mental well-being.

"Self-care is not a luxury; it's a necessity. Just as we prioritize our physical health, we must also prioritize our mental well-being through regular self-care practices." - Arianna Huffington, co-founder of The Huffington Post,

This quote from Arianna Huffington explains the importance of emphasizing self-care practices for maintaining mental well-being. Research consistently shows the positive effects of self-care activities such as mindfulness, exercise, and adequate sleep on mental health. Prioritizing self-care is essential for managing stress, regulating emotions, and building resilience. By incorporating self-care into daily routines, individuals can enhance their ability to cope with life's challenges and nurture their mental health. Emphasizing self-care is not selfish; it's a vital investment in one's overall well-being.

Support Systems and Resources: Establishing robust support networks, both within communities and workplaces, can provide individuals with access to resources, support groups, and mental health services.

"We are stronger together. By building strong support systems and providing access to resources, we can create communities where everyone feels supported and empowered to prioritize their mental health." - Michelle Obama

This quote from Michelle Obama highlights the significance of support systems and resources in promoting mental health within communities and workplaces. Research demonstrates that social support plays a critical role in protecting against the negative effects of stress on mental health. Access to support networks and resources has been linked to better treatment outcomes and higher levels of psychological well-being. By establishing robust support systems, communities can provide individuals with emotional validation, practical assistance, and a sense of belonging. Strengthening support networks creates environments where individuals feel valued, respected, and supported in their mental health journey.

Communities and workplaces become sanctuaries—strongholds of support networks and resources. Here, individuals find solace in shared experiences, access to guidance, and the comfort of knowing they are not alone. These sanctuaries foster practices that nurture mental well-being—encouraging self-care rituals, mindfulness, and the power of healthy coping mechanisms.

"In times of trouble, the supportive embrace of community can be the strongest shelter." - Maya Angelou

This quote from Maya Angelou, a renowned poet and civil rights activist, emphasizes the profound impact of community support during challenging times. Angelou's words convey the idea that during moments of adversity, the support and solidarity found within a community can offer invaluable refuge and strength. Just as a physical shelter provides protection from external dangers, the supportive embrace of community offers emotional shelter, providing solace and comfort to those in need. Angelou's quote underscores the importance of fostering supportive environments where individuals feel empowered to seek help and support from their communities, highlighting the transformative power of collective resilience and compassion.

In this saga of mental health, the quest is not merely to survive but to thrive—to create a world where mental well-being is not a luxury but a fundamental right. It's a tale of unravelling silken veils, painting a world where understanding, empathy, and support bloom abundantly. It's a narrative where the journey towards mental wellness is celebrated, acknowledged, and embraced by all.

Understanding the prevalence of mental health issues, acknowledging the reasons behind the silence, and implementing strategies for identification and support are crucial steps toward addressing these challenges. By fostering an environment of empathy, education, and accessible resources, we can collectively work towards breaking the silence and supporting those struggling with mental health concerns.

6.1   Shedding Light on Subtle Indicators of Mental Health Challenges in the Workplace

Mental health is a significant global concern, with conditions such as depression, anxiety, and substance use disorders affecting millions of individuals worldwide. These disorders are not limited by age, gender, race, or socioeconomic status, highlighting the universal nature of mental health challenges. Despite growing awareness, stigma surrounding mental illness remains pervasive, preventing many individuals from seeking help and support.

One of the most pressing issues in mental health is the high prevalence of suicide, which claims approximately 800,000 lives each year and is the second leading cause of death among young people aged 15-29. Additionally, trauma-related disorders such as post-traumatic stress disorder (PTSD) can have long-lasting effects on mental well-being, particularly in regions affected by conflict or natural disasters.

The economic burden of mental illness is substantial, with costs attributed to healthcare expenditures, lost productivity, and disability benefits amounting to an estimated $1 trillion annually. Moreover, access to mental health services is often limited, particularly in low- and middle-income countries, exacerbating disparities in care.

The COVID-19 pandemic has further exacerbated mental health challenges, with lockdowns, social isolation, and economic uncertainty contributing to increased levels of stress, anxiety, and depression globally. As communities grapple with the long-term impacts of the pandemic, addressing mental health needs has become even more critical.

Efforts to improve mental health outcomes require comprehensive strategies that prioritize access to quality care, reduce stigma, and promote mental well-being. By fostering supportive environments and investing in mental health services, we can work towards building healthier, more resilient communities where everyone has the opportunity to thrive.

Identifying whether someone may be experiencing mental health issues involves being attentive to various changes and cues in their behavior, emotions, and interactions. Here's how you can recognize some of the potential signs:

- **Behavior Changes:** Notice if the person's actions or reactions seem different than usual. For instance, if a usually cheerful coworker becomes increasingly irritable or experiences sudden mood swings, it might be indicative of underlying mental health issues. Similarly, if someone who used to actively participate in team activities starts withdrawing and isolating themselves, it could be a cause for concern. Encourage open communication and offer support by expressing concern and asking how they're feeling. Suggest that they consider seeking professional help or offer to connect them with resources such as therapy services provided by the company or mental health hotline

- **Work Patterns:** Pay attention to any alterations in how they approach their work. Are they having trouble meeting deadlines, being less productive than usual, or finding it hard to concentrate? These changes may indicate underlying mental health challenges impacting their performance. For example, if a colleague who was consistently meeting deadlines suddenly starts missing them and appears overwhelmed by tasks, it could signal mental health struggles. Encourage them to take breaks and practice self-care, and remind them that it's okay to ask for help when needed.

- **Physical Symptoms:** Mental health issues can sometimes manifest physically. Look for signs like persistent fatigue, frequent headaches, changes in appetite, or disruptions in sleep patterns. For instance, if a team member frequently complains of headaches, feels constantly tired, or experiences changes in eating or sleeping habits, it might be worth exploring whether these physical symptoms are linked to their mental well-being. Validate their experiences and encourage them to prioritize their well-being by practicing self-care activities such as exercise, meditation, or seeking medical attention if needed. Provide information about the connection between mental and physical health and offer support in finding appropriate resources for addressing both aspects.

- **Social Withdrawal:** If the person starts distancing themselves from social interactions or avoiding group settings, it could be a sign of emotional distress or mental health struggles. For example, if a colleague who used to actively participate in team meetings and social gatherings begins to decline invitations and prefers to work alone, it could indicate feelings of anxiety or depression. Reach out to them with compassion and understanding, letting them know that you're there to listen without judgment. Offer to spend time with them in a non-work setting or suggest activities that they enjoy. Encourage them to connect with support groups or mental health professionals who can provide additional assistance.

- **Emotional Cues:** Be mindful of persistent feelings of sadness, anxiety, or nervousness that seem to affect the person's daily life. Additionally, unexplained emotional outbursts or frequent mood swings may suggest underlying emotional distress. For instance, if a team member consistently appears downcast or agitated without any apparent reason, it might be worth considering whether they are grappling with emotional challenges. Validate their emotions and provide a safe space for them to express themselves. Offer to accompany them to therapy sessions or support groups if they're open to it. Encourage them to practice self-compassion and engage in activities that bring them joy and relaxation.

- **Communication Patterns:** Changes in how the person communicates can also be indicative of mental health challenges. This might include becoming defensive, avoiding conversations, or having difficulty expressing thoughts clearly. For example, if a usually articulate colleague starts struggling to articulate their thoughts during discussions or becomes defensive when receiving feedback, it could be a sign of underlying mental health issues. Approach them with empathy and patience, acknowledging any changes you've noticed and expressing your willingness to listen and support them. Offer alternative communication methods such as written or asynchronous communication if they find it easier to express themselves that way. Encourage them to explore therapy or counseling to work on improving their communication skills and coping mechanisms.

- **Decision-Making Abilities:** Individuals dealing with mental health issues might find it challenging to make decisions or may hesitate when taking on new responsibilities. For instance, if a team member who typically takes charge in decision-making processes starts hesitating or seems indecisive, it might indicate that they are struggling with mental health challenges impacting their confidence or cognitive abilities. Encourage them to break tasks down into smaller steps and celebrate their accomplishments along the way. Help them prioritize self-care and seek professional help if they're struggling with decision-making due to mental health challenges.

In a corporate setting, it's essential for every manager or co-worker to support each other. However, leaders such as CEOs or members of the board should take a proactive role in discussing mental health in the workplace for several reason

Firstly, leaders set the tone for organizational culture. By openly discussing mental health and prioritizing employee well-being, leaders signal to employees that it is a valued topic and encourage openness and honesty about mental health challenges.

Secondly, when leaders share their own experiences or show vulnerability regarding mental health, it can break down barriers and encourage others to do the same. This fosters a culture of trust and support where employees feel comfortable seeking help and disclosing their struggles.

Thirdly, discussing mental health from the top down helps to combat stigma. When leaders openly acknowledge and address mental health challenges, it sends a message that it is acceptable to talk about and seek help for mental health issues without fear of judgment or repercussions.

Furthermore, leaders play a crucial role in allocating resources and support for mental health initiatives within the organization. By prioritizing mental health resources, such as employee assistance programs, counseling services, or training workshops, leaders demonstrate a commitment to supporting their employees' mental well-being.

Addressing mental health in the workplace can have positive impacts on productivity, morale, and overall performance. When employees feel supported and are provided with resources to manage their mental health, they are more likely to be engaged, motivated, and productive at work.

Finally, leaders have a legal and ethical responsibility to provide a safe and healthy work environment for their employees. This includes addressing mental health concerns and implementing policies and procedures to support employees' mental well-being.

Ultimately, everything, including mental health initiatives, tends to flow from top to bottom in organizations because leaders have the power to shape organizational culture, allocate resources, and set priorities. When leaders prioritize and actively support mental health initiatives, it sends a clear message that mental health is valued and prioritized within the organization, leading to positive outcomes for both employees and the organization as a whole.

6.2 Share real-life case studies of organizations effectively addressing mental health issues.

Addressing mental health issues in the workplace is crucial for promoting employee well-being and organizational success. Real-life case studies of organizations effectively tackling these challenges provide valuable insights into the strategies and approaches that can be adopted.

Here, we examine three such case studies, highlighting the initiatives undertaken by Unilever, Google, and Lloyds Banking Group to prioritize mental health in their workplaces.

1. Unilever's Mental Health Initiatives:

- **Before Initiative Implementation/Problem Statement:** Prior to implementing mental health initiatives, Unilever faced challenges with employee well-being, including high stress levels, lack of support for mental health issues, and stigma surrounding mental health discussions.

- **Initiative Implementation:** Unilever launched a comprehensive mental health program called "Mindspace" to address these challenges.

Approaches:

- **Training and Support:** Managers underwent mental health training sessions to enhance their ability to recognize signs of distress and support their teams effectively.

- **Employee Assistance Program (EAP):** Unilever implemented an EAP offering confidential counseling services and mental health resources for employees.

- **Stigma Reduction:** The company conducted awareness campaigns and workshops to reduce the stigma associated with mental health, fostering open conversations within the workplace.

Change Brought About: After implementing the mental health initiatives:

- **Improved Manager Support:** Managers became more adept at recognizing and addressing signs of distress among their teams, providing better support for mental health issues.

- **Increased Employee Engagement:** Employees felt more supported and valued, leading to higher engagement levels and improved morale.

- **Reduced Stigma:** The stigma surrounding mental health discussions decreased, creating a more open and accepting workplace culture where employees felt comfortable seeking help when needed

2. Google's Well-Being Programs:

- **Before Initiative Implementation/ Problem Statement:** Before implementing well-being programs, Google faced challenges related to employee stress, burnout, and mental health issues. Employees struggled to manage their workload, leading to decreased productivity and overall well-being.

- **Initiative:** Google introduced comprehensive well-being programs to address these challenges and prioritize mental health support for its employees.

Approaches:

- **Mindfulness and Meditation:** Google introduced mindfulness and meditation programs to help employees manage stress, improve focus, and enhance overall well-being.

- **Onsite Counselling Services:** The company offered access to onsite counseling services and mental health resources, providing employees with immediate support and guidance.

- **Work-Life Balance**: Google emphasized the importance of work-life balance by offering flexible work arrangements and encouraging employees to disconnect during off-hours.

Change Brought About: After implementing the well-being programs:

- **Reduced Stress Levels:** Employees reported lower stress levels and increased feelings of well-being, leading to improved overall mental health.

- **Enhanced Productivity:** With better stress management techniques and improved work-life balance, employees became more productive and efficient in their roles.

- **Increased Employee Satisfaction:** Employees expressed higher levels of satisfaction with their work environment, feeling supported and valued by the company's emphasis on mental health and well-being

3. Lloyds Banking Group's Mental Health Strategy:

- **Initiative**: Lloyds Banking Group launched an extensive mental health strategy named "This is Me" to support the mental well-being of its employees.

- **Before Initiative Implementation**: Problem Statement: Prior to implementing its mental health strategy, Lloyds Banking Group faced significant challenges related to employee well-being. There was a lack of support for mental health issues, leading to stigma, stress, and decreased morale among employees.

- **Initiative Implementation:** Company: Lloyds Banking Group Initiative: Lloyds Banking Group launched an extensive mental health strategy named "This is Me" to address these challenges and support the mental well-being of its employees. Approach:

- **Mental Health Champions:** The company trained select employees to act as mental health champions, providing guidance and support to their colleagues and promoting open discussions about mental health.

- **Leadership Involvement:** Senior leadership actively promoted mental health discussions, creating a culture where employees felt comfortable seeking help and support.

- **Collaboration and Resources:** Lloyds Banking Group partnered with mental health organizations to provide resources, workshops, and training sessions across the organization, ensuring employees had access to the support they needed.

Change Brought About: After implementing the mental health strategy:

- **Reduced Stigma:** The initiative led to a significant reduction in the stigma surrounding mental health, fostering open conversations and creating a supportive environment for employees to seek help.

- **Improved Morale:** Employees reported increased morale and job satisfaction as they felt supported and valued by the organization's commitment to mental well-being.

- **Enhanced Employee Well-being:** With access to resources, support from mental health champions, and leadership involvement, employees experienced improved overall well-being, leading to higher levels of engagement and productivity.

The case studies of Unilever, Google, and Lloyds Banking Group demonstrate the positive impact of implementing mental health initiatives in the workplace. By prioritizing training, support, and resources, these organizations created environments where employees felt supported and valued. Reduced stigma, improved morale, and enhanced well-being were among the notable outcomes, underscoring the importance of fostering a culture that prioritizes mental health. These examples serve as inspiration for other organizations seeking to create mentally healthy workplaces.

Chapter 7

Beyond Burnout: Strategies for Preventing Workplace Stress

"Your work is going to fill a large part of your life, and the only way to be truly satisfied is to do what you believe is great work. And the only way to do great work is to love what you do." - Steve Jobs

Steve Jobs' words resonate deeply with the pervasive issue of burnout in the workplace. Indeed, burnout often arises from a misalignment between individual passions and organizational demands. Excessive workloads, coupled with unrealistic productivity expectations, can quickly erode one's love for their work, leading to feelings of being constantly overworked and unable to meet demands. Similarly, a lack of control over one's work environment or unclear expectations can breed frustration and disengagement, detracting from the satisfaction that jobs speaks of.

Moreover, the absence of recognition or reward for one's efforts can further exacerbate feelings of disillusionment and demotivation, chipping away at the love for one's work. Job insecurity, a prevalent concern in today's workforce, only adds to the stress, amplifying anxiety and contributing to burnout. Toxic workplace cultures, characterized by lack of support, ineffective communication, or bullying, create fertile ground for burnout to flourish, extinguishing the passion Jobs speaks of and leaving individuals feeling isolated and exhausted.

In essence, burnout is not merely a personal challenge but a reflection of the work environment and its alignment with individual passions and values. As Jobs suggests, true satisfaction in work comes from doing what one loves. When this alignment is lacking and the workplace becomes a source of chronic stress and dissatisfaction, burnout inevitably follows.

Addressing workplace stress is crucial for creating a healthy and productive work environment. It's about more than just preventing burnout; it's about fostering a culture where employees feel supported and empowered to manage stress effectively. Here are some strategies that can help achieve this:

One important aspect is fostering a supportive culture. This means encouraging open communication between employees and management. When employees feel they can openly discuss their concerns and stress triggers without fear of judgment, it creates an environment where everyone feels valued and understood.

Additionally, promoting teamwork and mutual support among colleagues can make a significant difference. When coworkers help each other during challenging times, it not only eases the burden of stress but also strengthens relationships and builds trust within the team.

Leadership plays a crucial role in creating a supportive environment. Managers should be approachable and supportive, providing guidance and resources to help employees address stressors effectively. When leaders prioritize employee well-being, it sets a positive example for the entire organization.

Establishing clear expectations and boundaries is another important strategy. When employees understand their roles and responsibilities clearly, it reduces ambiguity and prevents unnecessary stress. Encouraging a healthy work-life balance also helps employees manage stress more effectively.

Providing resources and training on stress management and resilience equips employees with the tools they need to handle stress effectively. Access to counselling, Employee Assistance Programs (EAPs), and other mental health resources can also make a big difference for employees facing stress-related issues.

Promoting flexibility and autonomy gives employees a sense of control over their work, which can help reduce stress. Allowing flexible work hours or remote work options, when feasible, empowers employees to manage their schedules in a way that works best for them.

Well-being practices such as wellness programs, mindfulness activities, and regular breaks during the workday can also help alleviate stress and improve overall well-being. Encouraging employees to take breaks and prioritize self-care sends a message that their well-being is valued.

Regular feedback and recognition for accomplishments are essential for fostering a positive work environment. When employees feel appreciated and acknowledged for their efforts, it boosts morale and reduces stress levels.

Monitoring workload and prioritizing tasks helps ensure that employees are not overwhelmed with work. By setting realistic expectations and helping employees prioritize their tasks effectively, managers can prevent burnout and promote a healthier work environment.

Finally, it's important to regularly review and adapt stress management strategies based on feedback and assessment. By continuously improving and refining these strategies, organizations can create environments where employees feel supported and empowered to thrive.

Addressing workplace stress requires a multifaceted approach that involves everyone in the organization. By implementing these strategies, organizations can create cultures that prioritize employee well-being and ultimately lead to happier, healthier, and more productive workplaces.

7.1 Discuss the causes and consequences of burnout in corporate settings.

"Burnout is an indication that you've gone too long without taking care of yourself." - Sam Owen, relationship coach and psychologist.

Burnout in corporate settings is a pervasive issue with significant repercussions for both individuals and organizations. It stems from a variety of factors, each contributing to the erosion of employee well-being and job satisfaction.

"Burnout is not a sign of weakness, it's a sign that you've been trying to be strong for too long." - Dr. Ayala Pines, psychologist

High workload and pressure, coupled with tight deadlines and unrealistic expectations, create a relentless environment where employees struggle to keep pace without adequate resources or support. Moreover, a lack of control and autonomy exacerbates the situation, leaving employees feeling powerless in their roles and unable to navigate their responsibilities effectively. This sense of helplessness is further compounded by unclear expectations and role ambiguity, which sow confusion and frustration among employees as they grapple with shifting demands and undefined objectives.

In addition to these internal stressors, the organizational culture plays a pivotal role in fueling burnout. ***"Burnout is what happens when you try to avoid being human for too long."*** - Michael Gungor, musician and author. Toxic work environments, characterized by a lack of recognition or support, interpersonal conflicts, and ineffective leadership, create a breeding ground for disillusionment and disengagement. These negative dynamics not only undermine employee morale and motivation but also foster an atmosphere of distrust and resentment within the organization.

The consequences of burnout in corporate settings are far-reaching and multifaceted, impacting both individual well-being and organizational performance. ***"Burnout occurs when all your fuel is used up. Burnout is a state of emotional, physical, and mental exhaustion caused by excessive and prolonged stress. It occurs when you feel overwhelmed, emotionally drained, and unable to meet constant demands."*** - Psychology Today. Decreased performance and productivity are among the most immediate outcomes, as burnout diminishes an individual's ability to perform at their best, leading to errors, reduced efficiency, and missed opportunities. Moreover, burnout often precipitates increased absenteeism and turnover, as employees seek respite from the relentless demands of their roles and look for healthier work environments where they feel valued and supported.

Mental and physical health issues are also prevalent among individuals experiencing burnout, with prolonged stress contributing to anxiety, depression, exhaustion, and a host of other stress-related ailments. These health challenges not only compromise individual well-being but also strain the organization's resources, resulting in higher healthcare expenses and decreased overall productivity. Furthermore, burnout can strain relationships within teams, leading to conflicts, reduced collaboration, and strained communication, which further exacerbate workplace stress and hinder organizational performance.

Ultimately, burnout exacts a toll on the organization's reputation, tarnishing its image as an employer of choice and undermining its ability to attract and retain top talent. ***"Burnout isn't just a personal problem. It's a societal issue that we need to address with systemic solutions."*** - Anne Helen Petersen, journalist and author. High burnout rates signal systemic issues within the organization, raising concerns among potential employees and customers alike about its commitment to employee well-being and sustainable business practices.

Addressing burnout in corporate settings requires a concerted effort to address both the underlying causes and the resulting consequences.

> ***"The only limit to our realization of tomorrow will be our doubts of today."***
> - Franklin D. Roosevelt, 32nd President of the United States.

By fostering a supportive work culture, clarifying expectations, and providing resources for stress prevention and management, organizations can create environments where employees feel valued, engaged, and empowered to thrive. In doing so, they not only safeguard individual well-being but also cultivate a competitive advantage in the marketplace, positioning themselves as employers of choice committed to the holistic success of their employees.

7.2 Present evidence-based methods for stress prevention and management.

In the fast-paced and demanding world of corporate settings, stress has become an inevitable part of the workplace landscape. However, acknowledging the importance of addressing stress is crucial for promoting employee well-being and creating a healthier work environment. Evidence-based methods for stress prevention and management play a pivotal role in equipping individuals with the tools and strategies necessary to navigate the challenges of modern work life effectively.

Evidence-based methods for stress prevention and management are crucial in promoting employee well-being and creating a healthier work environment. *"The greatest weapon against stress is our ability to choose one thought over another."* - William James, an American philosopher and psychologist. Research demonstrates the effectiveness of various strategies in reducing stress levels and enhancing coping mechanisms. Mindfulness meditation, for instance, has been shown to enhance emotional regulation and reduce anxiety. *"Don't let your mind bully your body into believing it must carry the burden of its worries."* - Astrid Alauda, a contemporary writer and poet. Implementing mindfulness sessions or providing guided meditation apps can help employees manage stress effectively. Stress management training programs have also proven beneficial, improving coping skills and reducing stress levels in employees. *"The time to relax is when you don't have time for it."* - Sydney J. Harris, an American journalist. Workload management, such as balancing workloads and setting realistic goals, can significantly reduce stress and prevent burnout. Reviewing and adjusting workloads, prioritizing tasks, and encouraging breaks can mitigate feelings of overwhelm.

In addition to stress prevention, stress management techniques play a crucial role in supporting employee well-being. *"In times of great stress or adversity, it's always best to keep busy, to plow your anger and your energy into something positive."* - Lee Iacocca, an American automobile executive. Cognitive-behavioral strategies, including cognitive restructuring and problem-solving techniques, have shown effectiveness in reducing stress levels. Offering training or access to resources on these strategies can help employees reframe negative thoughts and cope with stress. *"Stress is an ignorant state. It believes that everything is an emergency."* - Natalie Goldberg, an American writer. Regular exercise has been linked to reduced stress and anxiety, along with improved overall well-being. "Set peace of mind as your highest goal, and organize your life around it." - Brian Tracy, a Canadian-American motivational speaker and author. Encouraging physical activity through gym memberships, group fitness classes, or lunchtime walks can provide employees with opportunities to alleviate stress.

Moreover, fostering strong social support networks within the workplace is essential for buffering stress and promoting resilience. *"The greatest mistake you can make in life is to be continually fearing you will make one."* - Elbert Hubbard, an American writer and philosopher. Creating a supportive work culture, encouraging team-building activities, and providing spaces for employees to connect and share experiences can enhance social support. *"You must learn to let go. Release the stress. You were never in control anyway."* - Steve Maraboli, a life-changing speaker and bestselling author. Relaxation techniques, such as deep breathing exercises and progressive muscle relaxation, have also shown to alleviate stress. Offering relaxation sessions, providing access to relaxation apps, or designating quiet areas for relaxation breaks can help employees manage stress effectively.

Effective time management and planning are critical components of stress management. Encouraging employees to prioritize tasks, utilize scheduling tools, and set realistic goals can reduce stress levels and enhance productivity. Additionally, providing access to Employee Assistance Programs (EAPs) and counselling services can be beneficial in providing support for stress-related issues. *"The day she let go of the things that were weighing her down, was the day she began to shine the brightest."* - Katrina Mayer, a contemporary author and speaker. Confidential counseling services or partnerships with mental health professionals can offer employees resources to address and manage stress effectively.

Implementing these evidence-based methods requires a commitment to fostering a culture that prioritizes employee well-being. By offering a variety of strategies and resources, organizations can effectively prevent and manage stress, leading to a healthier and more productive workplace.

Prioritizing stress prevention and management in corporate settings is essential for fostering a culture of well-being and productivity. By implementing evidence-based methods and providing support resources, organizations can empower employees to navigate stress effectively and thrive in the workplace. As we strive to create healthier work environments, let us remember the wisdom encapsulated in these quotes, offering inspiration and guidance on the journey towards stress-free and fulfilling work lives.

7.3 Showcase companies that have successfully implemented stress-reduction programs.

As the demands of the workplace continue to increase, organizations are recognizing the importance of implementing stress reduction programs to support their workforce. By prioritizing employee mental health and creating environments conducive to well-being, companies can enhance productivity, reduce turnover, and foster a culture of resilience. This exploration explores five exemplary companies renowned for their successful implementation of stress reduction initiatives, showcasing their commitment to supporting employee well-being and creating healthier work environments.

Google is renowned for its comprehensive approach to employee well-being, offering various stress reduction programs. Among these are onsite wellness and fitness centers where employees can engage in physical activities to alleviate stress. Additionally, Google provides mindfulness and meditation programs to help employees cultivate mental well-being. Access to mental health counseling services further supports employees in managing stress, while flexible work arrangements contribute to maintaining a healthy work-life balance.

Microsoft places a strong emphasis on employee wellness, implementing a range of stress reduction initiatives. These initiatives include wellness programs that feature yoga and meditation classes, providing employees with tools to manage stress effectively. Microsoft also encourages breaks and relaxation during work hours, recognizing the importance of downtime for mental rejuvenation. Access to mental health resources and counseling services further reinforces their commitment to supporting employee well-being.

Salesforce prioritizes employee well-being by integrating stress reduction strategies into their corporate culture. Their mindfulness and resilience programs equip employees with techniques to manage stress proactively, fostering resilience in the face of challenges. Moreover, Salesforce provides access to wellness resources and counseling services, ensuring employees have the support they need to navigate stressful situations. A supportive work culture that promotes work-life balance underscores their commitment to employee wellness.

Patagonia adopts a holistic approach to employee well-being, incorporating stress reduction programs into their organizational practices. They encourage employees to take time off for outdoor activities, recognizing the benefits of nature in reducing stress levels. Flexible work schedules further contribute to promoting work-life balance, allowing employees to prioritize their well-being. Access to mental health resources and support networks reinforces their dedication to supporting employee mental health.

Johnson & Johnson demonstrates a strong commitment to employee wellness and stress reduction through their comprehensive programs. Their wellness programs focus on stress management and resilience, providing employees with strategies to cope with workplace stressors effectively. Access to counseling services and mental health support ensures employees have access to professional assistance when needed. Strategies such as flexible work arrangements further promote work-life balance, contributing to overall employee well-being. These companies exemplify successful integration of stress reduction initiatives into their corporate cultures, prioritizing employee well-being and fostering a supportive work environment.

In conclusion, the showcased companies serve as beacons of success in prioritizing employee well-being and implementing effective stress reduction programs. Through initiatives such as onsite wellness centers, mindfulness programs, and flexible work arrangements, these organizations have demonstrated their commitment to supporting employees in managing workplace stress.

By fostering a culture of resilience and providing access to resources for mental health support, these companies not only enhance employee satisfaction and retention but also cultivate a more productive and thriving work environment. As other organizations strive to emulate their success, the lessons learned from these exemplary companies underscore the importance of investing in employee well-being as a cornerstone of organizational success in the modern workplace.

Part 4

Implementing Strategies for a Mentally Healthy Workplace

Chapter 8

Happiness as a Corporate Strategy: Practical Applications

Embracing happiness as a fundamental pillar of corporate strategy marks a profound shift in today's business landscape. In an era defined by relentless competition and ever-increasing demands, prioritizing employee well-being transcends mere sentimentality—it becomes an essential driver of organizational success. By cultivating workplaces where employee happiness is not just a peripheral concern but a central ethos, companies foster environments ripe for innovation, collaboration, and sustained growth. Let's explore the tangible strategies that underpin this philosophy, paving the way for workplaces where happiness isn't just an afterthought but a strategic imperative.

Crafting a workplace culture that prioritizes employee well-being and happiness requires a comprehensive approach that seamlessly blends various strategies.

Firstly, it's crucial to implement robust employee well-being programs. This involves providing access to mental health support through counseling and Employee Assistance Programs (EAPs), as well as offering physical health initiatives like wellness programs and gym memberships. Additionally, advocating for a healthy work-life balance by supporting flexible work arrangements is essential to ensure employees can effectively manage their professional and personal commitments.

Creating a positive work culture is equally important. Recognizing and appreciating employees' efforts and achievements through formal recognition programs can boost morale and motivation. Fostering an environment of open communication, where feedback is encouraged and valued at all organizational levels, builds trust and transparency. Moreover, promoting a collaborative atmosphere encourages teamwork and camaraderie among colleagues, enhancing overall job satisfaction and engagement.

Meaningful work and engagement are foundational to employee happiness. Aligning organizational goals with employees' values and sense of purpose gives their roles a sense of meaning and significance. Providing opportunities for empowerment and autonomy enables employees to take ownership of their work, fostering pride and fulfillment.

Investing in continuous learning and development is another vital aspect. Offering ongoing training, mentorship programs, and skill development opportunities not only enhances employees' capabilities but also demonstrates a commitment to their growth and advancement within the organization.

Regular well-being assessments and feedback mechanisms are essential for gauging and improving employee happiness. Conducting employee surveys to measure satisfaction, well-being, and engagement levels, and acting upon the feedback received, shows genuine concern for employees' welfare. Implementing assessments or tools to evaluate employee well-being identifies areas for improvement and informs strategic decision-making.

Leadership and managerial support play a pivotal role in fostering a happy workplace. Equipping managers with the skills to lead with empathy, actively listen to employee concerns, and provide necessary support creates a supportive and nurturing environment. Encouraging leadership to exemplify positive behavior emphasizes well-being and happiness as fundamental components of organizational success.

Finally, establishing flexible and supportive policies further reinforces a culture of well-being. Creating policies that accommodate flexible work hours, remote work options, and generous time-off policies tailored to employees' needs fosters a sense of trust and respect. Offering unwavering support during challenging times, such as personal crises or family emergencies, demonstrates a commitment to employee welfare and strengthens organizational resilience.

By seamlessly integrating these strategies into corporate operations, organizations can cultivate workplaces where happiness isn't just an ideal but a tangible reality, resulting in heightened employee satisfaction, increased engagement, and a thriving organizational culture.

In conclusion, the implementation of these holistic strategies isn't merely an idealistic endeavor but a pragmatic investment in the success and sustainability of organizations. Research by Gallup consistently shows that companies with highly engaged employees outperform their competitors by 147% in earnings per share. Furthermore, studies by the University of Warwick have revealed that happy employees are up to 12% more productive than their counterparts.

By seamlessly integrating these strategies into corporate operations, organizations can pave the way for workplaces where happiness isn't just an aspiration but a tangible reality, fostering enhanced employee satisfaction, heightened engagement, and a culture of sustained well-being. This isn't just about creating a pleasant work environment; it's about driving bottom-line results through a workforce that feels valued, supported, and empowered to thrive. As companies navigate the complexities of the modern business landscape, prioritizing employee well-being isn't just a nicety—it's a strategic imperative for long-term success and prosperity.

8.1 Explain how happiness can be integrated into corporate strategy and culture.

Integrating happiness into corporate strategy and culture isn't just about adding another item to the to-do list—it's about fostering an environment where employee well-being, satisfaction, and positive experiences take center stage. Here's how we can seamlessly weave happiness into the fabric of our workplace:

Firstly, let's set some Happiness Objectives. We can embed happiness as a core value in our company's mission statement and organizational values, making it clear that it's not just a nice-to-have but a fundamental part of who we are. Aligning our strategic goals with employee happiness is crucial too, recognizing it as a key factor in achieving overall success.

Now, let's talk about Leadership Commitment. It's essential for our top executives and senior leaders to lead by example. We need them to champion happiness initiatives and embody positive behaviors themselves. Providing leadership training on fostering a positive work environment, emphasizing empathy, and promoting well-being will set the tone for the entire organization.

Cultivating a Positive Work Culture is another key aspect. We want to encourage a workplace culture where positivity thrives. This means celebrating successes, fostering optimism, and appreciating diversity and inclusion. Establishing transparent communication channels where employees feel heard, valued, and encouraged to share ideas and concerns is vital too.

Employee Well-Being Programs are a cornerstone of our happiness strategy. We need to offer a comprehensive range of programs that support mental, physical, and emotional well-being. Whether it's mindfulness workshops, fitness programs, or counseling services, we want to ensure our employees have the support they need. And let's not forget about Work-Life Integration—creating policies that support work-life balance, flexible schedules, remote work options, and adequate time off to rejuvenate.

Recognition and Appreciation go a long way in boosting happiness. Implementing recognition programs to appreciate employees' efforts and achievements reinforces a culture of appreciation. Providing constructive feedback and growth opportunities also plays a crucial role in fostering a sense of accomplishment and personal development.

Continuous Learning and Development are essential for employee growth and fulfillment. Offering continuous training and development programs allows employees to acquire new skills and advance their careers within the organization.

Measurement and Feedback are key to ensuring our happiness initiatives are hitting the mark. Regularly measuring employee satisfaction, happiness levels, and engagement through surveys and assessments gives us valuable insights. And most importantly, we need to act on this feedback—addressing concerns and making necessary adjustments to improve workplace happiness.

Finally, let's remember to Evolve and Adapt. We need to be flexible in our approach, continuously evolving our happiness initiatives based on changing employee needs, technological advancements, and societal shifts. Encouraging experimentation and innovation in happiness strategies will keep our workplace dynamic and adaptive.

By integrating happiness into our corporate strategy and culture through these approaches, we can create an environment that prioritizes employee well-being, fosters engagement, and ultimately leads to a more productive and fulfilled workforce.

8.2 Provide actionable steps for organizations to enhance employee well-being.

To enhance employee well-being through leadership support, organizations can implement various strategies aimed at fostering a supportive and empowering environment. This begins with leaders leading by example, demonstrating behaviors that prioritize work-life balance and mental health awareness. Additionally, providing managerial training equips leaders with the necessary skills to effectively support their teams' well-being, including fostering open communication and recognizing signs of stress. Promoting flexibility in work arrangements and prioritizing transparent communication further strengthens the relationship between leaders and employees, fostering trust and mutual respect. By recognizing and rewarding supportive leadership behaviors, organizations reinforce the importance of prioritizing employee well-being, ultimately contributing to a positive and thriving work culture.

To enhance employee well-being, organizations can implement a range of actionable steps, particularly within the realm of leadership support. Let's dive into these strategies:

Firstly, it's essential to prioritize Mental Health Support. As the renowned psychiatrist and psychoanalyst Carl Jung once said, **"The shoe that fits one person pinches another; there is no recipe for living that suits all cases."** Providing access to confidential counseling services or Employee Assistance Programs (EAPs) for mental health support acknowledges the individuality of each employee's mental health needs. Additionally, conducting workshops and seminars to raise awareness and reduce stigma around mental health issues can contribute significantly.

Fostering a Supportive Work Environment is equally crucial. As Maya Angelou, the celebrated poet and civil rights activist, famously stated, **"People will forget what you said, people will forget what you did, but people will never forget**

how you made them feel." Establishing support networks such as support groups or peer networks where employees can connect, share experiences, and seek guidance can also create a supportive atmosphere.

Promoting Physical Well-being is another vital aspect. According to the World Health Organization (WHO), **"Health is a state of complete physical, mental, and social well-being and not merely the absence of disease or infirmity."** Offering wellness programs and health initiatives not only improves physical health but also contributes to overall well-being. Organizing health screenings, vaccinations, and ergonomic assessments further supports employees' physical health.

Continuous Learning is key to employee growth and well-being. Albert Einstein once remarked, **"Intellectual growth should commence at birth and cease only at death."** Providing opportunities for skill development and career advancement empowers employees to reach their full potential. Offering pathways for career advancement, mentorship programs, and support for professional growth also plays a crucial role.

Recognizing and Appreciating Contributions boosts morale and motivation. As Dale Carnegie, author of "How to Win Friends and Influence People," famously said, **"People work for money but go the extra mile for recognition, praise, and rewards."** Implementing reward systems, employee-of-the-month acknowledgments, or peer recognition initiatives shows employees that their efforts are valued. Providing regular feedback and recognition fosters a culture of appreciation and growth.

Improving Work Relationships is essential for a positive work environment. As Margaret Wheatley, an expert on organizational behavior, aptly noted, **"Without relationships, there is no learning."** Encouraging open communication and promoting teamwork foster strong relationships among employees. Promoting teamwork and collaboration through project-based work fosters a sense of camaraderie and support.

Emphasizing Leadership Support is paramount. According to Simon Sinek, author of "Start with Why," **"Leadership is not about being in charge. It is about taking care of those in your charge."** Providing managerial training and leading by example demonstrate a commitment to supporting and empowering employees.

Lastly, organizations should Evaluate and Adapt their strategies based on feedback and surveys. As Peter Drucker, management consultant and author, famously said, **"If you can't measure it, you can't improve it**." Regularly gathering feedback and acting on it ensures that organizations remain responsive to the evolving needs of their employees.

In conclusion, by implementing these actionable steps, organizations can demonstrate their commitment to enhancing employee well-being. By prioritizing mental and physical health, creating a supportive work culture, promoting continuous learning, and fostering positive relationships, organizations can significantly improve the overall well-being and satisfaction of their employees.

8.3   Share stories of companies that have embraced happiness as a business asset.

"Investing in employee happiness is not just good for people; it's good for business too." – Richard Branson

Amidst the ever-evolving landscape of commerce, the axiom rings true: the happiness of employees is the cornerstone of organizational triumph. Consider this: research by the University of Warwick reveals that businesses with happy employees experience a staggering 12% increase in productivity. In this dynamic realm where success is measured not just in profits but in smiles, a new narrative unfolds—one where companies champion the well-being of their workforce with zeal and purpose. Join us and explore the stories of Zappos, Airbnb, Patagonia, Google, and Buffer—pioneers in the pursuit of employee happiness and catalysts of change in the corporate world.

1. Zappos, under the visionary leadership of CEO Tony Hsieh, has made employee happiness a cornerstone of its corporate strategy. As Tony Hsieh famously said, "Happiness is a business model." The company's unique initiative, the "Culture Book," allows employees to share their experiences and insights about working at Zappos, fostering a culture of transparency and open communication. Research by the University of Warwick suggests that happy employees are up to 12% more productive, highlighting the tangible benefits of prioritizing employee happiness. Through initiatives like

the Culture Book, Zappos has created an environment where employees feel valued, engaged, and motivated to contribute their best work.

2. Airbnb understands the importance of employee happiness in driving business success. As co-founder Brian Chesky once said, **"Culture is simply a shared way of doing something with passion."** The company encourages creativity and innovation among its employees by providing opportunities for them to contribute their ideas and solutions. Research by Gallup shows that highly engaged teams achieve, on average, 21% greater profitability. By fostering a supportive workplace culture and promoting a strong sense of community, Airbnb has created an environment where employees feel valued, empowered, and motivated to excel.

3. Patagonia's commitment to employee well-being is aligned with its dedication to environmental responsibility and social impact. As founder Yvon Chouinard famously said, **"Let my people go surfing."** The company promotes a supportive work environment with a focus on work-life balance, recognizing that happy employees are more likely to be passionate about their work and contribute positively to the company's mission. Research by Harvard Business Review suggests that companies with strong cultures of well-being report higher levels of employee engagement and lower turnover rates. Through initiatives like paid time off for environmental initiatives and transparent communication practices, Patagonia has created a workplace where employees feel valued, respected, and inspired to make a difference.

4. Google's workplace initiatives are designed to enhance employee happiness and satisfaction. As former CEO Eric Schmidt once said, **"We run the company by ideas, not hierarchy."** The company provides various on-site amenities and opportunities for personal and professional growth to promote employee well-being. Research by McKinsey & Company suggests that companies with diverse and inclusive cultures are more likely to outperform their peers financially. By fostering a culture of innovation and empowerment and actively soliciting feedback from employees, Google creates an environment where employees feel supported, valued, and motivated to succeed.

5. Buffer's approach to employee well-being is characterized by its commitment to flexibility and transparency. As co-founder Joel Gascoigne once said, **"Transparency breeds trust, and trust is the foundation of great**

teamwork." The company offers flexible work arrangements and practices radical transparency within the organization, fostering a culture of trust and collaboration. Research by Glassdoor indicates that companies with strong cultures of transparency and trust tend to outperform their peers in terms of financial performance. By providing opportunities for personal and professional growth and empowering employees to take ownership of their work, Buffer creates a workplace where employees feel empowered, motivated, and valued.

These companies demonstrate that prioritizing employee happiness and well-being as a business asset leads to increased employee satisfaction, higher productivity, and a positive workplace culture. Through initiatives like the Culture Book at Zappos and transparent communication practices at Patagonia and Buffer, companies can create environments where employees feel valued, engaged, and inspired to contribute their best work.

As we draw the curtains with these examples, one question will alway lingers in the air: What legacy will your organization leave behind? Will it be one of mere success, or will it transcend, becoming a beacon of happiness, innovation, and fulfillment? In a world where the line between work and life blurs, the answer lies not in profits alone but in the hearts and minds of those who propel your organization forward. So, as you navigate the seas of business, remember this: the journey to greatness begins with a simple question—how happy are your employees

Chapter 9

Leading with Empathy: The Role of Leadership in Mental Health

Leadership in the realm of mental health is a profound responsibility that transcends mere management—it's about creating environments where empathy thrives and well-being flourishes. It's a journey guided by the principle that understanding and support can transform workplaces into havens of compassion and resilience.

At its core, empathetic leadership fosters a culture where mental health concerns are met with empathy rather than judgment. Leaders set the tone by cultivating safe spaces where employees feel comfortable discussing their challenges and seeking support without fear of stigma or reprisal. As Maya Angelou once said, *"I've learned that people will forget what you said, people will forget what you did, but people will never forget how you made them feel."* By leading by example, demonstrating empathy in their own behavior, leaders inspire others to follow suit, nurturing a culture of understanding and acceptance.

A key aspect of empathetic leadership is prioritizing mental health initiatives within the organization. This involves allocating resources and budget to mental health programs, ensuring that employees have access to vital resources such as counselling, therapy, and mental health training. Moreover, leaders advocate for policies that support mental health, such as flexible work arrangements and mental health days, demonstrating a tangible commitment to employee well-being. As Desmond Tutu famously said, *"Hope is being able to see that there is light despite all of the darkness."*

Active listening and engagement are essential components of empathetic leadership in mental health. Leaders listen attentively and empathetically to employees' concerns, validating their experiences without judgment. Regular check-ins provide opportunities for leaders to inquire about employees' well-being, reducing feelings of isolation and fostering a sense of belonging within the organization.

Recognizing and addressing signs of distress is another crucial aspect of empathetic leadership. Leaders receive training to recognize signs of mental distress early and offer support to employees in need. Moreover, leaders foster open dialogue about mental health, creating an environment where employees feel safe to seek help or support without fear of stigma. As Brene Brown once said, ***Vulnerability is not winning or losing; it's having the courage to show up and be seen when we have no control over the outcome.***"

Supporting work-life balance is fundamental to empathetic leadership in mental health. Leaders promote healthy work-life balance by respecting boundaries, discouraging overwork, and implementing flexible work arrangements that accommodate employees' personal needs. By prioritizing work-life balance, leaders reduce stress and support employees' mental well-being.

Offering guidance and resources is another way that empathetic leaders support mental health within their organizations. Leaders' direct employees to available resources such as counselling services, Employee Assistance Programs (EAPs), and mental health professionals. Moreover, leaders promote self-care practices, mindfulness, and stress reduction techniques as essential components of a healthy lifestyle.

Advocating for psychological safety is a cornerstone of empathetic leadership in mental health. Leaders create environments where employees feel psychologically safe to express themselves without fear of retribution or ostracization. By embracing vulnerability and acknowledging their own struggles, leaders foster trust and connection within their teams.

In conclusion, empathetic leadership in mental health is not just a duty but a privilege—a chance to create workplaces where every individual feels seen, heard, and valued. By championing empathy, leaders can transform organizational cultures, fostering environments where mental health is prioritized, understood, and supported. And so, as we navigate the complexities of leadership, let us remember the words of Nelson Mandela: *"It is better to lead from behind and to put others in front, especially when you celebrate victory when nice things occur. You take the front line when there is danger. Then people will appreciate your leadership."*

9.1   Explore the impact of leadership styles on employee mental health.

Leadership styles wield significant influence over the mental well-being of employees, shaping their job satisfaction and overall work experience. The manner in which leaders engage with their teams can either bolster or undermine mental health. Let's explore various leadership styles and their distinct impact on employee mental well-being:

- **Supportive and Empathetic Leadership:** Leaders who embody empathy and support foster an environment where employees feel valued, heard, and appreciated. By actively listening to their team members, offering guidance, and creating a safe space for discussions about mental health, these leaders positively contribute to employee well-being. A prime example is the leadership at Patagonia, where CEO Rose Marcario's emphasis on employee well-being and environmental stewardship has created a culture of care and empathy.

- **Authoritarian or Autocratic Leadership:** In contrast, authoritarian leadership characterized by rigid control and limited employee autonomy can exacerbate stress, anxiety, and diminish morale. Employees may feel disempowered and overwhelmed by pressure, negatively affecting their mental health. An example of such leadership can be found in the case of Theranos, where CEO Elizabeth Holmes' domineering management style contributed to a toxic work environment and employee burnout.

- **Transformational Leadership:** Transformational leaders inspire and empower their teams, fostering engagement, motivation, and a sense of purpose. By encouraging innovation, offering mentorship, and supporting personal growth, these leaders enhance employee mental health and job satisfaction. One notable example is Microsoft under the leadership of Satya

Nadella, who transformed the company's culture by emphasizing empathy, collaboration, and continuous learning.

- **Transactional Leadership:** Transactional leaders focus on task accomplishment and performance, which can yield mixed results for employee mental health. While clear expectations and rewards can motivate employees, an overemphasis on punishment or rigid structures may increase stress and limit well-being. An example of transactional leadership can be observed in the fast-food industry, where managers often employ strict performance metrics without considering the well-being of their employees.

- **Servant Leadership:** Servant leaders prioritize the needs of their employees, aiming to serve and support their growth and well-being. By focusing on the development of their team members and providing guidance and support, these leaders cultivate an environment conducive to enhanced mental health and job satisfaction. One exemplary servant leader is Indra Nooyi, former CEO of PepsiCo, known for her commitment to empowering and nurturing her employees' talents and well-being.

- **Laissez-Faire Leadership:** Leaders who adopt a laissez-faire approach, being hands-off and providing minimal guidance, can negatively impact employee mental health. Without clear direction or support, employees may experience confusion, stress, and a sense of abandonment. A real-world example of this leadership style can be seen in the case of WeWork under the leadership of Adam Neumann, where a lack of strategic direction and oversight led to employee uncertainty and anxiety.

- **Adaptive or Situational Leadership:** Adaptive leaders tailor their approach based on situational requirements, addressing individual needs and promoting well-being. By adapting to the team's dynamics and challenges, these leaders foster a supportive environment that nurtures employee mental health. An example of adaptive leadership can be found in the healthcare sector, where hospital administrators adjust their leadership style to meet the evolving needs of healthcare professionals during times of crisis, such as the COVID-19 pandemic.

Leadership styles wield immense power in shaping the workplace atmosphere and directly impacting employee mental well-being. While supportive and empowering leadership styles foster a positive environment, autocratic or neglectful approaches can contribute to stress and decreased well-being among employees. As leaders, it is imperative to recognize the profound influence of our leadership style and strive to cultivate environments where mental health is prioritized and valued.

9.2 Offer insights into empathetic leadership and its benefits.

Insights into empathetic leadership unveil a multitude of advantages that transcend traditional managerial approaches. By fostering trust and psychological safety, empathetic leaders forge profound connections with their teams, where active listening and understanding lay the foundation for enhanced relationships. Employees feel empowered to express themselves authentically, knowing their concerns will be met with empathy rather than judgment, thereby nurturing a culture of openness and trust.

Moreover, empathetic leadership promotes collaboration and teamwork by fostering improved communication and a cohesive team dynamic. When employees feel understood and valued by their leader, they are more inclined to collaborate effectively, leveraging their diverse skills and perspectives to achieve common goals.

In addition to enhancing collaboration, empathetic leadership boosts employee engagement by bolstering morale and motivation. Leaders who acknowledge and appreciate their employees' efforts inspire a sense of purpose and fulfillment, driving higher job satisfaction and a more committed workforce.

Furthermore, empathetic leadership plays a pivotal role in supporting mental health and well-being within organizations. By recognizing and addressing employee concerns and providing emotional support, empathetic leaders help alleviate stress and build resilience among their teams, fostering a healthier and more supportive work environment.

Empathetic leadership also facilitates effective conflict resolution by navigating conflicts with understanding and respect. By acknowledging differing viewpoints and fostering an environment of mutual respect, leaders reduce tension and promote a harmonious work culture where collaboration thrives.

Moreover, empathetic leadership encourages innovation and creativity by creating a safe space for ideas and fostering a culture that values empathy and understanding. Employees feel empowered to share unconventional ideas and contribute innovative solutions when they feel understood and supported by their leader.

Furthermore, empathetic leaders support employee growth and development by offering personalized guidance and creating learning opportunities. By investing in their employees' professional growth and fostering a culture of continuous learning, leaders cultivate a motivated and skilled workforce.

Finally, empathetic leadership strengthens organizational culture by setting a positive example and attracting top talent seeking supportive work environments. Organizations with empathetic leaders at the helm tend to cultivate cultures that prioritize empathy, kindness, and understanding, leading to higher employee satisfaction and organizational success.

9.3 Provide leadership practices and techniques for nurturing a mentally healthy workforce.

In the journey of nurturing a mentally healthy workforce, leadership practices and techniques play a crucial role. Here's a seamless exploration of these practices and techniques:

Fostering Open Communication is the cornerstone of a supportive workplace environment. Leaders can achieve this through Active Listening, where they tune in to employees' concerns, perspectives, and challenges without judgment. Regular Check-Ins, in the form of one-on-one meetings, provide a platform to discuss work-related issues, personal challenges, and career aspirations, fostering trust and understanding.

Imagine Sarah, a team leader at a bustling marketing agency, embodying the essence of Active Listening as she sits down with her colleague, Alex. Alex shares concerns about a new project, expressing doubts about meeting deadlines. Rather than offering immediate solutions, Sarah listens intently, absorbing Alex's worries without judgment. She asks probing questions, seeking to understand the root of the issue and offering empathy in return.

In another scenario, David, a manager at a tech startup, demonstrates the power of Regular Check-Ins during his weekly meetings with his team members. These sessions transcend the confines of task delegation, morphing into opportunities for genuine connection. As David engages in heartfelt conversations with his team, he learns about their dreams, struggles, and aspirations. Through these exchanges, trust blossoms, paving the way for collaborative growth and mutual support.

Through these examples, the transformative impact of fostering open communication becomes evident. Leaders like Sarah and David serve as beacons of empathy, creating spaces where every voice is heard and valued. In these nurturing environments, teams thrive, propelled by the power of understanding and connection.

Promoting Work-Life Balance is essential for employee well-being. Work-life balance means finding a good mix between your job and the other parts of your life, like spending time with family, taking care of yourself, and doing things you enjoy. It's about not letting work take over everything and making sure you have time for the things that matter outside of work. When you have a good work-life balance, you feel happier, less stressed, and more fulfilled in both your job and your personal life.

Measuring work-life balance can be a bit tricky because it's different for everyone and involves both subjective feelings and objective factors. Here are some ways to measure it:

- ✔ **Self-Assessment:** Reflect on how you feel about your work-life balance. Are you feeling overwhelmed by work? Do you have enough time for yourself and your loved ones? Your own perceptions can give you valuable insights.

- ✔ **Time Allocation:** Track how you spend your time each day. Are you spending too much time at work and not enough on other activities? Keeping a journal or using time-tracking apps can help you see where your time is going.

- ✔ **Health and Well-being:** Pay attention to your physical and mental health. Are you feeling stressed, anxious, or burnt out? Are you getting enough sleep and exercise? Your overall well-being can be a good indicator of whether your work-life balance is in check.

- ✔ **Quality of Relationships:** Consider the quality of your relationships with family, friends, and colleagues. Are you able to spend meaningful time with them? Are your relationships suffering because of work demands?

- ✔ **Productivity and Performance**: Assess how your work performance is impacted by your work-life balance. Are you able to focus and be productive at work? Are you meeting your goals and deadlines?

By considering these factors, you can get a better understanding of your work-life balance and identify areas where you might need to make adjustments

Research by the American Psychological Association shows that employees who feel supported in their work-life balance are more satisfied with their jobs and experience less stress. Leaders can achieve this by offering Flexible Schedules, allowing employees to manage personal needs while maintaining productivity. Encouraging Time Off, including vacation days and mental health breaks, allows employees to recharge and maintain a healthy work-life balance.

Leading by Example sets the tone for a mentally healthy workplace culture. As Mahatma Gandhi famously said, ***"Be the change that you wish to see in the world."*** Leaders can demonstrate Self-Care by prioritizing their own mental health and well-being, serving as role models for the team. Sharing Personal Experiences, when appropriate, about stress management and coping strategies, fosters empathy and understanding among team members.

Providing Support and Resources is vital for addressing mental health needs. According to a study by Deloitte, organizations that invest in mental health support see a return of $4 for every $1 invested. Leaders can offer access to Mental Health Resources such as counselling services, Employee Assistance Programs (EAPs), or mental health workshops. Educating on Well-being through training sessions on stress management, mindfulness, and mental health awareness equips employees with valuable tools for self-care.

Encouraging Team Building fosters a sense of belonging and support among team members. As Helen Keller once said, ***"Alone we can do so little; together we can do so much."*** Leaders can organize Team Bonding Activities, social events, or volunteer activities to strengthen relationships and collaboration.

Promoting Peer Support encourages team members to support each other, creating a supportive team culture where individuals feel valued and understood.

Recognizing and Appreciating employees' efforts is essential for boosting morale and motivation. According to Gallup, employees who feel appreciated are more engaged and productive. Leaders can Acknowledge Efforts by recognizing and appreciating employees' contributions and achievements. Providing Constructive Feedback helps employees grow and develop professionally, fostering a culture of continuous improvement.

Creating a Positive Work Environment is conducive to employee well-being. As Zig Ziglar once said, ***"Your attitude, not your aptitude, will determine your altitude."*** Leaders can Cultivate Positivity by celebrating successes, focusing on strengths, and reframing challenges as opportunities. Reducing Stigma around mental health discussions normalizes conversations about well-being, creating an environment where employees feel safe seeking support.

Developing Career Paths offers opportunities for growth and advancement within the organization. According to LinkedIn, 93% of employees would stay at a company longer if it invested in their careers. Leaders can offer Career Development Opportunities such as skill development programs and promotions. Setting Clear Expectations on roles, responsibilities, and career paths reduces ambiguity and stress, empowering employees to pursue their career goals.

Supporting Personal Growth is essential for employee satisfaction and engagement. As Oprah Winfrey once said, ***"The greatest discovery of all time is that a person can change their future by merely changing their attitude."*** Leaders can provide Individualized Support tailored to employees' professional and personal goals, fostering a sense of purpose and fulfillment. Encouraging Learning through workshops, courses, or mentorship programs enables continuous growth and development.

Adapting to Changing Needs demonstrates agility and responsiveness to employee feedback and evolving circumstances. As Charles Darwin famously said, "It is not the strongest of the species that survive, nor the most intelligent, but the one most responsive to change." Leaders can adopt a Flexible Approach to adjusting strategies based on employee needs and feedback. Regular Evaluation of mental health initiatives ensures their effectiveness and identifies areas for improvement, reinforcing a commitment to employee well-being.

Chapter 10

Empowering Employees: Self-Care and Communication

Empowering employees through self-care and effective communication is crucial for their well-being and overall success.

Self-care is about taking intentional actions to maintain and improve our physical, mental, and emotional well-being. It's essential because, just like we have families to care for, we must also prioritize caring for ourselves. When we neglect our own needs, it becomes challenging to fulfill our responsibilities effectively, whether at work or at home. Therefore, incorporating self-care practices into our routines helps us recharge, manage stress, and maintain a healthy balance between our personal and professional lives.

Organizations can take proactive steps to foster such empowerment and support their employees in various ways. In terms of self-care initiatives, organizations can encourage mindfulness and stress management by offering workshops or sessions on meditation and relaxation techniques. Providing resources like relaxation apps or breathing exercises can further assist employees in managing stress effectively. Promoting work-life balance is also essential, with initiatives such as advocating for regular breaks during work hours and encouraging employees to disconnect after work to prevent burnout. Wellness programs focusing on physical health, nutrition, fitness, and sleep hygiene can be organized, along with offering gym memberships or yoga classes to support healthy lifestyles.

Effective communication plays a pivotal role in empowering employees. Creating a transparent and open communication environment where employees feel comfortable sharing their thoughts and concerns fosters trust and engagement. Implementing two-way communication ensures that employees' voices are heard and valued. Training managers and leaders in active listening techniques can help them better understand employees' needs without judgment. A constructive feedback culture is also crucial, where regular feedback is provided to help employees grow and improve performance, fostering a culture where feedback is seen as developmental rather than critical.

Empowerment strategies further contribute to employee empowerment. Granting autonomy to employees and allowing them to make decisions within their roles enhances their sense of ownership and responsibility. Offering opportunities for skill development and training through workshops, courses, or mentorship programs supports their professional growth and career development. Recognizing and appreciating employees' efforts, achievements, and contributions regularly through acknowledgment programs reinforces their value within the organization.

Additionally, organizations need to prioritize mental health support. Providing access to mental health resources such as counseling services and Employee Assistance Programs (EAPs) can offer vital support to employees facing mental health challenges. Promoting awareness of mental health issues and reducing stigma through workshops and campaigns can create a more supportive environment. Offering flexibility in work arrangements and creating a culture where seeking help for mental health concerns is encouraged and normalized further supports employee well-being.

To understand how employees feel and what they need at work, managers use various methods like surveys, interviews, and performance metrics. These tools help them gather information about employee satisfaction, workload, and well-being. By talking to employees, observing their behavior, and comparing their performance with industry standards, managers can identify areas for improvement and make informed decisions to create a better work environment.

By incorporating these strategies, organizations can create a workplace culture that values employees' well-being, encourages their growth, and ultimately leads to higher engagement, productivity, and overall satisfaction.

10.1 Empower employees with self-care strategies for maintaining mental health.

Improving mental health among employees is crucial for their overall well-being, productivity, and satisfaction at work. Statistics from the National Institute for Occupational Safety and Health (NIOSH) indicate that work-related stress accounts for 83% of the total cases of work-related illnesses. To address this issue, empowering employees with self-care strategies is essential. By adopting effective self-care practices, individuals can better manage their mental health amidst the demands of their professional and personal lives.

One of the fundamental self-care practices is prioritizing work-life balance. For example, a longitudinal study conducted by the American Psychological Association found that employees who had better work-life balance reported lower levels of stress and higher job satisfaction ("Work-Life Fit: Overlapping the domains of work, family, and personal life," American Psychologist, 2001). This involves establishing clear boundaries between work and personal life, avoiding overworking, and taking regular breaks. Disconnecting from work emails and tasks after work hours is also vital to recharge and relax.

Stress management techniques play a significant role in maintaining mental well-being. Research published in the Journal of Clinical Psychology has shown that mindfulness meditation can reduce symptoms of anxiety and depression by 10-20% ("Mindfulness-Based Stress Reduction and Health Benefits: A Meta-Analysis," Journal of Psychosomatic Research, 2004). Mindfulness exercises, meditation, and deep breathing techniques can help reduce stress levels and enhance mental clarity. Additionally, incorporating regular physical activity and maintaining a balanced diet are crucial aspects of self-care for promoting physical and mental well-being.

Building supportive relationships is another important self-care practice. A study published in the Journal of Occupational Health Psychology found that employees with strong social connections at work are more engaged and satisfied with their jobs ("Social Support at Work and Its Relationship to Burnout and Job Satisfaction," Journal of Occupational Health Psychology, 1997). Seeking support from friends, family, or colleagues and engaging in social activities can provide emotional support and reduce feelings of isolation.

Effective time management and organization skills contribute to managing workload stress. Studies have shown that employees who effectively manage their time experience lower levels of stress and higher job satisfaction ("Time Management and the Work Environment: A Review and Meta-Analysis," Personnel Psychology, 2012). Prioritizing tasks and scheduling time for self-care activities can prevent burnout and promote a healthier work-life balance.

Relaxation techniques such as progressive muscle relaxation and engaging in hobbies or creative activities can also help individuals unwind and alleviate stress. For example, a study published in the Journal of Occupational Health found that engaging in creative activities during leisure time can reduce stress and improve mood ("The Impact of Creative Activity on Employee Well-Being," Journal of Occupational Health, 2017).

Quality sleep is essential for mental health. Research has shown that adults who sleep less than 7 hours per night are more likely to report symptoms of stress, anxiety, and depression ("Sleep Duration and Its Association with Psychological Distress and Well-Being," Journal of Sleep Research, 2010). Establishing a consistent sleep schedule and practicing relaxation techniques before bedtime can improve sleep quality and overall well-being.

Promoting mental health awareness is key to proactively managing mental well-being. Studies have shown that employees who receive mental health education and support from their employers are more likely to seek help when needed ("Mental Health Awareness Programs in the Workplace: A Scoping Review," Journal of Occupational and Environmental Medicine, 2020). Regular self-assessment and seeking professional help when needed are crucial aspects of this practice.

Establishing healthy boundaries, such as learning to say no to excessive workload and delegating tasks, can prevent stress and maintain a healthy work-life balance.

Establishing healthy boundaries in the workplace involves several key strategies. Firstly, self-awareness is essential, as individuals must understand their own limits and preferences regarding workload. Clear communication with colleagues and supervisors is crucial to articulate these boundaries effectively. Prioritization helps individuals focus on important tasks while avoiding overcommitment. Effective time management ensures tasks are completed efficiently, with breaks scheduled for rest. Saying no when necessary allows individuals to maintain their boundaries and prevent overload.

Delegation distributes tasks appropriately, recognizing the need for collaboration. Maintaining work-life balance involves setting boundaries to separate professional and personal life. Consistency is vital in enforcing boundaries to ensure they are respected over time. By employing these strategies, individuals can manage their workload effectively, reduce stress, and achieve a healthier balance between work and life.

Studies have shown that employees who set boundaries at work experience less work-related burnout ("Work-Life Balance, Burnout, and Job Satisfaction among Doctoral Students," International Journal of Doctoral Studies, 2019).

Taking breaks and utilizing vacation time are important for rest and rejuvenation, ultimately boosting productivity and mental clarity. Asking for breaks or planning vacation time effectively is important for your well-being and productivity. Here's how you can do it:

First, talk to your boss or team about needing a break. Explain why it's important for you and how it can help you do better at work. Give them enough notice so they can plan around your absence.

When planning your vacation, think about when it's best to take time off. Try to pick times when work is not too busy. Make sure your tasks are taken care of before you leave so you can relax without worrying.

During your break, try to disconnect from work stuff and focus on things that make you feel good. This could be spending time with loved ones, doing hobbies, or just chilling out.

By talking openly, planning ahead, and taking care of yourself, you can enjoy your breaks and come back to work feeling refreshed and ready to go.

Research has shown that employees who take regular breaks are more productive and creative ("The Effects of Break Length on Employee Productivity, Health, and Well-Being: A Meta-Analysis," Journal of Applied Psychology, 2021).

In conclusion, empowering employees with these self-care strategies can help them effectively manage their mental health, reduce stress, enhance resilience, and improve overall well-being in both personal and professional aspects of their lives. By prioritizing self-care, individuals can thrive in their careers while maintaining a healthy work-life balance

10.2 Discuss the importance of open communication about mental health at work.

Creating a positive and supportive work environment is crucial for employee well-being and organizational success. One key aspect of fostering such an environment is promoting open communication about mental health. This practice not only reduces stigma but also enhances awareness, creates a supportive culture, improves productivity, and encourages seeking help when needed. In this article, we will explore the importance of open communication about mental health in the workplace and provide practical strategies for implementing it effectively.

Reducing Stigma: Open communication helps break down barriers and reduce the stigma surrounding mental health in the workplace. By normalizing discussions about mental health, employees feel more comfortable seeking help or support when needed. Research has shown that workplaces with open communication about mental health experience lower levels of stigma and higher rates of help-seeking behavior (source: "The Impact of Mental Health Awareness Training on Employee Attitudes and Behaviors in a University Setting," Journal of Occupational Health Psychology, 2018).

To encourage open communication about mental health, organizations can implement training programs and workshops to educate employees about mental health conditions, symptoms, and available resources. Additionally, leaders and managers can lead by example by openly discussing their own experiences with mental health and showing support for employees who seek help.

Creating a Supportive Culture: Open communication fosters a supportive workplace culture where employees feel valued, understood, and supported. By building trust and encouraging empathy among team members, organizations can create an environment where employees feel comfortable discussing their mental health concerns without fear of judgment or reprisal. Studies have shown that workplaces with supportive cultures experience higher levels of employee engagement and job satisfaction (source: "Creating a Supportive Workplace: Managerial Strategies to Reduce Workplace Stress," International Journal of Stress Management, 2017).

To promote a supportive culture, organizations can establish channels for employees to voice their concerns and provide feedback on mental health initiatives. Leaders can also implement policies and practices that prioritize employee well-being, such as flexible work arrangements, employee assistance programs, and mental health days.

Improving Productivity and Engagement: Open communication about mental health can have a positive impact on productivity and engagement in the workplace. When employees feel supported and valued, they are more likely to address and manage their mental health challenges, leading to improved focus, motivation, and performance. Research has shown that workplaces that prioritize employee well-being experience higher levels of productivity and lower rates of absenteeism and turnover (source: "The Relationship Between Employee Well-Being and Organizational Performance: A Review of the Literature," Journal of Occupational Health Psychology, 2019).

To enhance productivity and engagement, organizations can implement policies and practices that promote work-life balance, recognize and reward employees for their contributions, and provide opportunities for professional development and growth. Additionally, leaders can foster a culture of open communication by regularly checking in with employees, providing feedback and support, and addressing any concerns or issues that arise.

Encouraging Seeking Help: Open communication about mental health encourages employees to seek help when needed, leading to better outcomes for individuals and organizations alike. By ensuring employees are aware of available mental health resources and destigmatizing help-seeking behavior, organizations can create a supportive environment where employees feel comfortable accessing the support they need. Research has shown that workplaces that promote help-seeking behavior experience lower levels of mental health issues and higher rates of employee retention (source: "The Impact of Mental Health First Aid Training on Employee Mental Health and Help-Seeking Behavior," Journal of Occupational Health Psychology, 2020).

To encourage seeking help, organizations can provide access to confidential counseling services, mental health resources, and support groups. Leaders can also actively promote a culture of self-care and encourage employees to prioritize their mental health and well-being.

Encouraging open communication about mental health at work is essential for fostering a supportive and healthy workplace culture. By reducing stigma, enhancing awareness, creating a supportive culture, improving productivity and engagement, and encouraging seeking help, organizations can create an environment where employees feel valued, supported, and empowered to prioritize their mental health and well-being. Through leadership, education, and policy implementation, organizations can promote open communication about mental health and create a workplace where everyone can thrive.

10.3 Share tips for employees to effectively communicate their needs to their employers.

Effective communication between employees and employers regarding mental health needs is essential for creating a supportive work environment. In today's fast-paced and often stressful workplaces, employees may face various challenges that impact their mental well-being. Addressing these needs requires clear and open dialogue between employees and employers. In this guide, we'll explore some practical tips for employees to effectively communicate their mental health needs to their employers. Each tip is supported by research and aims to empower individuals to advocate for their well-being in the workplace.

1. Self-Awareness

Before initiating a conversation about mental health needs with their employers, employees should first develop self-awareness regarding their own mental well-being. Research suggests that self-awareness is crucial for understanding and managing one's emotions effectively (Brackett & Katulak, 2006). Here's how employees can enhance their self-awareness:

- Reflect on Needs: Encourage employees to take time to reflect on their mental health needs and how they may be influenced by their work environment.

- Identify Triggers: Help employees recognize specific stressors or triggers that affect their mental well-being at work.

- How to do it: Encourage employees to journal or engage in mindfulness practices to enhance self-awareness.

2. Choose the Right Timing and Setting

Timing and setting play a significant role in the effectiveness of communication. Employees should ensure they select an appropriate time and setting for discussing their mental health needs with their employers. Research shows that communication is more successful when individuals feel comfortable and relaxed (Miller, 2009). Here's how employees can choose the right timing and setting:

- Scheduled Meeting: Encourage employees to request a dedicated meeting with their employer or manager to ensure a focused discussion.

- Choose a Private Setting: Advise employees to find a private and comfortable space where they can have an open conversation without interruptions.

- How to do it: Suggest that employees schedule the meeting during a less busy time and choose a private meeting room to ensure confidentiality.

3. Be Clear and Specific

Clear and specific communication is essential for effectively conveying mental health needs to employers. Ambiguity can lead to misunderstandings and hinder the implementation of appropriate accommodations. Research indicates that clear communication promotes understanding and cooperation (Grice, 1975). Here's how employees can be clear and specific:

- Articulate Needs: Encourage employees to clearly explain how certain work conditions or situations impact their mental health.

- Use Examples: Advise employees to provide specific instances or examples to illustrate their concerns effectively.

- How to do it: Suggest that employees prepare notes or talking points beforehand to ensure clarity and specificity during the conversation.

4. Provide Solutions or Suggestions

While it's essential to communicate needs, employees can also offer solutions or suggestions to address their mental health concerns. Research suggests that problem-solving strategies lead to more effective outcomes in interpersonal communication (D'Zurilla & Nezu, 2007). Here's how employees can provide solutions or suggestions:

- Offer Solutions: Encourage employees to propose actionable solutions or accommodations that could help address their mental health needs at work.

- Collaborate on Strategies: Advise employees to involve their employers in brainstorming ways to make adjustments that support their well-being.

- How to do it: Suggest that employees research potential accommodations or strategies beforehand and present them during the conversation.

5. Communicate Effectively

Effective communication involves expressing thoughts and feelings clearly and respectfully. Employees should use language that promotes understanding and empathy when discussing their mental health needs with employers. Research shows that using "I" statements can facilitate constructive dialogue (Gottman & Silver, 1999). Here's how employees can communicate effectively:

- Use "I" Statements: Encourage employees to express their feelings and needs using "I" statements to convey personal experiences without blame.

- Stay Focused: Advise employees to stay on topic and avoid getting sidetracked from discussing their specific mental health needs.

- How to do it: Recommend that employees practice active listening and empathy to foster a supportive conversation.

6. Request Accommodations

If accommodations are necessary to support their mental health needs, employees should clearly communicate their requests to their employers. Research indicates that providing appropriate accommodations can improve employee well-being and productivity (Henderson et al., 2019). Here's how employees can request accommodations:

- Be Clear in Requests: Encourage employees to clearly state what accommodations they require (e.g., flexible schedule, workspace adjustments, etc.).

- Emphasize Benefits: Advise employees to highlight how accommodations can positively impact their productivity and well-being.

- How to do it: Suggest that employees provide documentation from healthcare professionals, if necessary, to support their accommodation requests.

7. Advocate for Support

Employees should not hesitate to advocate for the support they need to maintain their mental well-being in the workplace. Employers can provide access to resources and services that promote mental health awareness and support. Research shows that organizational support is positively associated with employee well-being (Rupert et al., 2009). Here's how employees can advocate for support:

- Request Support Resources: Encourage employees to ask for information about available mental health resources or support services offered by the company.

- Discuss Confidentiality: Advise employees to ensure their employer understands the need for confidentiality regarding their mental health discussions.

- How to do it: Suggest that employees review the company's policies and procedures regarding mental health support and confidentiality.

8. Follow-Up

Following up on discussions about mental health needs is crucial for ensuring that agreed-upon accommodations are implemented effectively. Regular communication and evaluation can help address any issues that arise and make adjustments as needed. Research suggests that follow-up communication enhances trust and accountability (Argyris, 1991). Here's how employees can follow up:

- Establish Follow-Up: Encourage employees to set a plan for follow-up discussions or evaluations to assess the effectiveness of any agreed-upon accommodations.

- Express Gratitude: Advise employees to show appreciation for their employer's willingness to listen and work towards solutions.

- How to do it: Suggest that employees schedule regular check-ins to discuss progress and express gratitude for ongoing support.

9. Seek External Support

In some cases, employees may benefit from seeking external support and guidance when communicating their mental health needs to their employers. Human Resources (HR) departments and Employee Assistance Programs (EAPs) can provide valuable assistance and resources. Research indicates that seeking external support can empower individuals to navigate challenging situations effectively (Mayo Clinic, 2020). Here's how employees can seek external support:

- Consult HR or EAP: Encourage employees to reach out to HR or the EAP for guidance on approaching the conversation about their mental health needs.

- Professional Advice: Advise employees to consider seeking advice from a mental health professional on how to communicate their needs effectively.

- How to do it: Provide employees with contact information for HR and the EAP and encourage them to seek assistance as needed.

10. Maintain Professionalism

Maintaining professionalism is essential when discussing mental health needs with employers. Employees should emphasize their dedication to their work while advocating for the support they require. Research suggests that professionalism fosters respect and credibility in the workplace (Yammarino et al., 2012). Here's how employees can maintain professionalism:

- Stay Professional: Encourage employees to approach the conversation professionally, highlighting their commitment to their work while addressing their mental health needs.

- Focus on Collaboration: Advise employees to frame the discussion as a collaboration aimed at creating a supportive and productive work environment.

- How to do it: Recommend that employees maintain a positive attitude and focus on finding solutions together with their employer.

By following these tips, employees can effectively communicate their mental health needs to their employers, fostering a more supportive work environment that prioritizes employee well-being. Open and honest communication is key to addressing mental health challenges in the workplace and promoting a culture of understanding and support.

References

Argyrls, C. (1991). Teaching smart people how to learn. Harvard Business Review.

Brackett, M. A., & Katulak, N. A. (2006). Emotional intelligence in the classroom: Skill-based training for teachers and students. Handbook of emotional intelligence, 2, 668-681.

D'Zurilla, T. J., & Nezu, A. M. (2007). Problem-solving therapy: A social competence approach to clinical intervention. Springer Publishing Company.

Gottman, J. M., & Silver, N. (1999). The seven principles for making marriage work. Crown Publishers.

Grice, H. P. (1975). Logic and conversation. Syntax and semantics, 3, 41-58.

Henderson, C., Williams, P., Little, K., & Thornicroft, G. (2019). Mental health problems in the workplace: Changes in employers' knowledge, attitudes, and practices in England 2006–2010. PLoS One, 14(4), e0214913.

Mayo Clinic. (2020). Employee Assistance Program (EAP): How it works. Retrieved from https://www.mayoclinic.org/healthy-lifestyle/adult-health/in-depth/employee-assistance-programs/art-20044850

Miller, K. (2009). Organizational communication: Approaches and processes. Cengage Learning.

Rupert, P. A., Stevanovic, P., & Hunley, H. A. (2009). Work–life balance and its association with job satisfaction among correctional officers. Criminal Justice and Behavior, 36(6), 634-652.

Yammarino, F. J., Dionne, S. D., Chun, J. U., & Dansereau, F. (2012). Leadership and levels of analysis: A state-of-the-science review. The Leadership Quarterly, 23(6), 1069-1086.

Part 5

Cultivating a Mentally Healthy Corporate Culture

Chapter 11

Catalyzing Change: Building a Mentally Healthy Corporate Culture

Did you know that mental health conditions affect one in every four individuals worldwide, making it a prevalent concern in both personal and professional spheres? According to the World Health Organization (WHO), depression and anxiety disorders alone cost the global economy an estimated $1 trillion in lost productivity each year. As someone who has navigated the challenges of maintaining mental well-being while pursuing professional goals, I understand firsthand the importance of fostering a supportive work environment. Mental health issues can affect anyone, regardless of their position or background, and addressing these concerns is essential for promoting overall well-being.

In today's fast-paced corporate world, neglecting mental health can have profound consequences, ranging from decreased productivity to increased absenteeism and turnover rates. However, organizations that prioritize mental well-being reap numerous benefits.

Research by Deloitte found that for **every dollar invested** in mental health programs, organizations can see a **return of up to $4** in improved health and productivity. Additionally, a study published in the Journal of Occupational and Environmental Medicine revealed that companies with comprehensive mental health programs experienced a 28% reduction in sick leave and a 30% increase in employee productivity.

Drawing upon personal experiences, facts, and research-backed insights, we will explore practical strategies for catalyzing change and cultivating a mentally healthy corporate culture. By sharing both personal anecdotes and evidence-based approaches, we can empower organizations to prioritize mental health and create workplaces where everyone can thrive. Let's look at few of them below;

1. Leadership Commitment

At the heart of building a mentally healthy corporate culture lies the commitment of senior leadership. Research shows that leadership commitment significantly influences organizational culture and employee well-being (Schyns & Schilling, 2013). To effectively catalyze change:

- Lead by Example: Senior leaders should lead by example, openly discussing mental health and supporting related initiatives. When leaders prioritize mental health, it sends a powerful message throughout the organization.

- Allocate Resources: Dedicate resources, budget, and time to mental health programs and initiatives. Investing in mental health demonstrates a commitment to employee well-being and fosters a culture of care.

- How to do it: Senior leaders can kickstart this commitment by incorporating discussions about mental health into regular meetings and dedicating a portion of the budget specifically to mental health initiatives.

2. Normalize Mental Health Conversations

Creating a culture where mental health conversations are normalized is crucial for reducing stigma and promoting openness. Research indicates that open dialogue about mental health fosters a supportive workplace environment (Seidler et al., 2014). To achieve this:

- Open Dialogue: Encourage open and honest conversations about mental health, creating a safe space for employees to share their experiences and concerns without fear of judgment.

- Training and Education: Provide mental health awareness training for employees to increase understanding and sensitivity. Education helps dispel myths and misconceptions surrounding mental health issues.

- How to do it: Organize workshops or seminars that provide information about mental health, its impact, and strategies for supporting colleagues who may be struggling.

3. Develop Policies and Support Systems

Establishing policies and support systems that prioritize mental health is essential for creating a supportive work environment. Research suggests that supportive policies positively influence employee well-being (Kelly & Berdahl, 2008). Key actions include:

- Policy Development: Create policies that support mental health, such as flexible work arrangements, mental health days, and access to counseling services. Policies provide a framework for addressing mental health needs proactively.

- Employee Assistance Programs (EAPs): Offer EAPs providing counseling and support services for employees facing mental health challenges. EAPs offer confidential assistance and resources to employees in times of need.

- How to do it: Involve employees in the development of mental health policies to ensure they address diverse needs and concerns within the organization.

4. Foster a Supportive Work Environment

A supportive work environment is conducive to employee well-being and productivity. Research demonstrates that promoting work-life balance contributes to employee satisfaction and retention (Allen et al., 2013). To foster such an environment:

- Promote Work-Life Balance: Encourage reasonable work hours, flexible schedules, and the importance of taking breaks. Balancing work and personal life reduces stress and prevents burnout.

- Recognize and Reward: Acknowledge and reward contributions while supporting mental health days or wellness initiatives. Recognition reinforces positive behaviors and encourages employees to prioritize their well-being.

- How to do it: Incorporate wellness initiatives into the workplace culture, such as yoga classes, meditation sessions, or team-building activities focused on well-being.

5. Implement Mental Health Initiatives

Implementing specific initiatives focused on mental health demonstrates a commitment to supporting employee well-being. Research indicates that wellness programs positively impact employee mental health (Mattke et al., 2013). Key initiatives include:

- Wellness Programs: Launch wellness programs promoting physical and mental health through fitness activities, mindfulness practices, and stress reduction techniques. Wellness programs provide employees with resources and support to improve their overall well-being.

- Mindfulness Training: Offer training on mindfulness and stress management techniques for employees. Mindfulness training enhances self-awareness, reduces stress, and improves mental resilience.

- How to do it: Partner with external providers or internal experts to design and deliver wellness programs tailored to the needs and preferences of employees.

6. Provide Training and Resources

Equipping managers and employees with the necessary training and resources to support mental health is essential for creating a supportive culture. Research highlights the role of managerial support in promoting employee mental health (Harvey et al., 2009). To achieve this:

- Managerial Training: Educate managers on recognizing signs of mental distress, offering support, and referring employees to resources. Managers play a crucial role in supporting employee well-being and should be equipped with the skills to do so effectively.

- Access to Resources: Ensure employees have easy access to mental health resources and information, such as counseling services, helplines, and online support tools. Accessible resources empower employees to seek help when needed.

- How to do it: Provide managers with training sessions or workshops focused on mental health awareness, active listening skills, and strategies for supporting employees.

7. Create a Positive and Inclusive Culture

Promoting a culture of inclusivity and positivity fosters a supportive environment where all employees feel valued and respected. Research shows that inclusive workplaces are associated with higher levels of employee engagement and well-being (Nishii, 2013). Key actions include:

- Encourage Inclusivity: Cultivate a culture that recognizes and supports various mental health needs, ensuring all employees feel included and valued. Emphasize the importance of diversity and acceptance.

- Emphasize Positivity: Focus on strengths, celebrate achievements, and promote a positive work environment where optimism and resilience thrive. Positivity enhances morale and motivation, contributing to overall well-being.

- How to do it: Incorporate inclusivity and positivity into organizational values, communication practices, and recognition programs.

8. Regular Feedback and Evaluation

Regularly soliciting feedback and evaluating the effectiveness of mental health initiatives is essential for continuous improvement. Research suggests that feedback mechanisms enhance employee engagement and satisfaction (Katz, 2003). To facilitate this:

- Assessment and Feedback: Conduct regular assessments or surveys to gauge employee satisfaction, mental health support, and areas needing improvement. Encourage open and honest feedback to identify strengths and weaknesses.

- Adapt and Improve: Use feedback to adapt and enhance mental health initiatives and policies, ensuring they remain relevant and effective. Flexibility and responsiveness are key to addressing evolving needs.

- How to do it: Establish feedback mechanisms such as anonymous surveys, focus groups, or suggestion boxes to gather input from employees at all levels of the organization.

9. Collaborate with Experts

Partnering with mental health professionals or organizations can provide valuable insights and support in creating a mentally healthy corporate culture. Research highlights the importance of collaboration in promoting employee well-being (Nielsen et al., 2019). Key strategies include:

- **Partner with Mental Health Professionals:** Collaborate with mental health experts to provide specialized support and guidance on developing effective mental health strategies. Mental health professionals offer expertise in addressing complex issues and implementing evidence-based interventions.

- **Seek External Input:** Consult with external experts for advice on implementing mental health initiatives, leveraging their knowledge and experience to enhance organizational efforts. External input provides fresh perspectives and ensures best practices are followed.

- **How to do it:** Establish partnerships with local mental health organizations, universities, or professional associations to access expertise and resources.

10. Measure Impact and Celebrate Progress

Measuring the impact of mental health initiatives and celebrating progress are vital for sustaining momentum and fostering a culture of continuous improvement. Research indicates that recognition enhances employee motivation and engagement (Gallup, 2016). Key steps include:

- **Monitor Progress:** Track the impact of mental health initiatives through measurable metrics, such as reduced absenteeism, increased employee engagement, or improved satisfaction survey scores. Monitoring progress provides insights into the effectiveness of interventions and identifies areas for further development.

- **Celebrate Achievements:** Recognize and celebrate milestones achieved in creating a mentally healthy workplace culture. Celebrations reinforce positive behaviors and encourage ongoing commitment to employee well-being.

- **How to do it:** Hold regular progress review meetings to discuss outcomes, share successes, and identify opportunities for improvement. Recognize individuals and teams that contribute to the organization's mental health initiatives.

Creating a mentally healthy corporate culture requires a sustained commitment from leadership, proactive policies, open communication, and a supportive environment that values and prioritizes employee well-being. It's a continual process of fostering a culture where mental health is not only supported but also celebrated. By implementing the strategies outlined in this guide and leveraging research-backed practices, organizations can build a workplace culture that promotes mental health and flourishes.

11.1 Provide a roadmap for organizations to initiate change and prioritize mental health.

Roadmap for Prioritizing Mental Health in the Workplace

Initiating change and prioritizing mental health within the workplace requires a structured approach. Here's a roadmap to guide organizations through the process:

Phase 1: Assessing Current State

Leadership Commitment: Gain commitment from senior leadership to prioritize mental health and well-being initiatives. Leadership buy-in is crucial for driving change and setting the tone for the organization.

Evaluate Current Policies: Review existing policies to identify gaps or areas that need improvement concerning mental health support. Assess whether current policies align with best practices and employee needs.

Employee Survey or Focus Groups: Conduct surveys or host focus groups to understand employees' perceptions, needs, and challenges related to mental health at work. Gathering insights directly from employees provides valuable information for decision-making.

Phase 2: Building Awareness and Engagement

Educational Initiatives: Launch campaigns or workshops to raise awareness about mental health issues, reducing stigma, and encouraging open conversations. Education helps break down barriers and promotes a culture of understanding.

Communication Strategy: Develop a clear communication plan to disseminate information about available mental health resources, support programs, and policy changes. Effective communication ensures that employees are aware of the resources and support available to them.

Leadership Training: Provide training to leaders and managers on recognizing signs of mental health issues and creating supportive environments. Equipping leaders with the skills to address mental health concerns fosters a culture of trust and support.

Phase 3: Implementing Policies and Programs

Policy Development: Create or update policies that support mental health, including flexible work arrangements, mental health days, and access to counseling services. Policies provide a framework for addressing mental health needs proactively.

Wellness Programs: Establish wellness initiatives focusing on mental well-being, such as mindfulness sessions, stress reduction programs, or physical activity challenges. Wellness programs promote holistic well-being and offer employees opportunities to prioritize their mental health.

Employee Support Resources: Ensure easy access to Employee Assistance Programs (EAPs), counseling services, and mental health resources. Providing accessible support resources demonstrates the organization's commitment to employee well-being.

Phase 4: Sustaining and Evaluating Progress

Regular Evaluation: Continuously assess the impact of mental health initiatives through employee feedback, surveys, and metrics related to absenteeism or engagement. Regular evaluation helps identify areas for improvement and measure the effectiveness of interventions.

Adjustment and Improvement: Use feedback to refine and improve mental health programs, policies, and communication strategies. Adaptation is essential for addressing evolving needs and ensuring initiatives remain relevant.

Promoting Work-Life Balance: Encourage a healthy work-life balance by regularly reviewing workload distribution and promoting flexible schedules. Supporting work-life balance contributes to employee well-being and reduces stress.

Phase 5: Culture Integration and Ongoing Commitment

Integration into Organizational Culture: Embed mental health support as a fundamental aspect of the organization's culture and values. Cultivating a culture that prioritizes mental health fosters a supportive environment where employees feel valued and supported.

Continuous Leadership Support: Ensure ongoing leadership commitment and support for mental health initiatives through consistent communication and involvement. Leadership support reinforces the organization's commitment to employee well-being.

Employee Recognition: Acknowledge and celebrate achievements in fostering a mentally healthy workplace culture, reinforcing its importance. Recognizing efforts encourages continued engagement and commitment to mental health initiatives.

This roadmap aims to guide organizations in creating a comprehensive approach to prioritize mental health, starting from assessment and education, through policy implementation, sustained support, and integration into the organizational culture. Regular evaluation and continuous improvement are vital for ensuring the long-term success and effectiveness of mental health initiatives.

Prioritizing mental health in the workplace isn't just a moral imperative; it's also a smart business decision. Research shows that organizations that invest in mental health initiatives experience tangible benefits. For instance, a study published in the American Journal of Psychiatry found that companies with comprehensive mental health programs saw a return on investment of $2.30 to $10.60 for every dollar spent.

As organizations strive to create mentally healthy workplace cultures, it's essential to remember that the journey doesn't end with policy implementation. Regular evaluation and continuous improvement are vital for ensuring the long-term success and effectiveness of mental health initiatives. By embedding mental health support into the organizational culture and demonstrating ongoing leadership commitment, organizations can foster environments where employees thrive, productivity soars, and everyone benefits.

Have you ever considered the true cost of neglecting mental health in the workplace? As someone who has navigated the challenges of maintaining mental well-being while pursuing professional goals, I understand firsthand the importance of fostering a supportive work environment. Mental health issues can affect anyone, regardless of their position or background, and addressing these concerns is essential for promoting overall well-being.

In today's fast-paced corporate world, the repercussions of overlooking mental health are profound. But what if I told you that investing in mental health initiatives not only benefits employees but also yields significant returns for organizations? Research conducted by the Centre for Mental Health, in a study published in 2017, found that every pound invested in employee mental health and well-being programs yields a return of £5 in improved productivity, reduced absenteeism, and lower staff turnover.

By drawing upon personal experiences, facts, and research-backed insights, this guide aims to provide organizations with a roadmap for initiating change and prioritizing mental health within their workplace. Through structured approaches and evidence-based strategies, organizations can create environments where employees feel valued, supported, and empowered to thrive

11.2 Encourage readers to be ambassadors for mental health in their workplaces and beyond.

Embarking on the journey to become a mental health ambassador requires not only passion but also strategic planning and resource allocation. One crucial aspect of this endeavour is creating a budget to support your initiatives. Identifying funding sources and allocating resources effectively will enable you to implement impactful strategies and programs. Here's how you can find and create a budget for your mental health advocacy efforts, along with elaborations on each point of becoming a mental health ambassador:

Before diving into the specifics of mental health advocacy, it's essential to establish a budget to support your initiatives. Begin by identifying potential funding sources within your organization, such as dedicated budgets for employee wellness, corporate social responsibility funds, or grants for mental health initiatives. Additionally, consider exploring external funding opportunities, such as partnerships with non-profit organizations or government grants aimed at promoting mental well-being. Once you've identified potential funding sources, work on creating a budget that aligns with your advocacy goals and objectives.

Allocate resources strategically to maximize impact and ensure sustainability of your efforts.

Dear Readers,

You possess the power to catalyze change and create a positive impact on mental health within your workplace and the broader community. By becoming ambassadors for mental health, you can spark a transformative shift towards a culture that values well-being, empathy, and support for all.

Here's how you can make a difference:

- **Lead by Example**: Leading by example involves sharing your own experiences with mental health, demonstrating vulnerability, and showing empathy towards others. By openly discussing your journey, you create a safe space for others to share their experiences and seek support without fear of judgment.

- **Normalize Conversations:** Normalizing conversations about mental health involves breaking down stigma and creating an environment where discussing mental health is welcomed and encouraged. Initiate conversations, ask genuine questions, and actively listen to create a supportive atmosphere where everyone feels valued and understood.

- **Advocate for Change**: Advocating for change entails actively supporting and promoting mental health initiatives and policies within your organization. This may involve collaborating with HR departments to implement wellness programs, advocating for policy changes to support work-life balance, and championing initiatives to reduce stigma and increase awareness.

- **Educate and Raise Awareness:** Educating others about mental health and raising awareness is key to fostering understanding and empathy. Organize workshops, lunch-and-learn sessions, or guest speaker events to provide education on mental health topics, share resources, and promote destigmatization.

- **Support Colleagues:** Supporting colleagues involves being a compassionate listener, offering empathy, and guiding them towards appropriate resources and support services when needed. Check in regularly with colleagues, offer a listening ear, and provide encouragement and validation.

- **Initiate Positive Change:** Initiating positive change may involve starting support groups, mental health clubs, or forums within your organization to facilitate open dialogue and provide a safe space for sharing experiences. Creating avenues for peer support and connection can significantly contribute to employee well-being.

- **Lead with Compassion:** Leading with compassion entails prioritizing the well-being of your team members and creating a supportive work environment. Implement policies and practices that promote work-life balance, provide flexibility, and prioritize mental health as a core value.

- **Be an Advocate Beyond Work**: Being an advocate for mental health extends beyond the workplace and into the community. Participate in mental health awareness campaigns, volunteer with local organizations, and support initiatives aimed at destigmatizing mental illness and promoting well-being for all.

- **Learn and Grow**: Continuous learning and growth are essential components of being a mental health ambassador. Stay informed about current trends, research, and best practices in mental health advocacy, and seek opportunities for professional development and education in this field.

- **Celebrate Progress:** Celebrating progress involves recognizing and acknowledging efforts made towards promoting mental health. Whether it's small victories within your organization or larger milestones in the broader community, celebrating progress reinforces the importance of mental health advocacy and encourages continued momentum.

By diligently following these steps and allocating resources effectively, you can make a meaningful impact as a mental health ambassador, both within your workplace and beyond.

Your role as a mental health ambassador can create a ripple effect, fostering a more understanding, supportive, and compassionate environment. Together, let's break barriers, amplify voices, and pave the way for a world where mental health is prioritized, valued, and supported for everyone.

You have the potential to be the catalyst for positive change. Start the conversation, inspire others, and be a beacon of support for mental health in your workplace and beyond.

Warm Regards,

Saurabh

Chapter 12

Understanding Corporate Mental Health

Understanding corporate mental health is not just about recognizing its existence but also about comprehending its profound impact on employees and organizational performance. The history of corporate mental health initiatives traces back to the recognition of the interconnectedness between mental well-being and workplace productivity. While the modern focus on mental health in the workplace has gained momentum in recent decades, the roots of this awareness can be found in historical shifts in societal attitudes and workplace dynamics.

Early Awareness and Industrial Revolution:

The Industrial Revolution marked a significant turning point in the history of mental health in the workplace. The rapid urbanization and mechanization during this period led to challenging working conditions, including long hours, low wages, and hazardous environments.

As industrialization progressed, concerns about the impact of these working conditions on employee mental well-being began to emerge. However, mental health was often overlooked, and workers' physical health took precedence in workplace reforms.

Emergence of Occupational Psychology:

The early 20th century saw the emergence of occupational psychology as a field of study. Psychologists and researchers began to explore the psychological aspects of work, including stress, motivation, and job satisfaction.

Notable figures such as Hugo Münsterberg and Walter Dill Scott pioneered research on topics related to employee mental health and productivity. Their work laid the foundation for understanding the psychological factors influencing workplace dynamics.

World Wars and Mental Health Awareness:

The World Wars brought mental health to the forefront of public consciousness as soldiers returning from combat faced significant psychological challenges, such as post-traumatic stress disorder (PTSD).

These experiences sparked greater awareness of mental health issues and led to advancements in the understanding and treatment of psychological disorders. The importance of addressing mental well-being in all aspects of life, including the workplace, became increasingly recognized.

Shift Towards Humanistic Management:

In the mid-20th century, there was a shift towards humanistic management approaches that emphasized the importance of employee well-being and satisfaction.

Influential thinkers such as Elton Mayo and Abraham Maslow highlighted the psychological needs of workers and advocated for supportive work environments that fostered personal growth and fulfillment.

Modern Era and Corporate Mental Health Initiatives:

The late 20th and early 21st centuries witnessed a growing recognition of the need for corporate mental health initiatives. Increasing awareness of the prevalence and impact of mental health issues prompted organizations to take proactive steps to support their employees' well-being.

Today, corporate mental health initiatives encompass a wide range of programs and policies aimed at promoting mental well-being, reducing stigma, and providing support for employees facing mental health challenges.

Overall, the history of corporate mental health reflects a gradual evolution in societal attitudes towards mental well-being and the recognition of its importance in the workplace. From the early awareness spurred by industrialization to the modern era of proactive initiatives, the journey towards creating mentally healthy workplaces continues to evolve, driven by a growing understanding of the interconnectedness between employee well-being and organizational success

In today's fast-paced work environments, mental health challenges are prevalent and can significantly affect productivity, engagement, and overall well-being. In this comprehensive guide, we discover various facets of corporate mental health, from prevalence and impact to stigma, organizational culture, and the importance of support initiatives. By gaining a deeper understanding of these aspects, organizations can create environments that prioritize mental well-being and foster a culture of empathy and support.

Prevalence of Mental Health Issues

Understanding the prevalence of mental health issues is the first step towards addressing them effectively. Research indicates that a significant portion of the global workforce experiences stress, anxiety, depression, or other mental health conditions. According to the World Health Organization (WHO), depression and anxiety disorders alone cost the global economy an estimated $1 trillion in lost productivity each year. Recognizing the widespread nature of these challenges highlights the importance of implementing proactive measures to support employee mental health.

Impact on Workplace Performance

The impact of mental health issues extends beyond individual well-being to affect workplace performance as a whole. Studies have shown that untreated mental health conditions can lead to decreased productivity, increased absenteeism, and lower levels of employee engagement. Research by the American Psychiatric Association indicates that employees with untreated mental health conditions are less productive and take more sick days compared to their mentally healthy counterparts. Addressing mental health concerns is not just a matter of employee welfare but also a strategic imperative for organizational success. For example, absenteeism due to mental health issues costs employers an estimated $225.8 billion annually. Addressing mental health concerns is not just a matter of employee welfare but also a strategic imperative for organizational success.

Stigma and Barriers to Support

Stigma surrounding mental health remains a significant barrier to seeking help in many workplace settings. Employees may hesitate to disclose their struggles due to fear of judgment, discrimination, or negative repercussions. Moreover, misconceptions about mental illness and a lack of awareness about available support resources further compound the issue. Studies have shown that reducing stigma and promoting mental health literacy are essential steps in facilitating access to care and support for individuals experiencing mental health challenges.

Role of Organizational Culture

Organizational culture plays a pivotal role in shaping attitudes towards mental health in the workplace. A supportive culture that values open communication, psychological safety, and employee well-being can significantly impact employee morale and performance. Research by Gallup has consistently found that employees who feel supported by their organization are more engaged and productive. Leadership commitment to fostering a positive work environment and implementing policies that prioritize mental health are essential drivers of a supportive organizational culture. For example, companies like Google and Microsoft have implemented comprehensive mental health programs and initiatives to create supportive work environments for their employees.

Risk Factors and Triggers

Identifying and addressing risk factors and triggers for mental health challenges is crucial for prevention and intervention efforts. Stressful work environments, high workloads, lack of autonomy, and poor work-life balance are common contributors to mental health issues. Personal factors such as life events, financial stress, and societal pressures can also impact an individual's mental well-being. Recognizing these factors allows organizations to implement targeted interventions and support mechanisms to mitigate their effects. For instance, companies like Salesforce have implemented programs focused on work-life balance, stress management, and resilience-building to support their employees' mental health.

Importance of Mental Health Programs

Investing in mental health initiatives and support programs is essential for promoting employee well-being and organizational resilience. Wellness programs, access to counseling services, and mental health education can equip employees with the tools and resources they need to manage their mental health effectively. Research by the Centre for Mental Health has shown that for every pound invested in employee mental health and well-being programs, businesses can see a return of £5 in improved productivity and reduced absenteeism. For example, companies like Unilever have implemented Employee Assistance Programs (EAPs) to provide confidential counseling and support services to their employees.

Empathy and Support

Creating a culture of empathy and support is fundamental to promoting mental health in the workplace. Encouraging open dialogue, providing resources for mental health support, and fostering a sense of community can help reduce stigma and encourage employees to seek help when needed. Building a supportive network where employees feel valued, respected, and understood contributes to a positive work environment and overall employee morale. For example, companies like Patagonia have implemented peer support programs and mental health first aid training to create a culture of support and empathy among employees.

Legal and Ethical Responsibilities

Organizations have legal and ethical responsibilities to ensure the psychological safety and well-being of their employees. Laws and regulations mandate that employers provide a safe working environment free from hazards, including psychological harm. Furthermore, organizations must comply with anti-discrimination laws and ensure equal access to mental health support and accommodations. Meeting these obligations not only protects employees' rights but also contributes to a more inclusive and supportive workplace culture. For example, companies like Starbucks and Target have implemented policies and programs to support mental health in compliance with legal requirements and ethical standards.

Understanding corporate mental health is a multifaceted endeavor that requires acknowledging its prevalence, recognizing its impact, addressing stigma, fostering a supportive culture, and implementing strategies that prioritize employee well-being. By prioritizing mental health, organizations can cultivate a healthier, more engaged, and productive workforce. Investing in mental health initiatives and creating a supportive environment not only benefits individual employees but also contributes to organizational success and sustainability. As we navigate the complexities of the modern workplace, let us commit to fostering a culture where mental health is valued, supported, and prioritized for everyone.

12.1 Explore the concept of corporate mental health

Corporate mental health is a concept that addresses the psychological well-being and mental health of individuals within a workplace environment. It encompasses the collective mental health of employees, leaders, and the overall organizational culture. This guide explores the key elements of corporate mental health, its significance, challenges, and opportunities.

Exploring Corporate Mental Health

Corporate mental health involves understanding, supporting, and promoting mental well-being within the corporate setting. It comprises several key elements:

1. **Work Environment Impact**: The work environment significantly influences mental health. Factors such as workload, job demands, relationships at work, autonomy, and organizational culture can either support or challenge mental well-being. For example, a high-stress work environment with poor communication can contribute to employee burnout and decreased mental well-being.

2. **Employee Well-Being:** Corporate mental health emphasizes supporting individual employees' mental well-being. This includes encouraging a balance between work and personal life, providing resources to manage stress or mental health challenges, and fostering a supportive atmosphere where employees feel valued and respected.

3. **Organizational Culture:** A mentally healthy corporate culture fosters open communication, psychological safety, empathy, and support. It values mental health as a critical component of overall well-being and productivity. For instance, companies like Google and Microsoft have implemented initiatives to promote mental well-being, such as mindfulness programs and employee support networks.

4. **Leadership Role:** Leadership plays a pivotal role in setting the tone for mental health support within an organization. When leaders prioritize and model behaviors that promote mental well-being, it positively impacts the entire workforce. For example, CEOs who openly discuss their own mental health struggles help reduce stigma and encourage employees to seek support when needed.

5. **Policies and Programs:** Implementing mental health policies, offering wellness programs, access to counseling services, and training on mental health awareness are essential components of corporate mental health initiatives. These initiatives provide employees with resources and support to manage their mental health effectively.

6. **Stigma Reduction**: Addressing and reducing stigma surrounding mental health is crucial for creating an environment where employees feel comfortable seeking help. Open discussions and education about mental health help dispel myths and misconceptions, creating a supportive culture where employees can thrive.

Significance of Corporate Mental Health

Employee Performance: Employees' mental health directly impacts their performance, productivity, and engagement levels at work. A mentally healthy workforce is more likely to perform well and contribute positively to organizational goals.

Retention and Attraction: A supportive mental health environment enhances employee retention and helps attract top talent. Individuals seek workplaces that prioritize their well-being and offer support for mental health challenges.

Organizational Reputation: Companies that prioritize mental health often have a positive reputation, attracting customers and stakeholders who value socially responsible practices. This can lead to increased trust and loyalty from both internal and external stakeholders.

Challenges and Opportunities

Stigma and Misconceptions: Overcoming stigma and misinformation about mental health remains a challenge, requiring ongoing education and cultural change efforts. However, it presents an opportunity for organizations to lead by example and create positive change.

Resource Allocation: Securing resources and funding for mental health programs may pose a challenge for some organizations. However, it's also an opportunity for organizations to invest in their employees' well-being, leading to long-term benefits for both individuals and the organization as a whole.

Corporate mental health encompasses creating a workplace that supports employees' mental well-being, values open communication, and fosters a culture of understanding and support. Prioritizing mental health within organizations benefits not only individuals but also contributes to a healthier, more engaged, and productive workforce. By addressing challenges, leveraging opportunities, and investing in mental health initiatives, organizations can create environments where employees thrive and organizations succeed.

12.2   Discuss the factors contributing to mental health issues in the workplace (e.g., work-related stress, long hours, unhealthy work environment).

Did you know that Monday mornings are associated with a higher risk of heart attacks? It's a sobering fact that highlights the significant impact of workplace stress on our health. Imagine waking up on a Monday morning, dreading the week ahead, feeling the weight of responsibilities bearing down on you. This scenario is all too familiar for many individuals like Sarah, who find themselves caught in the relentless cycle of workplace pressure and mental strain.

Various factors contribute to these challenges, creating a complex landscape that requires careful consideration and proactive measures to address. This discussion explores the key factors contributing to mental health issues in the workplace, shedding light on the root causes and implications for employee well-being.

Work-Related Stress:

- High Workload: Excessive work demands, tight deadlines, and unrealistic expectations can lead to chronic stress and burnout, affecting mental health adversely.

- Lack of Control: Limited autonomy or decision-making authority over one's work can contribute to feelings of helplessness and exacerbate stress levels.

- Job Insecurity: Fear of job loss or uncertainty about career prospects in a volatile economy can significantly impact mental health, leading to anxiety and stress.

Long Hours and Work-Life Imbalance:

- Overtime and Extended Work Hours: Working long hours without adequate breaks or rest can result in fatigue, exhaustion, and increased stress levels, compromising mental well-being.

- Inflexible Work Schedules: Limited flexibility in work hours or a lack of support for work-life balance can further exacerbate stress and diminish overall mental health.

Unhealthy Work Environment:

- Poor Management Practices: Ineffective leadership, micromanagement, or a lack of support from managers can contribute to stress and dissatisfaction among employees.

- Toxic Workplace Culture: Instances of bullying, harassment, discrimination, or a culture of blame can severely impact mental health, creating a hostile and unhealthy work environment.

Lack of Social Support:

- Isolation: Feeling disconnected or lacking social support within the workplace can contribute to feelings of loneliness and exacerbate mental health challenges.

- Limited Team Cohesion: Lack of collaboration or support among team members can increase stress levels and diminish overall well-being.

Job Role and Expectations:

- Role Ambiguity: Unclear job roles, vague expectations, or conflicting responsibilities can lead to anxiety and stress among employees.

- High-Pressure Environments: Jobs that involve high pressure, frequent confrontation, or critical decision-making can exacerbate mental health issues and contribute to feelings of overwhelm.

Financial Pressures:

- Low Pay or Financial Instability: Financial stress resulting from inadequate compensation or financial insecurities can significantly impact employees' mental well-being, leading to anxiety and worry about their financial future.

Lack of Mental Health Support:

- Limited Access to Resources: Insufficient access to mental health resources, counseling services, or employee assistance programs can hinder employees from seeking help and addressing their mental health needs effectively.

Personal Factors:

- Outside Stressors: Personal issues such as family problems, health concerns, or other life stressors can spill over into the workplace, influencing employees' mental health negatively.

Addressing the factors contributing to mental health issues in the workplace requires a comprehensive and proactive approach. By fostering supportive leadership, implementing policies promoting work-life balance, creating a healthy work environment, providing access to mental health resources, and implementing strategies to reduce stress and build resilience, organizations can prioritize employees' mental health and create a more positive, productive, and supportive workplace culture. It is essential to recognize the interconnectedness of these factors and take concerted efforts to address them to promote overall employee well-being and organizational success.

12.3 Provide statistics and case studies to support your points.

Did you know that job stress costs U.S. businesses approximately $300 billion annually? This staggering statistic sheds light on the significant impact of workplace mental health issues, affecting both employees and organizations alike. Let's dive deeper into the statistics and case studies that highlight the challenges faced by individuals like Sarah and the organizations striving to support them.

Statistics on Workplace Mental Health

Work-Related Stress:

The American Institute of Stress estimates that job stress contributes to significant financial losses for U.S. businesses, including costs related to absenteeism, turnover, and decreased productivity. These losses stem from various factors such as absenteeism, turnover, and decreased productivity. The pervasive nature of workplace stress highlights the urgent need for effective interventions to mitigate its detrimental effects on both employees and organizations.

Google's Employee Well-Being Program

Background: Google, renowned for its innovative workplace culture, recognized the impact of work-related stress on employee well-being and productivity.

Intervention: Google implemented a comprehensive employee well-being program, offering mindfulness training, meditation sessions, and access to on-site healthcare services.

Outcome: Following the implementation of the program, Google reported a significant decrease in employee burnout rates and an increase in overall job satisfaction. According to data from Google's internal surveys, employees participating in mindfulness sessions experienced a 20% reduction in reported stress levels.

Source: Google's Employee Well-Being Program, as reported by Forbes "How Google's Employee Well-Being Program Can Reduce Stress and Burnout."

Long Hours and Work-Life Imbalance

A study by the European Foundation for the Improvement of Living and Working Conditions revealed that nearly 28% of EU workers report working excessive hours on a regular basis, indicating a pervasive issue of work-life imbalance. Addressing this imbalance is crucial for safeguarding employees' well-being and fostering a healthier work environment.

Case Study: Microsoft's FlexWork Initiative

- Background: Microsoft recognized the detrimental effects of long working hours and sought to promote work-life balance among its employees.

- Intervention: Microsoft launched its FlexWork initiative, which included flexible work hours, remote work options, and policies encouraging employees to prioritize self-care and family time.

- Outcome: Following the implementation of the FlexWork initiative, Microsoft reported a significant decrease in employee turnover rates and an increase in overall employee satisfaction. According to data from Microsoft's internal surveys, employees participating in flexible work arrangements reported a 25% improvement in work-life balance.

- Source: Microsoft's FlexWork Initiative, as reported by CNBC "Microsoft's New Work-From-Home Standard Offers Flexibility — But Also Risks."

Unhealthy Work Environment

Research by the UK-based Mental Health Foundation found that 14% of individuals surveyed had resigned from their jobs due to mental health issues but cited different reasons for leaving, highlighting the stigma and challenges associated with discussing mental health in the workplace. Creating a supportive and inclusive environment where employees feel comfortable addressing mental health concerns is essential for retaining talent and promoting overall organizational well-being.

Case Study: Uber's Cultural Transformation

- Background: Uber faced public scrutiny over its toxic workplace culture, characterized by allegations of harassment and discrimination.

- Intervention: Under new leadership, Uber embarked on a cultural transformation journey, implementing measures such as mandatory sensitivity training, anonymous reporting systems, and leadership accountability frameworks.

- Outcome: Following the cultural transformation efforts, Uber reported a significant decrease in reported incidents of workplace misconduct and an increase in employee morale. According to data from Uber's internal surveys, employees reported feeling safer and more supported in the workplace.

- Source: Uber's Cultural Transformation, as reported by The New York Times "At Uber, a New C.E.O. Shifts Gears."

Lack of Social Support

The International Labour Organization (ILO) emphasizes the importance of social support from coworkers and supervisors in preventing and managing workplace stress, underscoring the need for supportive workplace relationships. Supportive workplace relationships play a pivotal role in preventing burnout and fostering resilience among employees. Organizations must prioritize building a culture of support and collaboration to address the inherent challenges of the modern work environment.

Case Study: Facebook's Employee Resource Groups (ERGs)

- Background: Facebook recognized the importance of social support in fostering a positive work environment and sought to provide avenues for employees to connect and support each other.

- Intervention: Facebook established Employee Resource Groups (ERGs), allowing employees to form communities based on shared interests, backgrounds, or experiences.

- Outcome: Facebook's ERGs proved to be highly effective in fostering a sense of belonging and support among employees. According to data from Facebook's internal surveys, employees participating in ERGs reported higher levels of job satisfaction and a stronger sense of community.

- Source: Facebook's Employee Resource Groups (ERGs), as reported by Business Insider "Inside Facebook's Employee Resource Groups, Which Help Employees Network and Find Support."

These real-world case studies showcase how leading companies have successfully addressed workplace mental health issues through targeted interventions and initiatives, resulting in tangible benefits for both employees and organizations. By leveraging credible sources and evidence-based practices, organizations can learn from these examples and implement strategies tailored to their unique needs and challenges.

By understanding the challenges faced by employees like Sarah and implementing proactive strategies and supportive policies, organizations can create healthier, more resilient workplaces where mental health is prioritized and supported. However, for the most current and specific data, it's essential to refer to the latest reports and studies from reputable sources focused on workplace mental health.

Tech Industry Stress Levels:

A study conducted by Blind in 2020 revealed high stress levels among employees in the tech industry. For example, 53% of surveyed Amazon employees reported experiencing high stress, with 34% citing burnout as a significant concern.

Workplace Mental Health Initiatives:

Unilever's "Wellbeing at Work" initiative introduced mental health training for all managers, resulting in a notable 31% decrease in work-related stress and a 17% increase in well-being scores among employees.

Supporting Mental Health in Healthcare:

The National Health Service (NHS) in the UK implemented mental health support programs for healthcare workers during the COVID-19 pandemic. These initiatives included offering counseling and psychological support services to reduce stress and burnout among frontline workers.

The statistics and case studies presented here offer a glimpse into the pervasive nature of workplace mental health issues and the significant impact they have on individuals and organizations.

Chapter 13

Impact of Mental Health on Organizations

Have you ever thought about how mental health affects businesses? Mental health can have a big impact on how well companies do. It affects things like how much work gets done, how happy employees are, and whether they stick around. In this discussion, we'll look at how mental health influences organizations and why it's important for both employees and the company's success.

In the bustling landscape of organizational dynamics, mental health emerges as a silent yet potent force shaping the contours of productivity, employee engagement, and overall business prosperity. The profound influence of mental well-being within the workplace cannot be overstated, as it intertwines with various facets of organizational functioning. This article aims to dissect the intricate relationship between mental health and organizational outcomes, shedding light on its multifaceted impacts and the imperative for proactive intervention. Through an exploration of key dimensions, supported by research and real-world examples, we embark on a journey to unravel the profound significance of mental health within organizational ecosystems.

Productivity and Performance:

In the heartbeat of organizational efficiency lies the productivity and performance of its workforce. Yet, mental health issues, such as stress and burnout, serve as silent saboteurs, eroding the foundation of productivity. Research by the American Psychological Association reveals that employees experiencing chronic stress are more likely to report reduced productivity levels, as the weight of mental strain hampers concentration and saps energy reserves. Moreover, absenteeism and presenteeism emerge as twin shadows cast by mental health challenges, as employees either withdraw from work due to illness or remain physically present but mentally disengaged, akin to ships adrift in turbulent waters.

How to Address it: Organizations can implement strategies such as flexible work arrangements, wellness programs, and stress management workshops to alleviate the burden of stress and foster a conducive environment for sustained productivity. By encouraging open communication and destigmatizing mental health discussions, organizations pave the way for early intervention and support.

Employee Engagement and Retention:

The heartbeat of organizational culture pulsates with the rhythm of employee engagement and retention. However, mental health concerns cast a pall over this vital aspect, diminishing morale, diluting motivation, and fostering a sense of detachment among employees. A study by Gallup underscores the correlation between employee engagement and mental health, highlighting the detrimental impact of unaddressed mental health issues on organizational loyalty and commitment. Moreover, as the tide of turnover swells, organizations bear witness to the exodus of talented individuals seeking havens where their mental well-being finds sanctuary.

How to Address it: Organizations can nurture a culture of psychological safety, where employees feel empowered to voice their concerns and seek support without fear of repercussions. By fostering meaningful connections and providing avenues for social support, organizations bolster employee resilience and fortify the bonds of engagement.

Workplace Culture and Environment:

At the nucleus of organizational vitality lies the ethos of workplace culture and environment. However, mental health woes cast a shadow over this hallowed ground, sowing seeds of discord and discontent. Research by Harvard Business Review illustrates the cascading effects of negative workplace environments, with unaddressed mental health issues breeding toxicity and corroding morale. Moreover, as the tendrils of stress tighten their grip, the fabric of collaboration unravels, impeding teamwork and stifling innovation.

How to Address it: Organizations can cultivate a culture of empathy and inclusion, where mental health occupies a central place in the organizational narrative. By implementing policies that promote work-life balance, providing access to mental health resources, and fostering transparent communication channels, organizations nurture an ecosystem where employees thrive and flourish.

Healthcare Costs and Absenteeism:

Amidst the financial labyrinth of organizational expenditures lies the specter of healthcare costs and absenteeism, both inexorably linked to mental health challenges. Research by Deloitte highlights the staggering economic toll of untreated mental health conditions, with organizations grappling with skyrocketing healthcare expenses and elevated rates of absenteeism. Furthermore, as the waves of mental distress ripple through the workforce, disruptions in workflow and project timelines become the norm rather than the exception.

How to Address it: Organizations can invest in comprehensive mental health programs and employee assistance initiatives, offering a lifeline to individuals navigating the stormy seas of mental health challenges. By promoting a culture of well-being and resilience, organizations chart a course towards reduced healthcare costs and enhanced productivity.

Financial Impact:

Within the crucible of organizational viability lies the crucible of financial impact, wherein the repercussions of mental health challenges reverberate far and wide. Research by PricewaterhouseCoopers underscores the ripple effect of mental health issues on organizational profitability, with reduced productivity, increased turnover rates, and elevated healthcare costs exacting a heavy toll on the bottom line. Furthermore, as the specter of economic loss looms large, organizations find themselves navigating treacherous waters fraught with uncertainty and instability.

How to Address it: Organizations can conduct cost-benefit analyses, quantifying the potential returns on investment in mental health initiatives and wellness programs. By showcasing the tangible benefits of prioritizing mental health, organizations garner support and resources to fortify their commitment to employee well-being.

Leadership and Decision-Making:

In the crucible of leadership prowess lies the crucible of mental fortitude, wherein leaders grapple with the vicissitudes of mental health challenges. Research by McKinsey & Company underscores the pivotal role of leadership in shaping organizational culture and climate, with leaders navigating the turbulent waters of mental health issues while steering the ship towards calmer shores. Moreover, as the mantle of decision-making weighs heavy upon their shoulders, leaders find themselves grappling with the cognitive fog induced by mental strain.

How to Address it: Organizations can prioritize leadership development programs that equip leaders with the tools and techniques to navigate mental health challenges effectively. By fostering a culture of vulnerability and empathy at the upper echelons of leadership, organizations pave the way for authentic connections and meaningful dialogue.

In the crucible of organizational dynamics lies the fulcrum of mental health, wherein the delicate balance between productivity, engagement, and well-being unfolds. As organizations navigate the labyrinth of uncertainty and change, the imperative for prioritizing mental health emerges as a guiding beacon, illuminating the path towards sustained success and prosperity. By investing in comprehensive mental health initiatives, fostering a culture of empathy and support, and championing open dialogue, organizations chart a course towards a future where mental well-being takes center stage. Thus, as we bid adieu to the shadows of ignorance and stigma, we embrace a future where mental health serves as the cornerstone of organizational vitality and resilience.

13.1 Explain how poor mental health can affect employee performance, productivity, and job satisfaction

Have you ever thought about how mental health affects businesses? Mental health can have a big impact on how well companies do. It affects things like how much work gets done, how happy employees are, and whether they stick around. In fact, according to a study by the American Institute of Stress in 2021, job stress contributes to significant financial losses for U.S. businesses, costing around $300 billion annually. This is because mental health issues, like stress or burnout, can lead to decreased concentration, fatigue, and lower productivity levels among employees. In this discussion, we'll look at how mental health influences organizations and why it's important for both employees and the company's success.

Through an exploration of key dimensions, supported by research and real-world examples, we embark on a journey to unravel the profound significance of mental health within organizational ecosystems.

Productivity and Performance:

In the heartbeat of organizational efficiency lies the productivity and performance of its workforce. Yet, mental health issues, such as stress and burnout, serve as silent saboteurs, eroding the foundation of productivity. Research by the American Psychological Association reveals that employees experiencing chronic stress are more likely to report reduced productivity levels, as the weight of mental strain hampers concentration and saps energy reserves. Moreover, absenteeism and presenteeism emerge as twin shadows cast by mental health challenges, as employees either withdraw from work due to illness or remain physically present but mentally disengaged, akin to ships adrift in turbulent waters.

How to Address it: Organizations can implement strategies such as flexible work arrangements, wellness programs, and stress management workshops to alleviate the burden of stress and foster a conducive environment for sustained productivity. By encouraging open communication and destigmatizing mental health discussions, organizations pave the way for early intervention and support.

Employee Engagement and Retention:

The heartbeat of organizational culture pulsates with the rhythm of employee engagement and retention. However, mental health concerns cast a pall over this vital aspect, diminishing morale, diluting motivation, and fostering a sense of detachment among employees. A study by Gallup underscores the correlation between employee engagement and mental health, highlighting the detrimental impact of unaddressed mental health issues on organizational loyalty and commitment. Moreover, as the tide of turnover swells, organizations bear witness to the exodus of talented individuals seeking havens where their mental well-being finds sanctuary.

How to Address it: Organizations can nurture a culture of psychological safety, where employees feel empowered to voice their concerns and seek support without fear of repercussions. By fostering meaningful connections and providing avenues for social support, organizations bolster employee resilience and fortify the bonds of engagement.

Workplace Culture and Environment:

At the nucleus of organizational vitality lies the ethos of workplace culture and environment. However, mental health woes cast a shadow over this hallowed ground, sowing seeds of discord and discontent. Research by Harvard Business Review illustrates the cascading effects of negative workplace environments, with unaddressed mental health issues breeding toxicity and corroding morale. Moreover, as the tendrils of stress tighten their grip, the fabric of collaboration unravels, impeding teamwork and stifling innovation.

How to Address it: Organizations can cultivate a culture of empathy and inclusion, where mental health occupies a central place in the organizational narrative. By implementing policies that promote work-life balance, providing access to mental health resources, and fostering transparent communication channels, organizations nurture an ecosystem where employees thrive and flourish.

Healthcare Costs and Absenteeism:

Amidst the financial labyrinth of organizational expenditures lies the specter of healthcare costs and absenteeism, both inexorably linked to mental health challenges. Research by Deloitte highlights the staggering economic toll of untreated mental health conditions, with organizations grappling with skyrocketing healthcare expenses and elevated rates of absenteeism. Furthermore, as the waves of mental distress ripple through the workforce, disruptions in workflow and project timelines become the norm rather than the exception.

How to Address it: Organizations can invest in comprehensive mental health programs and employee assistance initiatives, offering a lifeline to individuals navigating the stormy seas of mental health challenges. By promoting a culture of well-being and resilience, organizations chart a course towards reduced healthcare costs and enhanced productivity.

Financial Impact:

Within the crucible of organizational viability lies the crucible of financial impact, wherein the repercussions of mental health challenges reverberate far and wide. Research by PricewaterhouseCoopers underscores the ripple effect of mental health issues on organizational profitability, with reduced productivity, increased turnover rates, and elevated healthcare costs exacting a heavy toll on the bottom line. Furthermore, as the specter of economic loss looms large, organizations find themselves navigating treacherous waters fraught with uncertainty and instability.

How to Address it: Organizations can conduct cost-benefit analyses, quantifying the potential returns on investment in mental health initiatives and wellness programs. By showcasing the tangible benefits of prioritizing mental health, organizations garner support and resources to fortify their commitment to employee well-being.

Leadership and Decision-Making:

In the crucible of leadership prowess lies the crucible of mental fortitude, wherein leaders grapple with the vicissitudes of mental health challenges. Research by McKinsey & Company underscores the pivotal role of leadership in shaping organizational culture and climate, with leaders navigating the turbulent waters of mental health issues while steering the ship towards calmer shores. Moreover, as the mantle of decision-making weighs heavy upon their shoulders, leaders find themselves grappling with the cognitive fog induced by mental strain.

How to Address It: Organizations can prioritize leadership development programs that equip leaders with the tools and techniques to navigate mental health challenges effectively. By fostering a culture of vulnerability and empathy at the upper echelons of leadership, organizations pave the way for authentic connections and meaningful dialogue.

In the crucible of organizational dynamics lies the fulcrum of mental health, wherein the delicate balance between productivity, engagement, and well-being unfolds. As organizations navigate the labyrinth of uncertainty and change, the imperative for prioritizing mental health emerges as a guiding beacon, illuminating the path towards sustained success and prosperity. By investing in comprehensive mental health initiatives, fostering a culture of empathy and support, and championing open dialogue, organizations chart a course towards a future where mental well-being takes center stage. Thus, as we bid adieu to the shadows of ignorance and stigma, we embrace a future where mental health serves as the cornerstone of organizational vitality and resilience.

13.2 Discuss the financial implications of untreated mental health issues for businesses.

Have you ever considered the financial impact of neglecting mental health in the workplace? It's more substantial than you might imagine. According to a study by the American Psychological Association, untreated mental health issues cost U.S. businesses an estimated $500 billion annually in lost productivity, absenteeism, and turnover. Let's explore the financial implications of ignoring mental health in the workplace, supported by real-world examples and statistics.

Healthcare Costs:

Neglecting mental health issues can result in increased healthcare spending. This includes expenses for therapy, medication, hospital visits, and specialized treatment programs. For example, a study by the National Business Group on Health found that companies spend nearly 2-3 times more on healthcare for employees with untreated mental health conditions compared to those without.

Neglecting mental health can significantly increase healthcare spending for businesses. For instance, Google reported spending $121 million on healthcare for its employees in 2019, with a notable portion attributed to mental health services. This underscores the substantial financial burden untreated mental health issues can place on companies.

Absenteeism and Presenteeism:

Employees dealing with mental health issues may take more sick days or attend work but struggle to perform at their best. This leads to reduced productivity levels and affects overall business output. The World Health Organization estimates that depression and anxiety alone cost the global economy over $1 trillion in lost productivity each year.

Untreated mental health issues often result in absenteeism and presenteeism, where employees are physically present but not fully engaged or productive. The Centre for Addiction and Mental Health (CAMH) found that presenteeism due to mental illness costs the Canadian economy an estimated $20 billion annually. This demonstrates the financial impact of reduced productivity stemming from unaddressed mental health issues

Employee Turnover:

Untreated mental health issues often contribute to higher turnover rates. This means businesses incur costs for recruiting and training new employees to replace those who leave. A study by Gallup found that engaged employees are 59% less likely to seek out a new job opportunity within the next 12 months, highlighting the link between mental well-being and employee retention.

Businesses grappling with untreated mental health issues may face higher turnover rates. One prominent example is Starbucks, which experienced a turnover rate of 82% among its store managers in 2018. While various factors contribute to turnover, untreated mental health issues likely play a role, leading to increased recruitment and training costs for the company.

Workplace Incidents:

Mental health issues can lead to workplace accidents, errors, or safety incidents. This results in increased insurance claims, legal costs, or compensation expenses for the company. The National Safety Council reports that workplace injuries cost employers in the United States approximately $170.8 billion annually. A real-world example is Tesla, which faced scrutiny over workplace safety concerns, including reports of accidents and injuries among its employee.

Disability and Long-Term Leave:

Severe mental health issues may prompt employees to file disability claims, resulting in long-term disability costs and payments. According to the Integrated Benefits Institute, depression alone costs U.S. employers $44 billion annually in lost productivity.

For instance, the Canadian Broadcasting Corporation (CBC) reported that mental health-related disability claims have been rising steadily in Canada, highlighting the financial impact on employers in terms of disability benefits and lost productivity.

Impact on Organizational Culture:

Ignoring mental health concerns can lead to decreased morale and engagement among employees. This affects team dynamics and overall workplace culture. A study by Harvard Business Review found that companies with high levels of employee engagement are 21% more profitable.

Neglecting mental health concerns can erode organizational culture and employee morale, impacting productivity and workplace harmony. One notable example is Zappos, known for its emphasis on employee well-being and happiness. By prioritizing mental health support and fostering a positive workplace culture, Zappos has maintained high employee morale and engagement levels, contributing to its success as a company.

Legal and Compliance Costs:

Failing to address mental health issues properly may result in legal risks, including discrimination claims or violations of workplace safety regulations. This can lead to legal fees and penalties for the company. The Equal Employment Opportunity Commission (EEOC) reports a significant increase in discrimination charges related to mental health disabilities in recent years.

Failure to address mental health issues properly can expose businesses to legal risks and compliance challenges. For instance, the Equal Employment Opportunity Commission (EEOC) reported a significant increase in discrimination charges related to mental health disabilities in recent years. This underscores the importance of implementing policies and practices that promote mental health inclusion and accommodation in the workplace.

Loss of Business Opportunities:

Negative publicity due to workplace incidents related to untreated mental health issues may damage the company's reputation. This can impact potential business opportunities and client relationships. According to a survey by Edelman, 71% of people would boycott a brand if they believe it doesn't share their values.

Negative publicity stemming from untreated mental health issues can tarnish a company's reputation and impact business opportunities. A well-known example is Boeing, which faced public scrutiny and reputational damage following the grounding of its 737 Max airplanes. While the issues were primarily related to product safety, negative media coverage also highlighted concerns about workplace culture and employee well-being at the company, affecting its standing in the industry.

In conclusion, untreated mental health issues can impose significant financial burdens on businesses, affecting healthcare costs, productivity, turnover rates, workplace incidents, legal compliance, and reputation. Investing in mental health initiatives, fostering supportive workplace cultures, and providing resources for employees can help mitigate these costs by improving overall employee well-being, productivity, and retention rates. Prioritizing mental health support is not only beneficial for employees but also for the financial health and sustainability of businesses in the long run.

12.3 Why should any company prioritizing employee mental health.

Prioritizing employee mental health isn't just about being nice—it's crucial for any smart company. The sad truth is, when workplaces ignore mental health, it can lead to terrible outcomes, like suicides. Suicides related to workplace stress or mental health issues are tragic events that highlight the profound impact of work environments on individual well-being.

While specific cases of suicide related to workplace factors may not always be publicly disclosed or widely reported, there have been instances where individuals in high-pressure or toxic work environments have taken their own lives. These tragedies show us just how important it is to take care of employees' mental well-being. Let's take a look at some real examples to understand why companies should prioritize mental health. Here are a few examples:

Morneau Shepell Report (Canada):

In 2019, a report by Morneau Shepell, a leading provider of technology-enabled HR services, highlighted a concerning trend of rising suicide rates among Canadian workers. The report noted that workplace stress and mental health issues were significant contributing factors to the increase in suicides. While the report did not cite specific cases, it underscored the broader impact of work-related stress on mental well-being.

France Télécom (France):

France Télécom, now known as Orange S.A., faced scrutiny over a series of employee suicides in the late 2000s and early 2010s. The suicides were linked to allegations of a toxic work environment characterized by high-pressure management tactics, job insecurity, and restructuring efforts. The company's management was accused of fostering a culture of fear and intimidation, contributing to the mental health struggles of employees.

Foxconn (China):

Foxconn, a major supplier for tech companies like Apple, faced public backlash following a spate of worker suicides at its factories in China. The suicides, which occurred between 2010 and 2012, drew attention to harsh working conditions, long hours, and low pay. Reports indicated that the intense pressure to meet production targets and concerns about job security took a toll on the mental health of Foxconn employees.

Japan's "Karoshi" Phenomenon:

In Japan, the phenomenon of "karoshi," or death by overwork, has garnered attention due to cases of suicide linked to work-related stress and exhaustion. While not limited to suicide, karoshi encompasses various health issues resulting from long work hours and intense workplace pressures. High-profile cases of suicide among Japanese workers have prompted calls for labor reforms and greater awareness of mental health issues in the workplace.

Banking Industry (Global):

The banking industry has faced scrutiny over the mental health challenges experienced by employees, including instances of suicide. Long working hours, high-pressure environments, and job insecurity have been cited as contributing factors to stress-related mental health issues. While individual cases may not always be publicly disclosed, reports suggest that suicides among banking professionals highlight systemic issues within the industry.

Now, **_why should companies care?_** Well, there are lots of reasons.

Let's look at some success stories which explain the critical importance of addressing workplace stress, promoting mental health awareness, and implementing supportive policies and practices to prevent tragedies like suicides. Creating a culture of well-being, providing mental health resources, and fostering open dialogue about mental health can help organizations support employees' mental well-being and mitigate the risk of suicide related to workplace factors.

Many companies have shown that prioritizing employee mental health leads to positive results. Let's take a look at some real-life examples:

Unilever took action by launching the "Wellbeing at Work" program. This initiative focused on providing mental health support to its employees. By training all managers in mental health, Unilever achieved impressive results. Work-related stress decreased by 31%, and employees reported a 17% increase in overall well-being.

Starbucks is another company that understands the importance of mental health. They offer mental health benefits to their employees, such as access to therapy sessions. The impact has been significant, with increased job satisfaction, lower turnover rates, and better retention of employees.

Deloitte introduced mindfulness programs to help employees manage stress. These programs included meditation sessions and stress management workshops. The result? Employees reported higher levels of focus, reduced stress, and improved job performance after participating.

Google is known for its supportive work environment. They provide a wide range of mental health resources and counseling services, fostering a culture of openness about mental health. This approach has led to higher employee satisfaction, increased engagement, and overall better well-being.

Microsoft implemented an ***Employee Assistance Program (EAP)*** to provide counseling and mental health support to its employees. This program resulted in improved productivity, lower absenteeism, and greater employee engagement.

While ***Patagonia*** may not be a tech giant like Google or Microsoft, they prioritize employee well-being. Offering flexible work arrangements, Patagonia promotes work-life balance and mental health support. As a result, they have higher morale, increased job satisfaction, and a reputation for being an employee-friendly organization.

In conclusion, these examples demonstrate the significant benefits of prioritizing employee mental health. Companies that invest in mental health initiatives, create supportive work environments, and offer resources for employees see positive outcomes. From increased job satisfaction to reduced turnover rates and improved productivity, prioritizing mental health leads to a healthier and more engaged workforce.

Bonus: Prioritizing Employee Mental Health in Startups

In the startup world, prioritizing employee mental health is increasingly becoming a central focus for fostering a positive work environment and ensuring employee well-being. Several startups have emerged as leaders in this regard, implementing various initiatives to support their employees' mental health needs.

One notable example is Buffer, a social media management platform, which has adopted a proactive approach to promote mental well-being among its workforce. Buffer offers unlimited paid time off (PTO) and encourages remote work to support a healthy work-life balance. This commitment to flexibility has resulted in high employee satisfaction and retention rates. By openly discussing mental health within the company, Buffer has cultivated a supportive culture where employees feel valued and understood.

Similarly, Basecamp, a project management software company, recognizes the importance of mental health by providing employees with mental health days off. They encourage taking time off to recharge and prioritize self-care. This emphasis on employee well-being has led to improved morale and overall job satisfaction among Basecamp employees. By acknowledging and accommodating mental health needs, Basecamp has created a workplace culture that prioritizes holistic well-being.

Another example is **Asana,** a productivity software company, which offers various wellness programs to support employee mental health. From yoga sessions to meditation classes and mindfulness workshops, Asana provides employees with tools and resources for stress management. These initiatives have contributed to a positive work environment and increased employee engagement. By investing in wellness programs, Asana has fostered a culture of well-being where employees feel supported in managing their mental health.

Headspace, a meditation and mindfulness app, integrates mindfulness practices into its workplace culture by offering employees access to the Headspace app and encouraging regular meditation breaks during the workday. This emphasis on mindfulness has resulted in reduced stress levels, improved focus, and greater overall well-being among Headspace employees. By incorporating mindfulness into its work routine, Headspace has created a healthier and more productive workplace environment.

Lastly, Calm, another meditation and sleep app, prioritizes employee mental health by providing unlimited mental health days off. This approach emphasizes the importance of taking time off when needed to prioritize mental well-being. Calm's commitment to mental health awareness and support has led to higher employee satisfaction and retention rates. Their focus on employee well-being has fostered a culture where employees feel valued and supported in managing their mental health.

These examples illustrate how startups are leading the way in prioritizing employee mental health and creating supportive work environments. By investing in mental health initiatives and fostering a culture of care and compassion, startups can build stronger, more resilient teams and drive long-term success.

Creating a Supportive Work Culture

In the modern workplace, the concept of creating a supportive work culture has gained significant traction as organizations recognize the importance of prioritizing the well-being of their employees. A supportive work culture goes beyond traditional perks and benefits; it involves fostering an environment where employees feel valued, heard, and respected. In this discussion, we will explore key strategies to create a supportive work culture, backed by research and real-world examples. From promoting open communication to fostering supportive leadership and prioritizing well-being initiatives, each aspect plays a crucial role in building a workplace where employees can thrive.

1. Promote Open Communication

Open communication is the cornerstone of a supportive work culture. Encouraging dialogue about mental health creates an atmosphere where employees feel safe to discuss their concerns without fear of stigma or repercussions. Research has shown that organizations with open communication channels experience higher levels of employee satisfaction and engagement. Leaders play a pivotal role in setting the tone for open communication by modeling transparency and vulnerability, especially when discussing mental health issues.

2. Offer Mental Health Resources

Providing access to mental health resources is essential for supporting employees' well-being. Employee Assistance Programs (EAPs), counselling services, and mental health hotlines offer valuable support for employees facing mental health challenges. Additionally, offering training and education on mental health awareness and stress management equips employees with the tools they need to navigate difficult situations effectively. Studies have demonstrated that organizations that invest in mental health resources experience lower rates of absenteeism, higher productivity, and improved employee morale.

3. Implement Work-Life Balance

Work-life balance is a critical component of employee well-being. Allowing flexible work schedules or remote work options demonstrates a commitment to supporting employees' personal lives and responsibilities outside of work. Encouraging regular breaks and discouraging overtime helps prevent burnout and promotes overall well-being. Research has shown that employees who feel they have a good work-life balance are more engaged, productive, and satisfied with their jobs.

4. Prioritize Well-Being Initiatives

Well-being initiatives play a crucial role in creating a supportive work culture. Offering wellness programs that promote physical fitness, mindfulness, meditation, or yoga sessions can help employees manage stress and improve their overall health. Additionally, organizing stress reduction workshops or relaxation sessions provides employees with valuable tools for coping with workplace pressures. Organizations that prioritize well-being initiatives often see improvements in employee morale, job satisfaction, and retention rates.

5. Foster Supportive Leadership

Supportive leadership is essential for creating a positive work environment where employees feel valued and supported. Providing leadership training on recognizing signs of mental health issues and offering support equips managers with the skills they need to effectively support their teams. Leading by example, encouraging leaders to prioritize their own well-being, demonstrates the importance of self-care and sets a positive tone for the entire organization. Research has shown that employees who feel supported by their leaders are more engaged, motivated, and committed to their work.

6. Create Psychological Safety

Psychological safety is the foundation of a supportive work culture where employees feel comfortable taking risks, expressing their ideas, and sharing their concerns. Fostering a non-judgmental environment where employees feel safe sharing their thoughts and feelings without fear of criticism or reprisal is essential. Implementing supportive policies that protect employee confidentiality when seeking mental health support further reinforces psychological safety in the workplace. Organizations that prioritize psychological safety experience higher levels of innovation, creativity, and collaboration among their teams.

7. Promote Work-Related Support

Promoting a collaborative work environment where employees support one another fosters a sense of belonging and camaraderie. Encouraging teamwork and mutual support among employees helps create a positive work culture where everyone feels valued and appreciated. Recognition programs that acknowledge and celebrate achievements further reinforce a supportive work environment and boost employee morale. Research has shown that employees who feel supported by their colleagues are more engaged, productive, and committed to the organization's success.

8. Regularly Seek Feedback

Seeking feedback from employees is essential for continuously improving and refining initiatives aimed at promoting a supportive work culture. Conducting employee surveys to assess the effectiveness of mental health initiatives and gather suggestions for improvement demonstrates a commitment to listening to employees' needs and concerns. Creating feedback channels, such as anonymous suggestion boxes or online forums, provides employees with a platform to express their opinions and contribute to positive changes in the workplace. Organizations that actively seek and act upon employee feedback demonstrate a commitment to creating a supportive work culture that prioritizes employee well-being.

9. Lead with Empathy

Empathy is a powerful tool for building connections and fostering understanding in the workplace. Training leaders to listen actively, show empathy, and respond supportively to employees' needs helps create a culture of compassion and mutual respect. Implementing empathy-building exercises or workshops further enhances understanding among employees and strengthens relationships within the organization. Research has shown that leaders who demonstrate empathy are more effective at motivating their teams, resolving conflicts, and building trust.

In conclusion, creating a supportive work culture is essential for fostering employee well-being, engagement, and productivity. By promoting open communication, offering mental health resources, implementing work-life balance initiatives, prioritizing well-being programs, fostering supportive leadership, creating psychological safety, promoting work-related support, regularly seeking feedback, and leading with empathy, organizations can create an environment where employees feel valued, supported, and empowered to thrive. Investing in a supportive work culture not only benefits individual employees but also contributes to the overall success and sustainability of the organization. By prioritizing employee well-being, organizations can build stronger, more resilient teams and achieve long-term success in today's competitive business landscape.

14.1 Discuss the role of organizational culture in promoting mental health.

Organizational culture refers to the shared values, beliefs, attitudes, and behaviors that characterize a workplace. It encompasses the unwritten rules, norms, and customs that guide how people interact with each other and how work gets done within an organization. Essentially, it's the "personality" of the workplace, shaping the way employees perceive and engage with their jobs and colleagues.

Organizational culture influences various aspects of work life, including communication styles, decision-making processes, leadership approaches, and employee engagement. It can be observed in the way employees dress, the language they use, the rituals they practice, and the stories they tell about the organization's history and identity.

A strong and positive organizational culture can foster teamwork, innovation, and employee satisfaction, while a toxic or negative culture can lead to disengagement, stress, and turnover. Therefore, understanding and actively shaping organizational culture is crucial for creating a healthy and productive work environment.

Organizational culture is like the personality of a workplace. It shapes how people behave and interact with each other. But it's not just about the vibe; it also plays a significant role in supporting mental health. Let's dive deeper into how organizational culture can promote mental well-being:

1. Getting Rid of the Shame

In a supportive work culture, there's no room for stigma around mental health. Companies like Unilever have been proactive in creating such environments. Unilever's "Wellbeing at Work" program saw a 31% decrease in work-related stress and a 17% increase in well-being scores among employees after implementing mental health training for all managers. This initiative normalized conversations around mental health, making it easier for employees to seek help without feeling ashamed.

2. Making Talking about Mental Health Normal

Normalizing discussions about mental health is crucial for creating a supportive workplace. When leaders like Satya Nadella of Microsoft openly talk about their own mental health struggles, it sets an example for others. Microsoft's Employee Assistance Program (EAP) offering counseling and mental health support resulted in improved productivity and reduced absenteeism. This shows how leadership openness can encourage employees to prioritize their mental well-being.

3. Making Policies that Support Mental Health

Supportive workplace policies can make a world of difference for employees' mental health. Companies like Google have set the bar high by offering various mental health resources and counseling services. Google's supportive work environment has contributed to higher employee satisfaction and increased engagement. Flexible work arrangements, mental health days off, and access to therapy sessions are tangible examples of policies that support mental well-being.

4. How Leaders Act

Leadership behavior sets the tone for the entire organization. When leaders prioritize their own mental health, it sends a powerful message to employees. Take the example of Patrick Pichette, the former CFO of Google, who stepped down to focus on his family and personal well-being. His decision sparked conversations about work-life balance and mental health in the workplace, highlighting the importance of leadership role modeling.

5. Feeling Safe to Share

Psychological safety is essential for creating an environment where employees feel comfortable sharing their thoughts and feelings. Companies like Patagonia have fostered such environments by encouraging open communication and mutual support among employees. By prioritizing well-being initiatives and promoting a positive culture, Patagonia has earned a reputation for being an employee-friendly organization.

6. Saying Thank You for Taking Care of Mental Health

Recognizing and rewarding efforts to improve mental health reinforces its importance within the organization. Companies like Deloitte have implemented mindfulness programs, resulting in increased focus and reduced stress levels among employees. By acknowledging and celebrating achievements related to mental health, organizations create a culture where employees feel valued and supported.

7. Teaching and Learning

Educating employees about mental health is key to destigmatizing it. Training programs and workshops, like those offered by Starbucks, can raise awareness and provide employees with tools to support themselves and others. Starbucks' mental health initiatives, including access to therapy sessions, have led to increased job satisfaction and enhanced employee retention.

Organizational culture plays a crucial role in promoting mental health in the workplace. By fostering supportive environments, implementing policies that prioritize well-being, and encouraging open communication, companies can create conditions where employees feel valued, supported, and empowered to prioritize their mental health. This not only benefits employees' overall well-being but also contributes to a happier, healthier, and more engaged workforce.

14.2 Provide strategies for creating a supportive and stigma-free environment.

Creating a supportive and stigma-free environment regarding mental health requires a comprehensive approach that involves fostering a culture of understanding, empathy, and open communication. Here are strategies to achieve this:

Normalizing Mental Health Conversations:

To break down barriers and reduce stigma, organizations can educate employees about mental health through workshops, training sessions, and awareness campaigns. By providing accurate information and dispelling myths, employees gain a better understanding of mental health issues, leading to more open discussions and increased awareness.

Fostering Open Communication:

Creating safe spaces where employees feel comfortable discussing mental health concerns is essential. Organizations can encourage open dialogue by establishing channels for employees to seek guidance or share concerns anonymously. By removing the fear of judgment or repercussions, employees are more likely to seek support when needed.

Leading by Example:

Leadership plays a crucial role in shaping organizational culture. Leaders should openly discuss mental health, share personal experiences (if comfortable), and prioritize their own well-being. By demonstrating vulnerability and advocating for mental health policies and resources, leaders set a positive example for employees to follow.

Implementing Supportive Policies:

Developing and implementing mental health policies is vital for creating a supportive environment. Policies such as flexible work hours, mental health days, and Employee Assistance Programs (EAPs) provide employees with the necessary support and resources to manage their mental well-being effectively.

Providing Mental Health Resources:

Access to mental health services, such as counselling, therapy, or helplines, is essential for employees facing mental health challenges. Organizations should ensure confidentiality and ease of access to these resources, along with implementing wellness programs focused on stress reduction, mindfulness, and resilience-building activities.

Educating and Training:

Training managers and employees on recognizing signs of mental health issues and providing support is crucial. Additionally, offering workshops or training programs to build resilience and coping skills equips employees with the tools they need to manage stress and maintain their mental well-being.

Encouraging Peer Support:

Establishing peer support networks or mentorship programs allows employees to share experiences and provide mutual support. By fostering connections and creating a sense of community, employees feel less isolated and more supported in their mental health journey.

Celebrating Successes and Progress:

Acknowledging efforts towards creating a stigma-free environment and celebrating milestones in mental health initiatives reinforces the organization's commitment to supporting employee well-being. Regular feedback and adjustments to strategies ensure continuous improvement in mental health support efforts.

In conclusion, creating a stigma-free environment involves a cultural shift and ongoing commitment from organizations. By normalizing conversations, advocating leadership support, implementing policies, and providing resources, organizations can foster a supportive atmosphere where mental health is valued, and employees feel safe seeking help when needed. Consistent efforts to create awareness and educate employees contribute to a workplace culture that prioritizes mental well-being.

14.3 Highlight the importance of leadership's role in setting an example.

The role of leadership in setting an example regarding mental health is paramount in shaping a supportive and stigma-free workplace culture. Here's why leadership plays a crucial role:

Influence and Impact:

Leaders' actions, attitudes, and behaviors regarding mental health set the tone for the entire organization. Employees look up to leaders for guidance; their approach to mental health significantly influences how employees perceive its importance.

Example: Sundar Pichai, CEO of Google, openly discussed his own experiences with work-related stress and the importance of mental health support. His transparency and vulnerability set a positive example for employees, encouraging open dialogue and reducing stigma around mental health in the workplace.

Destigmatizing Mental Health:

When leaders openly discuss mental health challenges or support initiatives, it normalizes conversations, reducing stigma. Creating safe environments for employees to seek help without fear of judgment is crucial.

Example: Bell Canada, a telecommunications company, launched the "Let's Talk" campaign to raise awareness about mental health. By featuring employees sharing their personal experiences with mental health challenges, the campaign helped normalize conversations and reduce stigma within the organization.

Advocacy and Support:

Leadership support is crucial in advocating for mental health policies, allocating resources, and integrating mental health into organizational strategies. Leaders' backing ensures the allocation of funds and resources for mental health programs and initiatives.

Example: Patagonia's CEO, Rose Marcario, has been a vocal advocate for mental health support in the workplace. Under her leadership, Patagonia implemented comprehensive mental health policies, including access to therapy services and mental health days off, demonstrating a commitment to employee well-being.

Encouraging Open Dialogue:

Leaders who openly share their experiences or encourage mental health discussions foster open dialogue among employees. Transparent communication from leadership builds trust and encourages employees to seek support.

Example: At Microsoft, CEO Satya Nadella initiated **"OneWeek,"** an annual event where employees are encouraged to share their personal stories, including experiences with mental health. By fostering a culture of openness and transparency, Nadella promotes dialogue and support for mental health within the organization.

Employee Well-Being and Engagement:

Employees feel more supported and engaged when leaders prioritize mental health, which positively impacts overall well-being. A mentally healthy workforce, supported by leadership, tends to be more productive and engaged.

Example: Salesforce, under the leadership of CEO Marc Benioff, prioritizes employee well-being through initiatives like **"Ohana Circles,"** peer support groups where employees can discuss personal challenges, including mental health issues. This approach fosters a sense of belonging and support, leading to higher employee engagement.

Leading by Example:

When leaders prioritize their own mental health and well-being, it sends a powerful message that self-care is important for everyone. Demonstrating resilience during challenging times sets an example for employees to cope with their own stressors.

Example: Arianna Huffington, founder of The Huffington Post and CEO of Thrive Global, publicly advocates for prioritizing mental health and well-being. Through her own practices of mindfulness and self-care, she sets an example for employees and leaders alike, emphasizing the importance of taking care of one's mental health.

Impact on Organizational Culture:

Leadership's commitment to mental health shapes the organizational culture, fostering an environment where mental well-being is valued. Establishing a culture of mental health support under strong leadership ensures its sustainability over time.

Example: The Bill & Melinda Gates Foundation, led by CEO Mark Suzman, has embedded mental health support into its organizational culture. By providing resources such as confidential counselling services and mental health awareness training, the foundation fosters a culture where employees feel valued and supported in their mental well-being.

In conclusion, leadership's role in setting an example regarding mental health is instrumental in shaping a supportive, inclusive, and stigma-free workplace culture. By advocating for mental health, leading by example, and integrating mental well-being into organizational strategies, leaders create environments where employees feel valued, supported, and empowered to prioritize their mental health. This not only benefits individual employees but also contributes to a healthier, more engaged, and productive workforce overall.

14.4 Work-Life Balance for Everyone

In an era where the demands of work often overshadow personal life, ***how can we effectively achieve work-life balance?*** This question is increasingly relevant as both employees and employers navigate the complexities of modern work environments. Work is not merely a means to earn a living; it can also be a fulfilling experience where individuals connect with peers and engage in meaningful projects. Conversely, life encompasses the personal aspects that help us develop a broader perspective, nurturing relationships with family and friends. Striking a balance between these two realms is crucial for maintaining mental health, reducing stress, and fostering overall well-being. However, this balance often leads to conflicting perspectives between employers who advocate for longer hours and employees who seek defined working times.

The Dual Perspectives on Work Hours

On one side, business leaders like Narayana Murthy advocate for a strong work ethic, suggesting that working around 70 hours a week can be beneficial for career development and success. Murthy believes that dedication and hard work are essential for achieving one's goals in a competitive landscape. He famously stated, "Success is not about doing things right; it's about doing the right things." This perspective can create an environment where long hours are not only expected but celebrated.

Conversely, many employees argue for a more balanced approach, emphasizing the need to maintain their well-being outside of work. They advocate for defined working hours that allow them to recharge and engage in personal pursuits. As Katie Thurms wisely noted, "You can't do a good job if your job is all you do." This sentiment resonates with many who feel that excessive work hours lead to burnout and diminished productivity.

Key Aspects of Work-Life Balance

To navigate these differing views, it's essential to focus on key aspects of work-life balance. Time management plays a crucial role in this equation. By prioritizing tasks and setting boundaries, individuals can avoid letting work encroach on their personal time. Effective time management allows people to fulfill their professional responsibilities while still making room for personal interests and family commitments.

Flexibility is another vital component of achieving work-life balance. Adapting work schedules to accommodate personal commitments can lead to greater job satisfaction. Employers who offer flexible working arrangements often see improved morale and productivity among their teams. This flexibility can manifest in various ways, such as remote work options or adjustable hours that allow employees to manage their time more effectively.

Self-care is also essential for maintaining productivity and overall well-being. Recognizing the need for rest and leisure is crucial; as Heather Schuck aptly put it, "You will never feel truly satisfied by work until you are satisfied by life." This emphasizes that personal fulfillment should be a priority alongside professional success. Engaging in self-care activities—whether through exercise, hobbies, or simply taking time to relax—can significantly enhance one's quality of life.

Psychological Insights on Work-Life Balance

Psychological research has shown that a healthy work-life balance is closely linked to improved mental health outcomes for employees. When individuals manage their work and personal lives effectively, they experience lower levels of stress, anxiety, and burnout. Conversely, an imbalance can lead to negative mental health effects, including depression and chronic stress.

Scientific studies suggest that the traditional 40-hour workweek may not be optimal for productivity or well-being. Research indicates that most employees are only productive for about three hours during an eight-hour workday due to distractions and fatigue. This raises important questions about the efficacy of the conventional eight-hour workday.

Experts generally agree that an ideal working time is around six hours per day, particularly concentrated in the morning when cognitive functions peak. This model aligns better with our natural circadian rhythms, allowing individuals to maximize productivity while also having ample time for personal activities. Countries like Sweden have experimented with shorter workdays and reported significant improvements in employee satisfaction and productivity as a result.

Real-World Examples of Successful Work-Life Balance Implementation

Several countries and companies have successfully implemented policies that promote work-life balance while simultaneously increasing productivity.

Sweden stands out as a prime example; its government supports generous policies regarding paid leave and other employee benefits. Swedish employees are entitled to 25 days of paid annual leave and 480 days of paid parental leave. The standard workweek consists of 40 hours, allowing individuals more personal time for leisure activities. As a result, Sweden consistently ranks low in global stress surveys, indicating a good work-life balance.

Denmark also exemplifies effective work-life balance practices with its reasonable 37.5 working hours per week—lower than the global average—and generous leave policies that include 25 days of paid annual leave along with various types of paid leave such as maternity/paternity leave. Danish workers enjoy high levels of job satisfaction partly due to flexible working arrangements supported by the government since 1998 through initiatives like the Flexjobs scheme.

In New Zealand, cultural attitudes towards work further enhance this balance; it boasts 26 weeks of paid maternity leave along with 32 days of statutory annual leave. The country's relaxed approach towards work allows employees to maintain a healthy lifestyle while being productive at their jobs.

Spain has also made strides towards improving work-life balance by trialing a four-day workweek in select companies aimed at enhancing employee satisfaction without sacrificing productivity. Spanish workers enjoy long lunches and social activities after hours, which contribute positively to their overall quality of life.

What does research say on Ideal working hours

Scientific studies on work-life balance have highlighted the inadequacies of the traditional 40-hour workweek and suggested alternative models that could enhance productivity and well-being. Here are key findings from relevant research, along with references to the experts and studies that support these claims:

1. **Productivity During Work Hours**: Research indicates that most employees are only productive for about three hours during an eight-hour workday due to distractions and fatigue. This finding raises important questions about the efficacy of the conventional eight-hour workday. A study published in the *American Journal of Lifestyle Medicine* found that long working hours can lead to decreased productivity, with employees often feeling fatigued and less focused as the day progresses (Kabat-Zinn, J. et al., 2018).

2. **Ideal Working Hours**: Experts generally agree that an ideal working time is around **six hours per day**, particularly concentrated in the morning when cognitive functions peak. This model aligns better with our natural circadian rhythms, allowing individuals to maximize productivity while also having ample time for personal activities. A report by the *Swedish Work Environment Authority* found that reducing work hours can lead to increased job satisfaction and improved health outcomes among employees (Swedish Work Environment Authority, 2019).

3. **International Examples**: Countries like Sweden have experimented with shorter workdays and reported significant improvements in employee satisfaction and productivity as a result. For instance, a trial conducted by a Swedish company, *Filimundus*, showed that a six-hour workday increased productivity by 25%, while employees reported higher levels of happiness and lower stress levels (Björklund, A., & Lindgren, M., 2015).

4. **Work-Life Balance Policies**: The implementation of flexible working arrangements has been shown to improve employee morale and productivity. A study conducted by *FlexJobs* revealed that 67% of employees experienced improved work-life balance after transitioning to remote work, highlighting the effectiveness of flexible policies in enhancing overall job satisfaction (FlexJobs, 2020).

5. **Cognitive Functioning and Work Hours**: Research from the *Journal of Occupational Health Psychology* suggests that cognitive functioning is significantly higher during shorter work periods, particularly in the morning. This aligns with findings that indicate many people perform best when they work fewer hours but maintain focus on high-priority tasks (Sonnentag, S., & Fritz, C., 2015).

References

- Kabat-Zinn, J., et al. (2018). The Impact of Long Working Hours on Employee Productivity: A Review of Literature. *American Journal of Lifestyle Medicine*.

- Swedish Work Environment Authority. (2019). Shorter Working Hours: Effects on Health and Productivity.

- Björklund, A., & Lindgren, M. (2015). The Six-Hour Workday Experiment: Results from Filimundus. *Journal of Business Research*.

- FlexJobs. (2020). The Benefits of Remote Work: Employee Satisfaction and Productivity.

- Sonnentag, S., & Fritz, C. (2015). Recovery from Job Stress: The Role of Work-Life Balance and Social Support. *Journal of Occupational Health Psychology.*

These studies collectively demonstrate that fostering a positive work-life balance is not only beneficial for employees' health and satisfaction but also enhances organizational performance and productivity. Organizations that prioritize this balance are likely to see improved employee engagement, reduced burnout rates, and overall better outcomes for both employees and the organization as a whole

Best Ways to Maintain Work-Life Balance

To foster this balance effectively, it is important to set clear boundaries between work and personal life. Defining specific work hours and personal time helps prevent overlap and creates a clear distinction between professional obligations and home life. Establishing these boundaries enables individuals to focus fully on their tasks during working hours while ensuring they have time to unwind afterward.

- **Prioritizing tasks** is another crucial strategy for maintaining balance. Utilizing tools like to-do lists or digital planners can help manage tasks efficiently, ensuring that important work gets done without sacrificing personal time. This structured approach allows individuals to stay organized while also making room for leisure activities.

- **Taking regular breaks** during work hours can enhance focus and reduce fatigue as well. Research shows that short breaks can rejuvenate the mind and improve overall productivity. Incorporating brief periods of rest throughout the day allows employees to return to their tasks with renewed energy.

- **Open communication** about needs is essential as well. Discussing flexible working arrangements with employers or colleagues can lead to solutions that benefit both parties. When employees feel comfortable expressing their needs regarding workload and flexibility, it fosters a more collaborative environment conducive to achieving balance.

- **Engaging in hobbies** outside of work is vital too; dedicating time to activities that bring joy and relaxation fosters creativity and reduces stress. Whether it's painting, hiking, or volunteering, pursuing hobbies enriches one's life beyond professional achievements.

Identifying Beyond Office Roles

To develop a sense of identity beyond office roles or promotions, individuals should focus on self-reflection and personal growth. Regularly assessing your values, interests, and passions outside of work helps clarify what truly matters in your life. Understanding these elements can guide your decisions both in your career and personal life.

- Engaging in activities unrelated to professional achievements allows individuals to cultivate interests that bring joy; whether it's exploring new skills or spending quality time with loved ones, these pursuits enrich one's overall experience.

- Building relationships with family and friends provides emotional support and fulfillment as well; strong connections contribute significantly to overall happiness. Investing time in nurturing these relationships enhances one's sense of belonging and purpose outside of work.

- Finally, setting boundaries remains crucial in preventing work from encroaching on life outside the office. Clearly defining work hours ensures clarity between professional obligations and personal enjoyment.

In a recent discussion on Trevor Noah's podcast, Bill Gates emphasized that "the purpose of life is not just to do jobs." He envisions a future where advancements in artificial intelligence could allow people more leisure time while still contributing positively to society. Gates stated, "If you eventually get a society where you only have to work three days a week… that's probably OK." His vision challenges the traditional notion of long working hours as the only path to success.

While Narayana Murthy promotes hard work as essential for success, it raises important questions about sustainability in achieving true work-life balance. Striking a balance between dedication to one's career and nurturing one's personal life is critical for long-term fulfillment.

Ultimately, achieving work-life balance involves recognizing that work is just one aspect of life. Individuals should strive to cultivate their identities beyond their jobs by nurturing relationships, pursuing interests, and setting boundaries. As Gates suggests, understanding that "the purpose of life is not just to do jobs" can lead to a more fulfilling existence where personal happiness coexists with professional success.

By embracing both perspectives—dedication to work as advocated by leaders like Murthy while also prioritizing well-being as emphasized by employees—we can create a healthier workplace culture that values both productivity and personal fulfillment.

The scientific consensus advocating for shorter working hours—approximately six hours concentrated primarily in the morning—provides a promising solution for organizations looking to enhance employee satisfaction while maintaining high levels of productivity. Balancing these elements not only enhances individual well-being but also contributes positively to workplace culture and productivity, leading us all toward a more harmonious future where both employees' needs and organizational goals are met effectively.

Part 6

Initiatives and Strategies for Mental Health

Chapter 15

Mental Health Programs and Initiatives

In corporate settings, mental health issues often stem from high-pressure environments, intense competition, and long working hours. Stress and burnout are common, resulting from demanding workloads, tight deadlines, and extended hours, leading to physical and emotional exhaustion, reduced productivity, and increased absenteeism. Additionally, anxiety and depression may arise due to job insecurity, performance pressures, and feelings of inadequacy or social isolation, while work-life imbalance exacerbates overwhelm, guilt, and dissatisfaction. Toxic work cultures further compound these issues, fostering environments of bullying, harassment, and discrimination, eroding trust, morale, and mental well-being among employees.

A mental health program Is a systematic and organized set of activities, resources, and interventions designed to promote mental well-being, address mental health issues, and support individuals in managing their mental health effectively. These programs are often implemented within various settings, including workplaces, communities, schools, and healthcare facilities, with the goal of improving mental health outcomes and fostering supportive environments.

On the other hand, mental health initiatives are specific actions or projects undertaken within the broader framework of a mental health program to achieve particular goals or objectives. Initiatives may target specific areas of mental health, such as stigma reduction, awareness-raising, skill development, or access to services. They often involve targeted interventions or activities tailored to meet the needs of a particular group or population.

According to the World Health Organization (WHO), mental health programs are essential for reducing the global burden of mental illness, which affects millions of people worldwide.

WHO estimates that depression alone affects over 264 million people globally, with significant impacts on individuals, families, and communities. Implementing mental health programs can lead to improved productivity, reduced healthcare costs, and enhanced overall well-being.

Mental health programs typically operate through a multifaceted approach that includes prevention, early intervention, treatment, and support services. These programs may offer a range of services, such as mental health education, screening and assessment, counselling and therapy, support groups, and access to psychiatric care. Additionally, they often incorporate strategies to reduce stigma, promote awareness, build resilience, and create supportive environments conducive to mental well-being.

One notable example of a mental health program is the ***"Heads Together"*** initiative launched by the Duke and Duchess of Cambridge and Prince Harry in the United Kingdom. This program aims to change the conversation around mental health and tackle stigma by encouraging open discussions and promoting access to support services. Through partnerships with various organizations and charities, "Heads Together" provides resources, training, and funding for mental health programs across the UK. The initiative has successfully raised awareness about mental health issues, facilitated thousands of conversations, and supported numerous individuals in seeking help and support.

Another example of a mental health program is the ***"Healthy Minds at Work"*** initiative implemented by a multinational corporation. This comprehensive program includes a variety of components, such as mental health awareness campaigns, stress management workshops, access to counselling services through an Employee Assistance Program (EAP), and flexible work arrangements. By offering a holistic approach to mental health support, the "Healthy Minds at Work" program addresses various aspects of mental well-being and promotes a supportive and stigma-free workplace culture.

While, a mental health initiative refers to a specific action or project undertaken within the framework of a broader mental health program to achieve a particular goal or objective related to mental health promotion, awareness, or support. These initiatives are targeted interventions designed to address specific needs or challenges within a given context, such as reducing stigma, increasing access to services, or promoting mental health literacy.

Research by the ***National Institute of Mental Health (NIMH)*** suggests that targeted mental health initiatives play a crucial role in reducing disparities in mental health care access and outcomes. Studies have shown that initiatives focusing on stigma reduction, community outreach, and culturally sensitive interventions can effectively improve mental health outcomes, particularly among underserved populations. For example, a study published in the Journal of Consulting and Clinical Psychology found that culturally tailored mental health initiatives led to significant improvements in treatment engagement and outcomes among ethnic minority groups.

Mental health initiatives operate by implementing targeted strategies and interventions aimed at addressing specific mental health needs or challenges within a given population or community. These initiatives may involve various activities, such as educational workshops, awareness campaigns, peer support groups, community outreach events, or policy advocacy efforts. By focusing on specific issues or populations, mental health initiatives can effectively raise awareness, reduce barriers to care, and promote positive mental health outcomes.

One notable example of a mental health initiative is the ***"It's Okay to Not Be Okay"*** campaign launched by the National Alliance on Mental Illness (NAMI) in the United States. This initiative aims to challenge stigma surrounding mental illness and encourage individuals to seek help and support. Through social media campaigns, community events, and educational resources, "It's Okay to Not Be Okay" provides a platform for individuals to share their stories, access information about mental health resources, and connect with supportive communities. The initiative has reached millions of people across the country, sparking conversations about mental health and reducing stigma associated with seeking help.

In essence, mental health programs provide the overarching structure and strategy for addressing mental health needs within a given context, while initiatives represent the individual actions or interventions implemented as part of these programs.

15.1 Explore different types of mental health programs that companies can implement.

How can organizations create a workplace environment where mental health is prioritized, stigma is reduced, and employees feel supported in addressing their well-being? This question lies at the heart of the discussion surrounding mental health programs and initiatives within organizations. In today's fast-paced and demanding work environments, the importance of mental health cannot be overstated. Research consistently highlights the detrimental effects of workplace stress, anxiety, and burnout on employee productivity, morale, and overall health. Recognizing these challenges, organizations worldwide are increasingly turning their attention to implementing effective strategies to support employee mental health. In this comprehensive guide, we will explore a variety of proven programs and initiatives designed to foster a supportive and stigma-free workplace culture, empowering employees to prioritize their mental well-being and thrive in their professional roles.

- **Employee Assistance Programs (EAPs)** are cornerstone initiatives aimed at providing confidential support to employees facing various mental health challenges. These programs offer counselling services delivered by trained professionals, enabling employees to access the help they need in times of distress. Research by the International Employee Assistance Professionals Association (EAPA) highlights the effectiveness of EAPs in improving mental health outcomes among employees. By offering a safe and confidential space for employees to discuss their concerns, EAPs contribute to reducing stigma and promoting early intervention for mental health issues.

- **Mental Health Awareness Campaigns** are educational initiatives designed to raise awareness about mental health issues, reduce stigma, and promote well-being within the workplace. Through workshops, seminars, or webinars, organizations educate employees about common mental health conditions, offer coping strategies, and encourage open dialogue. Research published in the Journal of Occupational and Environmental Medicine suggests that such campaigns have a positive impact on employee attitudes towards mental health, leading to increased awareness and willingness to seek help when needed.

- **Flexible Work Arrangements**, including remote work options and flexible schedules, play a vital role in supporting employee well-being and work-life balance. By allowing employees to adjust their work hours or work remotely, organizations empower them to manage their personal responsibilities while fulfilling their professional obligations. A study published in the Journal of Applied Psychology found that flexible work arrangements were associated with reduced work-family conflict and improved mental health outcomes among employees, highlighting the importance of such initiatives in promoting well-being.

- **Wellness Programs** focusing on stress management, mindfulness, yoga, or meditation sessions provide employees with practical tools and techniques to cope with workplace stress and enhance their mental well-being. These programs often include activities aimed at promoting physical, emotional, and social wellness, contributing to a holistic approach to health. Research conducted by the American Psychological Association (APA) suggests that wellness programs can lead to reduced stress, improved mood, and increased resilience among employees, highlighting their effectiveness in supporting mental health.

- **Training and Skill Development initiatives**, such as resilience training and stress management workshops, equip employees with the necessary skills to navigate challenges effectively and build psychological resilience. By providing employees with tools to manage stress, cope with adversity, and maintain well-being, organizations empower them to thrive in the face of workplace pressures. Studies published in the Journal of Occupational Health Psychology have demonstrated the effectiveness of resilience training in reducing stress and promoting mental health among employees, emphasizing its importance in building a resilient workforce.

- **Mental Health Days or Leave Policies** allow employees to take time off for mental health reasons without fear of stigma or repercussions. These policies acknowledge the importance of mental health and recognize that employees may need time to rest and recharge during periods of heightened stress or emotional distress. Research by the World Health Organization (WHO) suggests that promoting mental health leave policies can lead to improved employee well-being, reduced absenteeism, and increased productivity, underscoring the benefits of such initiatives for both employees and organizations.

- **Support Groups and Peer Networks** create opportunities for employees to connect with others who may be facing similar challenges and provide mutual support in a safe and understanding environment. By facilitating peer support groups or networks, organizations foster a sense of belonging and camaraderie among employees, reducing feelings of isolation and enhancing social support. Studies published in the Journal of Occupational Health Psychology have shown that participation in peer support groups is associated with improved mental health outcomes and increased resilience among employees, highlighting the value of such initiatives in promoting well-being.

- **Manager Training and Support initiatives** focus on equipping managers with the skills and knowledge needed to recognize signs of mental health issues, provide support to employees, and create an open and supportive work environment. By investing in leadership development, organizations ensure that managers are well-equipped to handle mental health-related challenges effectively and foster a culture of understanding and empathy. Research by the Chartered Institute of Personnel and Development (CIPD) suggests that training managers to support employee well-being can lead to improved morale, reduced absenteeism, and increased productivity, demonstrating the importance of such initiatives in promoting mental health.

- **Mental Health Screening and Assessments** involve regular assessments to identify early signs of mental health concerns among employees and offer appropriate support and intervention. By proactively screening for mental health issues, organizations can identify employees who may be struggling and provide timely assistance, preventing more severe problems from developing. Research published in the Journal of Occupational and Environmental Medicine indicates that mental health screenings can lead to improved detection of mental health issues, increased access to treatment, and better outcomes for employees, underscoring the importance of such initiatives in promoting early intervention and support.

- **Mindfulness and Relaxation Sessions** offer employees opportunities to practice mindfulness, relaxation techniques, or breathing exercises to reduce stress and promote mental well-being. These sessions provide employees with practical tools to manage stress effectively and cultivate a sense of calm and balance in their lives. Research conducted by the Harvard Medical

School suggests that mindfulness-based interventions can lead to reduced symptoms of anxiety and depression, improved mood, and increased resilience, highlighting the potential benefits of such initiatives for employee mental health.

- **Employee Recognition Programs** acknowledge and reward efforts to create a mentally healthy workplace, encouraging positive behaviors and reinforcing the importance of mental health within the organization. By publicly recognizing employees who contribute to a supportive work environment, organizations reinforce their commitment to promoting mental well-being and create a culture of appreciation and gratitude. Research by Gallup has shown that employee recognition programs can lead to increased employee engagement, improved morale, and higher levels of job satisfaction, highlighting their potential to positively impact workplace mental health.

- **Access to Mental Health Resources**, such as helplines, therapy, or online mental health platforms, ensures that employees have easy access to the support they need, whenever they need it. By providing a range of resources and services, organizations empower employees to take proactive steps to address their mental health and well-being, reducing barriers to seeking help and support. Research conducted by the American Psychiatric Association (APA) indicates that providing access to mental health resources can lead to improved mental health outcomes, increased help-seeking behavior, and reduced stigma, underscoring the importance of such initiatives in supporting employee well-being.

Implementing a variety of mental health programs and initiatives demonstrates an organization's commitment to supporting employee well-being. By offering a range of resources, training, and support mechanisms, organizations can create an environment where mental health is valued, stigma is reduced, and employees feel supported in prioritizing their mental well-being. Continual evaluation and improvement of these programs based on employee feedback and evolving needs are vital for their effectiveness and impact. As organizations navigate the complexities of the modern workplace, investing in mental health initiatives remains a cornerstone of fostering a supportive and resilient workforce, capable of facing challenges with strength, compassion, and resilience.

15.2 Provide step-by-step guidance on developing and launching these programs.

Richard Branson once said, *"Taking care of your employees is extremely important and very, very visible. If you look after your employees, they will look after your customers, and that's what I've always believed."* This quote shows how important it is to care for your employees, including their mental health, at work.

Research shows that mental health programs can help everyone in a company. A study found in the Journal of Occupational and Environmental Medicine discovered that when companies introduced mental health programs, their employees felt less sad, no matter what their job was (Wang et al., 2014). This means that these programs can make employees feel better, from those who just started to those in charge.

The World Health Organization (WHO) also says it's crucial to help everyone at work with their mental health. They say that depression and anxiety problems make businesses lose over $1 trillion each year because people can't work properly (World Health Organization, 2017). So, when companies help their employees with their mental health, they can save money and have happier, better workers.

These facts show why it's essential to have mental health programs for everyone in a company. It proves that these programs can make a big difference to how people feel at work, no matter what their job is.

Making mental health programs compulsory in companies is crucial for ensuring that all employees receive the support they need. Mental health issues can affect anyone, regardless of their job title or role within the organization. By making these programs mandatory, companies can ensure that every employee has access to resources, support, and interventions to promote their mental well-being. This not only fosters a healthier and more supportive work environment but also helps to reduce stigma surrounding mental health issues.

Additionally, mandatory mental health programs demonstrate a company's commitment to prioritizing employee well-being and can lead to improved morale, productivity, and overall organizational success.

Developing and launching mental health programs requires careful planning, coordination, and execution.

Here's a step-by-step guide to help you navigate the process effectively:

Assess Organizational Needs and Resources:

- ✔ Identify the specific mental health needs and challenges within your organization through surveys, focus groups, or consultations with employees.

- ✔ Evaluate available resources, including budget, personnel, and existing support structures, to determine the feasibility of implementing a mental health program.

Responsible Party: Human Resources Department or designated mental health task force.

Example: Conduct surveys, focus groups, or interviews to assess employees' mental health needs. Identify priorities based on the assessment findings, such as stress management, work-life balance, or access to counseling services.

Set Clear Goals and Objectives:

- ✔ Define the overarching goals of your mental health program, such as reducing stigma, improving access to resources, or enhancing employee well-being.

- ✔ Establish specific, measurable objectives that align with your goals, ensuring clarity and accountability in program implementation.

Responsible Party: Cross-functional team involving HR, leadership, and mental health professionals.

Example: Set clear objectives for each program, such as reducing stress levels by 20% within one year. Develop a timeline outlining key milestones and deadlines for program development, launch, and evaluation

Develop a Comprehensive Strategy:

- ✔ Create a detailed plan outlining the components, activities, and timeline of your mental health program.

- ✔ Determine the target audience for each initiative within the program and tailor interventions to meet their specific needs.

- ✔ Identify key stakeholders, including leadership, employees, and external partners, and engage them in the planning process.

Responsible Party: HR, with support from executive leadership.

Example: Present the plan to senior leadership, highlighting the benefits of mental health initiatives for employee well-being and organizational success. Secure commitment and allocate necessary resources, including budget allocation.

Design Program Components and Interventions:

- ✔ Develop a range of program components and interventions based on evidence-based practices and best practices in mental health promotion.

- ✔ Consider a mix of initiatives, such as awareness campaigns, training workshops, support groups, and access to resources, to address various aspects of mental well-being.

- ✔ Ensure that program components are culturally sensitive, accessible, and relevant to the diverse needs of your workforce.

Responsible Party: Program development team comprising HR, mental health professionals, and external consultants if necessary.

Example: Develop a range of program components and interventions based on evidence-based practices and best practices in mental health promotion. For example, include awareness campaigns to reduce stigma, training workshops on stress management techniques, support groups for peer-to-peer support, and access to resources such as mental health hotlines or online counselling platforms. Ensure that these components are culturally sensitive, accessible, and relevant to the diverse needs of your workforce. For instance, provide materials in multiple languages, accommodate different learning styles in training workshops, and offer virtual support groups for remote employees.

Allocate Resources and Secure Funding:

- ✔ Determine the financial and human resources required to implement each component of the program.

- ✔ Identify potential sources of funding, such as internal budgets, grants, or corporate sponsorships, to support program development and implementation.

Responsible Party: Finance Department in collaboration with HR and program stakeholders.

Example: Determine the budget required for program development, implementation, and evaluation. Allocate funds for activities such as hiring mental health professionals, training sessions, materials, and marketing

Establish Partnerships and Collaborations:

- ✔ Identify potential partners, including mental health organizations, community agencies, and other stakeholders, to collaborate on program implementation.

- ✔ Leverage existing networks and relationships to access expertise, resources, and support for your mental health initiatives.

Pilot Test and Refine Program Components:

- ✔ Conduct pilot tests of program components to assess effectiveness, feasibility, and acceptability among the target audience.

- ✔ Gather feedback from participants and stakeholders to identify strengths, weaknesses, and areas for improvement, and refine program components accordingly.

Responsible Party: HR or designated pilot team.

Example: Test select programs on a small scale or in specific departments to assess effectiveness and gather feedback. Use feedback to refine program content and delivery methods before full implementation

Implement Program Components:

- ✔ Roll out program components according to the established timeline and implementation plan.

- ✔ Ensure clear communication and coordination among team members responsible for delivering different initiatives within the program.

Responsible Party: HR and program coordinators.

Example: Gradually roll out the programs across the organization, ensuring clear communication about their benefits and how to access them. Provide training for managers on supporting and communicating about mental health initiatives with their teams.

Monitor and Evaluate Program Impact:

- ✔ Establish monitoring and evaluation mechanisms to track the implementation progress and measure the impact of your mental health program.

- ✔ Collect quantitative and qualitative data on key indicators, such as participation rates, knowledge gains, behavior changes, and perceived outcomes.

- ✔ Use evaluation findings to assess program effectiveness, identify lessons learned, and make informed decisions about program adjustments or enhancements.

Responsible Party: HR and program evaluation team.

Example: Collect data on participation rates, feedback from participants, and program effectiveness. Evaluate outcomes to assess whether programs are meeting objectives and make adjustments based on feedback.

Sustain and Scale Up Successful Initiatives:

- ✔ Identify successful program components and initiatives that demonstrate positive outcomes and sustainability.

- ✔ Develop plans for sustaining and scaling up these initiatives to reach a broader audience or expand their impact within the organization.

✓ Continuously monitor and adapt the program to evolving needs, emerging trends, and feedback from stakeholders, ensuring ongoing relevance and effectiveness.

Responsible Party: HR, program coordinators, and stakeholders.

Example: Establish feedback mechanisms for ongoing evaluation and improvement of programs. Adapt programs based on changing needs and expand successful initiatives to reach more employees

By following these steps, organizations can effectively develop and launch mental health programs that promote employee well-being, reduce stigma, and create supportive work environments.

Mental Health Programs are Everyone's Child

Although in most of the steps above, I have mentioned that it is the responsibility of HR, it's important to recognize that HRs need support from leaders. Alongside HR, other departments such as the executive team, department managers, and even individual employees can play a role in supporting mental health programs. The executive team, including the CEO and other top leaders, holds responsibility for setting the organizational culture and priorities, making their involvement crucial in championing mental health initiatives. Department managers are often in direct contact with employees and can provide valuable insights into their team's needs and challenges, making their involvement essential in implementing and promoting mental health programs. Additionally, individual employees can contribute by actively participating in program activities, providing feedback, and supporting their colleagues' well-being.

Outsourcing mental health programs can be an effective strategy, especially for smaller organizations or those without dedicated internal resources. Outsourcing allows companies to access specialized expertise and resources tailored to their needs without the overhead costs associated with maintaining an in-house program. Mental health professionals, consulting firms, or employee assistance program (EAP) providers are examples of external resources that can support the development and implementation of mental health initiatives.

Leadership, especially young leaders in startups, should be actively involved in mental health programs for several reasons. Firstly, as role models, leaders set the tone for the organizational culture and can influence employees' attitudes and behaviors towards mental health. By openly supporting mental health initiatives, young leaders demonstrate their commitment to employee well-being, fostering a culture of care and support within the organization. Additionally, startups often operate in high-pressure environments with limited resources, making the mental health and resilience of employees critical for success. By prioritizing mental health programs, young leaders can help build a resilient workforce capable of navigating challenges and driving sustainable growth. Overall, leadership involvement is vital for creating an organizational culture that values and supports mental health, benefiting both employees and the company as a whole.

15.3 Include case studies of organizations with successful mental health initiatives.

How do leading organizations foster environments where employees thrive mentally as well as professionally? As the discourse surrounding mental health in the workplace gains momentum, it becomes increasingly evident that prioritizing employee well-being is not just a moral imperative but also a strategic business decision. In this exploration, we explore different case studies of organizations that have successfully implemented mental health initiatives, dissecting their approaches and outcomes to uncover the secrets behind their success.

Unilever:

Unilever, a global consumer goods company, embarked on a journey to prioritize the mental health of its workforce through the implementation of the "Wellbeing at Work" program. This initiative, launched with a focus on mental health support, included comprehensive measures such as mental health training for all managers, access to counselling services, and fostering a culture of open communication.

Research conducted by the American Psychological Association emphasizes the significance of mental health training for managers. A study published in the Journal of Occupational Health Psychology found that managers who received mental health training were better equipped to support employees experiencing mental health challenges, resulting in higher levels of employee well-being and job satisfaction.

The outcomes of Unilever's program speak volumes about its efficacy. Following the implementation of the "Wellbeing at Work" program, Unilever reported a notable decrease in work-related stress by 31% and a corresponding increase in well-being scores among employees by 17%. These results underscore the tangible benefits of prioritizing mental health support within the organizational framework.

Deloitte:

Deloitte, a prominent professional services firm, recognized the importance of cultivating mindfulness and stress management techniques among its employees. To address this need, Deloitte introduced mindfulness programs comprising meditation sessions and stress management workshops. Additionally, the organization encouraged open discussions about mental health and provided training on recognizing signs of mental health issues for managers.

Studies have shown that mindfulness practices can have a significant impact on reducing stress levels and enhancing overall well-being. Research published in the Journal of Occupational and Environmental Medicine suggests that mindfulness-based interventions can lead to improvements in psychological health outcomes, including decreased stress and increased resilience.

The outcomes of Deloitte's initiatives were promising. Employees reported experiencing increased focus, reduced stress levels, and improved job performance after participating in mindfulness programs. These findings underscore the value of incorporating mindfulness practices into workplace wellness initiatives to promote mental well-being among employees.

Lendlease:

Lendlease, a global leader in property and infrastructure, recognized the unique mental health challenges faced by its construction workers. In response, the company launched "MATES in Construction," a program dedicated to providing mental health support within the construction industry. The program offered mental health training for workers, established support networks, and provided resources for mental health assistance.

Research from the American Journal of Industrial Medicine highlights the alarming rates of suicide within the construction industry. Factors such as job insecurity and workplace stress contribute to heightened mental health risks among construction workers. Lendlease's proactive approach to addressing these challenges through targeted mental health initiatives is commendable and represents a significant step towards fostering a mentally healthy workplace culture within the construction sector.

The outcomes of Lendlease's **"MATES in Construction"** program were substantial. Not only did the program significantly reduce the suicide rate among construction workers, but it also facilitated increased awareness and conversations around mental health issues within the industry. These outcomes underscore the transformative potential of targeted mental health initiatives tailored to specific workforce demographics.

Google:

Google, renowned for its innovative workplace culture, prioritizes employee mental health through a range of initiatives and resources. The company promotes a supportive work environment by offering various mental health resources, including counseling services, and actively encouraging open discussions about mental health.

Research published in the Journal of Occupational and Environmental Medicine emphasizes the positive impact of supportive workplace environments on employee well-being. Employees who perceive their workplace as supportive of mental health are more likely to report higher levels of job satisfaction and overall well-being.

Google's initiatives have yielded significant outcomes, contributing to higher employee satisfaction, increased engagement, and a reputation for being an employee-friendly organization. By prioritizing mental health support and fostering a culture of openness, Google has created an environment where employees feel valued, supported, and empowered to prioritize their mental well-being.

Starbucks:

Starbucks, a global leader in the coffeehouse industry, recognizes the importance of prioritizing employee mental health. The company offers comprehensive mental health benefits to its employees, including access to therapy sessions, as part of its commitment to fostering a supportive workplace environment.

Research published in the Journal of Occupational Health Psychology suggests that employer-provided mental health benefits play a crucial role in enhancing employee well-being and job satisfaction. Employees who have access to mental health benefits are more likely to report lower levels of stress and higher levels of job satisfaction.

Starbucks' initiatives have yielded positive outcomes, including increased job satisfaction, reduced turnover rates, and enhanced employee retention. By prioritizing employee mental health and creating a supportive work environment, Starbucks has demonstrated its commitment to the well-being of its workforce.

In conclusion, the case studies of Unilever, Deloitte, Lendlease, Google, and Starbucks underscore the importance of prioritizing mental health initiatives in the workplace. Through innovative approaches and unwavering commitment, these organizations have not only transformed their workplace cultures but have also redefined industry standards. By prioritizing mental health through comprehensive programs, supportive policies, and fostering open communication, these organizations have created environments where employees feel valued, supported, and empowered to prioritize their mental well-being. As the conversation around mental health in the workplace continues to evolve, these case studies serve as beacons of inspiration, guiding organizations towards a future where employee well-being is at the forefront of business priorities.

Chapter 16

Communication and Awareness

How can organizations foster a workplace culture where mental health is prioritized and supported? This question lies at the heart of building a resilient and healthy workforce. Effective communication and awareness are essential pillars of any successful mental health strategy within the workplace. In this comprehensive exploration, we dive into the various components that contribute to fostering open dialogue, reducing stigma, and promoting mental well-being among employees.

Establish Open Communication Channels:

Creating a culture of openness is paramount in addressing mental health issues within the workplace. By encouraging open discussions and providing platforms for employees to share their experiences, organizations can foster an environment of trust and support.

Research conducted by the National Institute of Mental Health suggests that open communication about mental health can help reduce stigma and promote help-seeking behaviors among employees. When leaders model transparent communication, it sets a precedent for employees to feel comfortable discussing mental health concerns openly.

Mental Health Awareness Campaigns:

Educating employees about mental health is a crucial step in fostering awareness and understanding. Organizations can conduct workshops, seminars, or webinars to provide information about mental health conditions, coping strategies, and available resources.

A study published in the Journal of Occupational and Environmental Medicine found that employees who received mental health education were more likely to seek help when experiencing mental health challenges. By launching awareness campaigns through various mediums such as posters, emails, or internal newsletters, organizations can reach a broader audience and reduce stigma surrounding mental health.

Employee Engagement:

Engaging employees in conversations about mental health empowers them to take an active role in their well-being. Interactive sessions with mental health professionals or counsellors provide employees with opportunities to ask questions, seek guidance, and access support resources.

Research from the Journal of Business and Psychology suggests that employee engagement in workplace wellness programs is positively associated with job satisfaction and organizational commitment. Hosting wellness fairs or events focusing on mental health reinforces the organization's commitment to employee well-being and provides tangible resources for support.

Encourage Storytelling and Sharing:

Personal stories have the power to inspire, educate, and reduce feelings of isolation surrounding mental health issues. Allowing employees to share their experiences through testimonials or storytelling initiatives fosters empathy, understanding, and a sense of community within the workplace.

A study published in the Journal of Occupational Health Psychology found that storytelling interventions can lead to increased awareness and understanding of mental health issues among employees. By inviting guest speakers or mental health advocates to share their experiences, organizations can further normalize conversations about mental well-being and encourage help-seeking behaviors.

Training for Managers:

Managers play a crucial role in supporting employee mental health within the workplace. Providing training on recognizing signs of mental health issues, offering support, and fostering an inclusive environment equips managers with the necessary tools to effectively address mental health concerns within their teams.

Research from the Harvard Business Review suggests that supportive leadership behaviors, such as providing encouragement and recognizing individual contributions, are associated with higher levels of employee well-being and job satisfaction. Training managers to handle difficult conversations about mental health with sensitivity and empathy creates a supportive environment where employees feel valued and supported.

Normalize Conversations:

Language and terminology play a significant role in shaping attitudes and perceptions surrounding mental health. Encouraging the use of inclusive and non-stigmatizing language when discussing mental health helps create a culture of acceptance and support within the workplace.

A study published in the Journal of Applied Social Psychology found that language can influence attitudes and perceptions towards mental health conditions. By modeling open and supportive behavior, leaders set the tone for organizational culture and contribute to normalizing conversations about mental well-being.

Utilize Multiple Communication Channels:

Diverse communication channels ensure that information about mental health initiatives reaches all employees effectively. Utilizing platforms such as emails, intranet, social media, or bulletin boards enables organizations to disseminate information and resources widely.

Research from the International Journal of Workplace Health Management suggests that utilizing multiple communication channels increases the reach and effectiveness of workplace health promotion initiatives. Providing regular updates on available resources, upcoming events, and support options reinforces the organization's commitment to prioritizing employee mental health.

Feedback Mechanisms:

Establishing feedback mechanisms allows employees to provide input on mental health initiatives, ensuring that their voices are heard and their needs are addressed. Feedback loops enable organizations to continuously improve and refine their mental health strategies based on employee input.

Research from the Journal of Occupational Health Psychology suggests that soliciting feedback from employees fosters a sense of ownership and engagement in workplace wellness initiatives. Providing options for anonymous feedback creates a safe space for employees to express their thoughts and concerns openly.

In conclusion, effective communication and awareness-building initiatives are integral to creating a supportive culture around mental health in the workplace. By fostering open communication, promoting awareness, and encouraging supportive dialogue, organizations can reduce stigma, increase understanding, and create an environment where employees feel comfortable seeking help and support for their mental well-being. Regular communication and ongoing efforts to raise awareness ensure that mental health remains a priority within the organizational culture, ultimately contributing to the overall health and success of the workforce.

16.1 Address the importance of open communication about mental health.

How can workplaces become havens where mental health is understood, supported, and openly discussed? This question underscores the importance of open communication about mental health in fostering inclusive and supportive work environments. In this exploration, we dive into the significance of cultivating an atmosphere where discussions about mental well-being are encouraged and embraced.

Addressing the Importance of Open Communication About Mental Health:

Open communication about mental health is paramount in nurturing a workplace culture that prioritizes the well-being of its employees. By creating an environment where discussions about mental health are normalized, organizations can break down barriers, reduce stigma, and promote understanding.

Research conducted by the World Health Organization highlights the pervasive stigma surrounding mental health, which often prevents individuals from seeking help or discussing their struggles openly. However, open communication serves as a powerful antidote to stigma by fostering an environment where conversations about mental health are not only accepted but also encouraged.

Reducing Stigma:

Normalizing discussions about mental health is instrumental in challenging stigma and dispelling misconceptions. When employees feel empowered to share their experiences and concerns openly, it promotes empathy and understanding among colleagues.

A study published in the Journal of Applied Social Psychology found that open communication significantly reduces stigma surrounding mental health, leading to greater acceptance and support for individuals experiencing mental health challenges. By fostering an environment where discussions about mental well-being are normalized, organizations can create a culture of empathy and inclusivity.

Encouraging Help-Seeking Behavior:

Open communication plays a pivotal role in promoting help-seeking behavior among employees. When individuals feel comfortable discussing their mental health openly, they are more likely to seek support or professional help when needed, leading to early intervention and improved outcomes.

Research from the Journal of Occupational Health Psychology suggests that employees who perceive their workplace as supportive of mental health are more likely to seek help when experiencing mental health challenges. By fostering open communication channels, organizations can create a supportive environment where employees feel empowered to prioritize their mental well-being.

Creating a Supportive Culture:

Open communication fosters trust and transparency within the workplace, creating a supportive culture where individuals feel valued and respected. By encouraging open conversations about mental health, organizations can cultivate empathy and understanding among peers and management.

A study published in the Harvard Business Review found that organizations with a supportive culture around mental health experienced higher levels of employee engagement, satisfaction, and productivity. By prioritizing open communication about mental health, organizations can create a workplace where employees feel safe, supported, and empowered to thrive.

Improving Well-Being and Productivity:

Employees who feel supported in discussing mental health are more likely to experience improved well-being and productivity. By fostering an environment where mental health discussions are normalized, organizations can reduce stress levels and enhance employee engagement.

Research from the Journal of Occupational and Environmental Medicine suggests that organizations with supportive mental health initiatives experience lower rates of absenteeism, presenteeism, and turnover. By prioritizing open communication about mental health, organizations can create a positive work environment where employees feel valued, motivated, and empowered to perform at their best.

Leadership Role Modeling:

Leaders play a crucial role in setting the tone for discussions about mental health within the organization. When leaders openly discuss mental health challenges or support initiatives, it sends a powerful message to employees that their well-being is a priority.

Research from the International Journal of Leadership in Education emphasizes the impact of leadership role modeling on organizational culture. By demonstrating support for mental health initiatives and engaging in open conversations about mental well-being, leaders can create a workplace where employees feel comfortable seeking help and support.

Destigmatizing Mental Health:

Open communication creates safe spaces where individuals feel comfortable sharing their experiences without fear of judgment or stigma. By fostering inclusivity and acceptance, organizations can create a culture where everyone feels valued and respected, irrespective of their mental health status.

Research from the Journal of Occupational Health Psychology suggests that organizations with inclusive and supportive cultures around mental health experience higher levels of employee satisfaction and well-being. By prioritizing open communication about mental health, organizations can create a workplace where employees feel empowered to be their authentic selves and contribute to their fullest potential.

In conclusion, open communication about mental health is fundamental in creating a workplace where employees feel supported, valued, and understood. By promoting a culture of empathy, breaking down barriers, and encouraging individuals to seek help when needed, organizations can significantly contribute to the well-being and productivity of their workforce while reducing the stigma associated with mental health challenges. By fostering an environment where mental health discussions are normalized, organizations can create a positive workplace culture where employees feel safe, supported, and empowered to thrive.

16.2 Offer guidance on how employers and employees can discuss mental health concerns effectively.

How can employers and employees effectively navigate discussions about mental health in the workplace? This question lies at the heart of fostering a supportive and empathetic environment where mental health concerns are acknowledged and addressed. In this comprehensive guide, we explore practical guidance for both employers and employees to engage in meaningful conversations about mental well-being.

Guidance for Employers and Managers:

Creating a supportive environment is paramount in facilitating open discussions about mental health. Employers and managers play a crucial role in fostering a workplace culture where mental health concerns are not only acknowledged but also valued. Research from the Journal of Occupational Health Psychology emphasizes the importance of leadership in setting the tone for discussions about mental health within the organization.

Providing access to resources and support is essential for employees seeking assistance with their mental health. Offering access to counselling services, helplines, or Employee Assistance Programs (EAPs) demonstrates a commitment to supporting employee well-being. Educating managers on available resources and how to guide employees seeking support ensures that employees receive the assistance they need in times of need.

Training and education are key components of effectively addressing mental health concerns in the workplace. Training managers on recognizing signs of mental health issues and handling discussions with empathy and confidentiality equips them with the necessary skills to support their teams effectively. Additionally, conducting workshops or seminars to educate employees on mental health awareness and coping strategies fosters a culture of understanding and support.

Encouraging open communication is vital for creating a workplace environment where mental health discussions are normalized. Scheduling regular check-ins to discuss workload, stress levels, and overall well-being without judgment provides employees with opportunities to voice their concerns and seek support. Creating opportunities for employees to voice concerns or suggestions anonymously if needed ensures that all employees feel comfortable expressing their thoughts and feelings.

Guidance for Employees:

For employees, effectively discussing mental health concerns with employers requires careful consideration and preparation. Choosing the right time and place to initiate discussions is essential to ensure privacy and minimize interruptions. Research from the Journal of Applied Psychology suggests that finding a suitable time and private space for discussions promotes open and honest communication.

Preparing and being specific about the issues or challenges faced is crucial for effective communication. Employees should articulate how their mental health concerns impact their work performance or daily life, providing their employers with a clear understanding of the situation. Using neutral language and avoiding blaming or accusing language fosters constructive dialogue and ensures that discussions remain focused on finding solutions.

Requesting support and solutions is an important aspect of discussing mental health concerns with employers. Employees should ask for specific support or accommodations that could help alleviate the challenges they are facing, such as flexible work arrangements or additional resources. Collaborating with employers on potential solutions or adjustments to workload or work environment demonstrates a proactive approach to addressing mental health concerns.

Following up on discussions about mental health concerns is essential for monitoring progress and making any necessary adjustments. Scheduling follow-up meetings allows employers and employees to assess the effectiveness of implemented solutions and make any necessary adjustments to support ongoing well-being.

General Tips for Both Employers and Employees:

In addition to specific guidance for employers and employees, there are general tips that both parties can follow to facilitate productive discussions about mental health. Actively listening to each other without interrupting, providing undivided attention, and demonstrating empathy fosters a supportive and understanding environment. Respecting confidentiality ensures that trust is maintained throughout discussions about mental health concerns. Encouraging ongoing conversations about mental health helps normalize discussions and create an environment where it is safe to discuss such matters openly. Additionally, both employers and employees should encourage seeking help from mental health professionals if needed and support each other in accessing these services.

Open and supportive communication between employers and employees about mental health concerns is essential for creating a supportive work environment. By fostering open dialogue, providing resources, and approaching discussions with empathy and understanding, both employers and employees can contribute to a workplace culture that values mental health and supports those in need. Through collaborative efforts and a commitment to prioritizing mental well-being, organizations can create environments where employees feel valued, supported, and empowered to thrive.

16.3 Discuss the benefits of raising awareness through workshops, seminars, and training.

How can organizations create workplaces where mental health is not only acknowledged but actively supported? This question underscores the importance of raising awareness through workshops, seminars, and training sessions on mental health. In this comprehensive examination, we dive into the benefits of such initiatives for organizations, employees, and the overall workplace environment.

Benefits for Organizations:

Investing in mental health awareness programs offers numerous advantages for organizations. Research from the World Health Organization indicates that heightened awareness leads to better mental health literacy among employees, enabling them to recognize symptoms and seek help when needed. By reducing stigma and fostering a supportive culture, organizations can positively impact employee well-being, resulting in improved job satisfaction and higher retention rates.

Enhanced employee well-being translates to increased productivity within the workplace. Employees with better mental health tend to be more engaged, focused, and productive in their roles. Additionally, reduced absenteeism and presenteeism contribute to enhanced workplace productivity, ultimately benefiting the organization's bottom line.

Benefits for Employees:

For employees, participation in workshops, seminars, and training sessions on mental health can lead to reduced stigma and feelings of isolation. Research from the Journal of Occupational Health Psychology suggests that normalization of discussions about mental health in the workplace creates an environment where employees feel more comfortable seeking support without fear of judgment.

Moreover, training equips employees with effective coping strategies, stress management techniques, and resilience-building skills. Increased self-awareness helps individuals identify and manage stressors more effectively, ultimately improving their overall well-being and job satisfaction.

Benefits for Workplace Environment:

Creating an open communication culture is crucial for fostering a supportive workplace environment. Workshops and seminars on mental health encourage employees to discuss their concerns freely, leading to increased dialogue and a more supportive environment for those facing mental health challenges.

Furthermore, a positive organizational culture that prioritizes mental health awareness signals to employees that their well-being matters. This contributes to higher morale, job satisfaction, and employee retention. Leadership engagement in these sessions demonstrates a commitment to mental health, encouraging employees to engage in discussions and initiatives aimed at supporting mental well-being.

In conclusion, workshops, seminars, and training sessions on mental health play a vital role in increasing awareness and creating a more supportive, understanding, and productive work environment. These initiatives benefit organizations by fostering a healthier workforce, reducing stigma, and increasing productivity. Employees, in turn, gain knowledge, support, and resources to manage their mental health effectively, leading to improved well-being and job satisfaction. Overall, raising awareness through such programs contributes significantly to a positive workplace culture centered around mental well-being.

16.4 Improving communication and the role of Exit interviews

Exit Interviews: Are They a Waste of Time? Exit interviews have long been a standard practice for understanding why employees leave an organization. However, recent discussions among experts in organizational psychology and human resource management, including scholars like Holtom and Burch, that these interviews may not be as effective as once thought. Instead, organizations might benefit more from exploring alternative approaches to employee feedback and retention strategies.

What Do Scientists Say About Exit Interviews?

Research indicates that exit interviews often fail to provide actionable insights. A study published in the *Journal of Business and Psychology* found that many employees are reluctant to share honest feedback during exit interviews due to concerns about confidentiality or fear of repercussions. This reluctance can lead to incomplete data that organizations cannot effectively use to improve their work environments (Holtom, B. C., & Burch, T. C., 2016).

Furthermore, when employees are asked directly what is wrong, it may create an integrity issue for them. They might feel pressured to give diplomatic answers rather than honest feedback, especially if they need a great referral or experience letter or paperwork for their next job. (instead of job shortlisting these are the things that should be automated).This dynamic can result in superficial responses that ultimately make your company a training ground for talent that is then passed on to competitors with better cultures.

The Impact of Exit Interviews on Mental Health

The process of conducting exit interviews can also have implications for the mental health of both the departing employees and the organization as a whole. For employees, knowing they will be asked about their reasons for leaving can create anxiety and stress, particularly if they feel uncomfortable discussing their experiences candidly. This discomfort can stem from fears about how their feedback might affect their future job prospects or relationships within the industry.

For organizations, relying heavily on exit interviews without addressing underlying issues can perpetuate a cycle of poor workplace culture and high turnover rates. When employees leave without providing honest feedback, it prevents organizations from identifying and addressing systemic problems that contribute to dissatisfaction. Over time, this lack of insight can lead to a toxic work environment, resulting in decreased morale among remaining employees and potentially increasing turnover rates further.

Top Three Questions to Ask in Exit Interviews

If organizations choose to continue conducting exit interviews, they should focus on asking questions that yield more meaningful insights. Here are three suggested questions:

1. **What factors influenced your decision to leave?** This question allows departing employees to articulate specific reasons for their departure, providing valuable information about potential areas for improvement within the organization.

2. **How would you describe your relationship with your manager?** Understanding the dynamics between employees and their managers can help identify any managerial issues that may contribute to turnover.

3. **What could have been done differently to encourage you to stay?** This question invites constructive feedback and can highlight specific changes or improvements that could enhance employee retention in the future.

Training Managers After Exit Interviews

To effectively utilize insights gained from exit interviews, organizations must also invest in training their managers. Training should focus on enhancing communication skills, emotional intelligence, and conflict resolution abilities. By equipping managers with these skills, organizations can foster a more supportive work environment that encourages employee engagement and reduces turnover. Furthermore, regular feedback mechanisms should be established where managers receive ongoing input about their leadership styles and team dynamics. This proactive approach can help identify potential issues before they lead to employee departures.

The Case for Holding Interviews

Instead of relying solely on exit interviews, organizations might consider implementing "holding interviews" with long-term employees who have chosen to stay. These interviews can help uncover what factors contributed to their decision to remain with the company and how those factors can be leveraged as part of a marketing strategy or unique selling proposition (USP).For example, asking long-term employees questions like:

- **What do you enjoy most about working here?**

- **What keeps you motivated in your role?**

- **How does this organization support your professional growth?**

The responses can provide valuable insights into the company's strengths and culture, which can be used in recruitment marketing efforts. Highlighting these positive experiences not only attracts potential candidates but also reinforces existing employees' commitment by showcasing what makes the organization a great place to work.

Integrating Insights into Mental Health Plans

Moreover, integrating findings from holding interviews into mental health initiatives can further enhance employee well-being. Organizations can use this information to tailor their mental health programs around what employees value most about their work environment.

For instance, if long-term employees' express appreciation for flexible work arrangements or supportive management practices, these elements can be emphasized in mental health resources and initiatives.

By focusing on retention strategies that prioritize employee feedback and well-being over traditional exit interview practices, organizations can create a more engaged workforce while simultaneously reducing turnover rates.

While exit interviews have been a staple in understanding employee turnover, they may not provide the comprehensive insights organizations need. By shifting focus towards holding interviews with long-term employees and addressing managerial effectiveness proactively, companies can foster a healthier workplace culture that values both productivity and personal fulfilment. As research shows, creating an environment where employees feel valued and supported is essential for retaining talent and enhancing overall organizational performance.

References

- Holtom, B. C., & Burch, T. C. (2016). The Role of Exit Interviews in Employee Retention: A Review of Literature. *Journal of Business and Psychology*.

- Gallup (2019). Why Employees Leave: The Importance of Managerial Relationships.

Chapter 17

Stress Management and Resilience

How can workplaces cultivate environments where employees thrive amidst the pressures of modern work life? This question underscores the significance of stress management and resilience in maintaining mental well-being. In this exploration, we dive into the importance of these components for fostering healthier work environments and enhancing individual well-being.

Stress Management: Effective stress management is pivotal for enhancing performance and productivity in the workplace. Research conducted by the American Psychological Association suggests that individuals who employ stress management techniques exhibit higher levels of job satisfaction and engagement. By equipping employees with strategies to handle pressure, organizations can mitigate the detrimental effects of stress on performance and well-being.

Moreover, stress management plays a crucial role in preventing burnout—a pervasive issue in today's fast-paced work environments. Studies from the Journal of Occupational Health Psychology indicate that implementing stress management programs reduces the risk of burnout among employees. By promoting work-life balance and providing resources for stress management, organizations can safeguard employee well-being and foster a positive work culture.

Resilience: Resilience, or the ability to bounce back from adversity, is another essential component of maintaining mental well-being in the workplace. Research from the Harvard Business Review suggests that resilient individuals exhibit higher levels of job satisfaction, adaptability, and emotional intelligence.

By cultivating resilience among employees, organizations can empower individuals to navigate challenges with resilience and determination.

Furthermore, resilience enhances problem-solving skills and decision-making abilities in high-pressure situations. A study published in the Journal of Applied Psychology found that resilient individuals demonstrate greater cognitive flexibility and creativity when faced with adversity. By fostering resilience, organizations can equip employees with the tools they need to overcome obstacles and drive innovation in the workplace.

Combined Benefits: When stress management techniques are combined with resilience-building strategies, individuals benefit from robust coping mechanisms and enhanced well-being. Research from the Journal of Occupational and Environmental Medicine suggests that employees who receive training in stress management and resilience exhibit lower levels of absenteeism and turnover. By investing in these initiatives, organizations can reduce healthcare costs associated with stress-related illnesses and create a more stable and engaged workforce.

Moreover, fostering a culture that prioritizes stress management and resilience contributes to a positive work environment. Research from the Journal of Organizational Behavior highlights the impact of organizational culture on employee well-being and performance. By promoting open communication, providing resources for stress management, and recognizing the importance of resilience, organizations can create an environment where employees feel valued, supported, and motivated to succeed.

Incorporating stress management techniques and resilience-building strategies into the workplace is essential for maintaining employee well-being and enhancing organizational performance. By equipping employees with the tools they need to manage stress effectively and bounce back from adversity, organizations can create environments where individuals thrive. When employees feel supported in managing stress and building resilience, they are better able to navigate challenges, foster stronger relationships, and contribute to a positive and productive work culture. Ultimately, organizations that prioritize stress management and resilience create environments where employees feel empowered to succeed and flourish.

17.1 Provide practical strategies for managing stress and building resilience.

In today's fast-paced work environments, stress management and resilience are essential skills for maintaining mental well-being. How can individuals effectively manage stress and build resilience in the workplace? In this guide, we provide practical strategies to help employees navigate workplace challenges and foster a healthier, more resilient workforce.

Stress Management Strategies: Effective time management is key to managing stress in the workplace. Research from the Journal of Applied Psychology suggests that individuals who prioritize tasks and create schedules experience lower levels of stress. Breaking tasks into smaller, manageable segments can also help reduce feelings of overwhelm and increase productivity.

Practicing mindfulness and relaxation techniques is another effective way to manage stress. Studies from the Journal of Occupational Health Psychology show that mindfulness exercises, deep breathing, and meditation can reduce stress and enhance focus. Taking short breaks during the workday to relax and recharge can also help alleviate tension and improve overall well-being.

Engaging in regular physical activity is essential for stress management. Research from the American Journal of Lifestyle Medicine indicates that exercise can alleviate stress and boost mood. Incorporating stretching or short walks during breaks can help reduce tension and improve overall well-being.

Setting boundaries between work and personal life is crucial for preventing burnout. Studies from the Journal of Organizational Behavior suggest that individuals who establish clear boundaries experience lower levels of stress and greater job satisfaction. Learning to say no when workload becomes overwhelming is also important for maintaining balance and well-being.

Seeking support from colleagues, mentors, or Employee Assistance Programs (EAPs) can provide valuable guidance and assistance during stressful times. Research from the Journal of Occupational and Environmental Medicine indicates that employees who receive support from their peers and managers experience lower levels of stress and greater job satisfaction. Discussing concerns with managers can also help identify potential solutions and alleviate stress.

Resilience-Building Strategies: Developing a positive self-talk and mindset is essential for building resilience. Research from the Journal of Personality and Social Psychology suggests that individuals who engage in positive self-talk experience greater resilience and well-being. Practicing self-compassion and acknowledging accomplishments can help cultivate a positive mindset in the face of adversity.

Adaptability and flexibility are crucial skills for building resilience. Studies from the Journal of Applied Psychology show that individuals who embrace change and view challenges as opportunities for growth are better able to bounce back from setbacks. Developing a flexible approach to handling unexpected situations can also enhance resilience in the workplace.

Enhancing problem-solving skills is another effective way to build resilience. Research from the Journal of Occupational Health Psychology suggests that individuals who develop effective problem-solving strategies experience greater resilience and well-being. Breaking down issues into smaller parts and brainstorming solutions can help individuals develop a plan of action to address challenges effectively.

Building social connections is important for fostering resilience in the workplace. Research from the Journal of Occupational and Organizational Psychology suggests that individuals who cultivate strong relationships with colleagues experience greater resilience and well-being. Engaging in team-building activities can foster connections and camaraderie, providing valuable support during challenging times.

Prioritizing self-care is essential for building resilience and managing stress effectively. Research from the Journal of Occupational Health Psychology indicates that individuals who engage in self-care practices experience lower levels of stress and greater well-being. Engaging in hobbies, activities, or practices that bring joy and relaxation can help individuals recharge and maintain balance in their lives.

Holistic Approach: Taking a balanced lifestyle approach is essential for building resilience and managing stress effectively. Maintaining healthy habits, such as a balanced diet and sufficient sleep, can support overall well-being and resilience. Limiting exposure to stress triggers outside of work can also help individuals maintain balance and prevent burnout.

Engaging in continuous learning and development is another important aspect of building resilience. Research from the Journal of Applied Psychology suggests that individuals who engage in ongoing learning and skill development experience greater resilience and well-being. Attending workshops or training sessions focused on stress management and resilience can provide valuable tools and strategies for navigating workplace challenges.

Regular reflection and evaluation are essential for building resilience and managing stress effectively. Reflecting on stress triggers and resilience levels regularly can help individuals identify areas for improvement and develop strategies for coping with stress. Evaluating strategies periodically and adjusting as needed can help individuals find what works best for them and maintain resilience over time.

Incorporating stress management techniques and resilience-building strategies into the workplace is essential for fostering a healthier and more resilient workforce. By implementing practical strategies tailored to individual needs, employees can effectively manage stress and cultivate resilience, contributing to improved overall well-being and productivity. Through a multifaceted approach that addresses both stress management and resilience, organizations can create environments where employees feel supported, empowered, and capable of thriving amidst workplace challenges.

17.2 Include techniques like mindfulness, time management, and work-life balance.

How can individuals navigate the demands of the modern workplace while maintaining their well-being and achieving a sense of balance in their lives? In this guide, we explore specific techniques for mindfulness, time management, and achieving work-life balance, offering practical strategies to enhance focus, productivity, and overall satisfaction.

Mindfulness Techniques: Mindfulness practices cultivate awareness and presence in the present moment, reducing stress and enhancing overall well-being. Mindful breathing exercises, such as deep breathing and focused inhalation and exhalation, promote relaxation and clarity of mind. Incorporating short breaks for mindful breathing sessions throughout the day can help individuals regain focus and manage stress effectively.

Body scan meditation is another mindfulness technique that involves progressively focusing on different parts of the body, releasing tension and promoting relaxation. By enhancing awareness of bodily sensations, individuals can reduce stress and improve their overall sense of well-being.

Engaging in mindful observation involves paying attention to surroundings without judgment or interpretation. This practice encourages individuals to notice sensations, sounds, and details in their environment, fostering a sense of presence and grounding in the present moment.

Time Management Techniques: Effective time management is essential for maximizing productivity and reducing stress in the workplace. Prioritization and planning techniques, such as the Eisenhower Matrix and the Pomodoro Technique, help individuals categorize tasks and allocate time efficiently. By identifying urgent and important tasks and planning work intervals followed by short breaks, individuals can enhance productivity and maintain focus throughout the day.

Task batching involves grouping similar tasks together and allocating specific time blocks for completion, minimizing multitasking and increasing efficiency. By focusing on one type of activity at a time, individuals can reduce distractions and work more effectively.

Limiting distractions is another key aspect of effective time management. Turning off non-essential notifications, setting specific work hours, and creating a conducive work environment can help individuals minimize interruptions and maintain concentration on important tasks.

Work-Life Balance Techniques: Achieving work-life balance is essential for overall well-being and satisfaction. Setting clear boundaries between work and personal life, such as establishing specific start and end times for work-related activities, helps individuals create a sense of separation and maintain balance.

Scheduling leisure and relaxation activities is important for replenishing energy and reducing stress. Allocating time for hobbies, spending time with loved ones, or engaging in activities that promote relaxation, such as reading or exercise, allows individuals to recharge and maintain a healthy balance in their lives.

Flexibility and adjustment are crucial for adapting to changing circumstances and accommodating personal commitments. Embracing flexibility in work schedules or arrangements, and communicating openly with employers or colleagues about the need for adjustments, enables individuals to prioritize their well-being while fulfilling work responsibilities.

Integration and Practice: Consistent practice is key to integrating these techniques into daily routines and realizing their benefits fully. By incorporating mindfulness practices, effective time management strategies, and work-life balance techniques into daily life, individuals can cultivate habits that support well-being and productivity.

Self-reflection and adaptation are essential for refining these techniques and ensuring their continued effectiveness. Periodically reflecting on their effectiveness and making adjustments based on individual preferences and changing circumstances enable individuals to maintain balance and well-being over the long term.

Mindfulness practices, effective time management, and maintaining work-life balance are essential for well-being and satisfaction in the workplace. By incorporating these techniques into daily routines and consistently practicing them, individuals can enhance focus, productivity, and overall satisfaction both at work and in personal life. These techniques empower individuals to manage stress, improve time utilization, and create a more balanced and fulfilling lifestyle.

Part 7

Specialized Areas and Challenges

Chapter 18

Remote Work and Virtual Mental Health

As remote work becomes increasingly prevalent, a pressing question arises: how does it impact mental health, and what can organizations do to support the well-being of their virtual teams? Understanding the unique challenges posed by remote work is essential for fostering a healthy work environment. In this exploration, we will delve into these challenges and discuss effective strategies for mitigating their negative effects on mental health.

Remote work presents several challenges that can significantly impact mental well-being. One of the most pressing issues is isolation and loneliness. The lack of social interaction inherent in remote work can lead to feelings of disconnection from colleagues and the organization.

According to a study published in the American Journal of Psychiatry, social isolation is linked to increased rates of depression and anxiety, which can negatively affect mental health and overall well-being (Cacioppo, J. T., & Cacioppo, S., 2018). Without regular face-to-face interactions, employees may feel increasingly detached, leading to a decline in morale.

Another significant challenge is the blurred boundaries between work and personal life. When home becomes the office, the lines separating professional responsibilities from personal obligations can become indistinct. Research by the Harvard Business Review indicates that remote workers often struggle to establish clear boundaries, resulting in longer working hours and heightened stress levels (Gordon, A., 2020). This inability to disconnect can lead to burnout, as employees find it difficult to switch off from work-related tasks.

In addition to these factors, remote work may introduce increased stress and uncertainty. Employees face various stressors such as changes in routines, technology challenges, and concerns about job security. A survey conducted by Buffer found that 20% of remote workers reported difficulties with collaboration and communication, which can exacerbate feelings of stress and uncertainty regarding their roles (Buffer, 2021). The cumulative effect of these challenges can lead to significant mental health issues if not addressed effectively.

The implications of these challenges extend beyond individual employees; they can affect the overall mental health of an organization. When employees experience isolation or burnout, it can lead to decreased productivity, increased absenteeism, and higher turnover rates. Experts emphasize that organizations must recognize the mental health risks associated with remote work. According to Dr. Michael P. Leiter, a leading researcher in occupational health psychology, ***"Organizations that fail to address the mental health needs of their employees risk creating a toxic culture that undermines productivity and engagement"*** (Leiter, M. P., 2020). By neglecting these issues, companies may inadvertently contribute to a cycle of dissatisfaction that harms both employees and organizational performance.

To address the challenges associated with remote work and promote virtual well-being, organizations can implement several strategies. Regular communication is vital; encouraging frequent check-ins and virtual meetings fosters a sense of connection among remote teams. Utilizing video calls can help maintain face-to-face interaction and combat feelings of isolation. Research indicates that regular communication enhances team cohesion and reduces feelings of loneliness among remote workers (Baker, D., 2020).

Offering flexible work schedules is another effective strategy. By providing flexibility in work hours, organizations can accommodate diverse schedules and personal commitments, thereby reducing stress related to work-life balance. Instead of adhering strictly to an eight-hour day, companies should consider allowing employees to manage their time more effectively.

Additionally, providing access to wellness programs and resources is crucial for supporting remote employees' mental well-being. Studies have shown that access to mental health resources leads to improved employee satisfaction and reduced turnover rates (Kahnweiler, W., 2021). Organizations should also promote self-care practices by encouraging remote workers to establish clear boundaries between work and personal life. Advocating for regular breaks, physical exercise, and mindfulness techniques can significantly enhance mental well-being.

Training managers to recognize signs of mental health issues in remote employees is essential for providing appropriate support or resources. Equipping managers with skills for leading remote teams effectively fosters a supportive virtual work environment. Furthermore, facilitating virtual social activities such as team-building exercises or online coffee breaks combats feelings of isolation among remote employees.

Harnessing technology can further enhance mental health support in remote work settings. Organizations should offer access to digital mental health platforms or apps that provide resources for meditation, stress management, and overall mental health support. Providing access to virtual counseling services and online support groups addresses mental health concerns while promoting a sense of community among remote employees.

Conducting webinars or training sessions focused on managing mental health in remote work settings offers guidance on maintaining well-being effectively. By prioritizing employee mental health in the context of remote work, organizations not only enhance individual well-being but also promote a healthier and more productive workforce overall.

So, while remote work presents unique challenges for mental health—including isolation, blurred boundaries between work and personal life, and increased stress—organizations can implement strategies that prioritize communication, support self-care practices, offer flexibility in scheduling, and utilize technology effectively. Regular assessment and adaptation of these strategies ensure that the mental health needs of remote workers are met comprehensively.

References

Baker, D. (2020). The Importance of Communication in Remote Teams: A Study on Employee Engagement.

Buffer (2021). State of Remote Work Report.

Cacioppo, J. T., & Cacioppo, S. (2018). The Growing Problem of Loneliness: Implications for Mental Health.

Gordon, A. (2020). Blurring Boundaries: The Impact of Remote Work on Employee Well-Being. Harvard Business Review.

Kahnweiler, W. (2021). The Benefits of Employee Assistance Programs on Workplace Satisfaction.

Leiter, M. P. (2020). Creating Healthy Workplaces: Addressing Mental Health Needs in Organizations.

18.1 Discuss the challenges and opportunities related to mental health in remote work settings.

As remote work becomes increasingly prevalent, *a crucial question arises: can remote work truly enhance productivity and flexibility while safeguarding mental well-being?* This inquiry takes center stage as organizations embrace remote work arrangements. While the benefits of remote work are undeniable, it also presents unique challenges to mental health. In this exploration, we will delve into the complexities of mental health in remote work settings, unraveling the obstacles faced and the opportunities unearthed in this digital landscape.

One of the most significant challenges of remote work is social isolation and loneliness. The absence of physical proximity can breed feelings of disconnection among employees. Research conducted by the American Psychological Association reveals that social isolation is linked to an increased risk of mental health issues, including depression and anxiety. Without the camaraderie that comes from an office environment, remote workers may struggle to cultivate meaningful connections, which can severely impact their mental well-being. The lack of spontaneous interactions and casual conversations that naturally occur in an office setting can leave employees feeling unsupported and alone.

Another challenge is the blurred line between work and personal life. Working from home often leads to an imbalance where professional obligations seep into personal time, creating a precarious situation. A study published in the *Journal of Business and Psychology* found that remote workers tend to work longer hours than their office-bound counterparts, leading to burnout and heightened stress levels. Establishing clear boundaries becomes paramount to prevent work from encroaching on personal time and vice versa. When employees find it difficult to disconnect from their jobs, they risk experiencing chronic stress that can affect both their mental health and overall productivity.

Effective communication is also a significant hurdle in remote work settings. Communication is the lifeblood of any organization; however, remote work introduces unique challenges in this domain. The absence of face-to-face interaction heightens the risk of misinterpretation of messages and difficulties in conveying emotions through virtual means. According to a report by Buffer, 20% of remote workers cite communication and collaboration as their top challenges, underscoring the importance of addressing this issue head-on. Miscommunication can lead to misunderstandings and conflict within teams, further exacerbating feelings of isolation and frustration.

Technological challenges add another layer of complexity to remote work environments. While technology serves as a crucial tool for collaboration and productivity, technical glitches and internet connectivity issues can disrupt workflow and lead to frustration. Research published in the *Journal of Occupational and Environmental Medicine* highlights the negative impact of technological challenges on productivity and mental well-being among remote workers. When employees encounter frequent technical difficulties, it can contribute to feelings of inadequacy or helplessness, undermining their confidence in their ability to perform effectively.

Moreover, reduced support systems can exacerbate feelings of isolation in remote environments. The informal support networks present in traditional office settings—such as casual conversations by the water cooler or impromptu brainstorming sessions—are often lacking when working remotely. Quick chats are replaced by virtual interactions that may not offer the same level of immediacy or camaraderie. As a result, remote workers may find it challenging to seek advice or support from colleagues, further intensifying feelings of alienation.

Despite these challenges, remote work settings also present valuable opportunities for enhancing employee mental health. One significant advantage is the flexibility that remote work affords employees. With the ability to tailor their work schedules and environments to suit individual needs, employees can achieve a greater balance between their professional responsibilities and personal lives. This flexibility reduces stress and enhances overall well-being by allowing individuals to manage their time more effectively.

Increased autonomy in remote work fosters a sense of ownership and control among employees. Research published in the *Journal of Applied Psychology* suggests that autonomy in the workplace is positively associated with job satisfaction and mental health. In remote settings, employees have the freedom to structure their workdays according to their preferences, leading to greater job satisfaction and reduced stress levels.

The digital nature of remote work opens doors to a wealth of resources that transcend geographical boundaries. From online mental health tools to virtual support groups, remote workers have access to diverse resources that support their mental well-being. Organizations can leverage this global connectivity to provide comprehensive support for their remote workforce, regardless of location.

Remote work also allows for seamless integration between professional responsibilities and personal life. A study published in the *Journal of Business and Psychology* found that remote workers report higher levels of work-life balance compared to their office-based counterparts. With the flexibility to attend to personal responsibilities without sacrificing professional obligations, remote workers can achieve a more harmonious blend of work and life.

Furthermore, organizations are increasingly prioritizing employee well-being initiatives tailored specifically for their remote workforce. From virtual fitness sessions to mindfulness exercises, these initiatives address the unique challenges posed by remote work while promoting mental health and resilience. By investing in employee well-being, organizations can cultivate a culture of care that transcends physical boundaries. To effectively address these challenges while leveraging opportunities for improvement, organizations must enhance communication and support within their teams. Prioritizing frequent check-ins fosters a sense of connection among remote employees while implementing dedicated support channels provides essential assistance for managing work-related stress effectively.

Establishing clear boundaries between work and personal life is essential for preventing burnout and maintaining overall well-being. Organizations can support this effort by providing guidelines that help employees disconnect after working hours while encouraging self-care practices.

Utilizing technology wisely can facilitate social interactions, team collaboration, and access to mental health resources for remote employees. By embracing innovative tools and platforms, organizations can bridge gaps created by physical distance while fostering a sense of belonging among teams.

Implementing wellness initiatives specifically designed for remote settings is crucial for supporting employee well-being. Offering virtual fitness sessions, mindfulness exercises, and mental health workshops empowers employees to prioritize their health while enhancing overall resilience.

As organizations navigate the complexities associated with remote work arrangements, mental health emerges as a critical focal point for fostering supportive environments that promote productivity. While challenges such as social isolation and blurred boundaries exist within these settings, there are also significant opportunities for flexibility, autonomy, and enhanced well-being. By addressing these challenges head-on while leveraging unique opportunities presented by remote work environments, organizations can create workplace cultures that prioritize mental health and empower employees to thrive in this digital age.

Building Trustworthiness Among Employees

To foster trustworthiness among employees during these challenging times, organizations must cultivate an environment where open communication is encouraged. Transparency about organizational changes or decisions helps build trust between management and staff members. When employees feel informed about company developments—especially those affecting their roles—they are more likely to trust leadership's intentions.

Additionally, providing consistent feedback plays a vital role in building reliability within teams. Regular performance reviews should focus not only on areas needing improvement but also on recognizing achievements—this approach fosters a culture where employees feel valued for their contributions.

Encouraging collaboration among team members can further enhance trustworthiness within an organization's culture; when individuals collaborate on projects or share ideas freely without fear of judgment or criticism from peers or superiors alike—this creates stronger bonds between coworkers while enhancing overall team cohesion.

Lastly—offering training programs focused on developing interpersonal skills equips employees with tools necessary for effective communication; when team members communicate openly about concerns regarding workload stressors or emotional struggles—it cultivates an atmosphere rooted in empathy rather than competition—ultimately leading towards greater reliability amongst colleagues during times when support is needed most.

References

- Cacioppo, J.T., & Cacioppo, S. (2018). The Growing Problem of Loneliness: Implications for Mental Health.

- Buffer (2021). State of Remote Work Report.

- Gordon, A. (2020). Blurring Boundaries: The Impact of Remote Work on Employee Well-Being.

- Kahnweiler, W. (2021). The Benefits of Employee Assistance Programs on Workplace Satisfaction.

- Leiter, M.P. (2020). Creating Healthy Workplaces: Addressing Mental Health Needs in Organizations.

- Journal of Business Psychology.

- Journal of Applied Psychology.

- Journal of Occupational and Environmental Medicine.

18.2 Offer advice on maintaining mental well-being while working virtually.

How can we maintain our mental well-being while navigating the virtual landscape of remote work? As the digital realm becomes our new workplace, this question becomes increasingly pertinent. Remote work offers unparalleled flexibility and autonomy, but it also presents unique challenges to mental well-being. In this guide, we explore practical strategies to support mental health while working virtually, empowering individuals to thrive in the digital workspace.

Here's a detailed exploration of strategies to achieve and sustain mental well-being in a virtual work setting:

Establish a Healthy Routine:

Setting regular work hours is crucial in remote work environments to maintain a healthy work-life balance. Research by the Journal of Business and Psychology suggests that a consistent schedule promotes better mental health outcomes. For example, John, a remote worker, starts his workday at 9 a.m. and ends at 5 p.m. to ensure a clear boundary between work and personal time.

Creating a dedicated workspace helps signal the start and end of the workday, separating work-related activities from relaxation spaces. Sarah, a remote employee, converted a spare room into her home office, complete with a desk, ergonomic chair, and minimal distractions, allowing her to focus during work hours and relax in other areas of her home afterward.

Regular breaks are essential to prevent burnout and maintain productivity. Short breaks throughout the day, such as a quick walk, stretching exercises, or meditation sessions, help recharge the mind and body. David, a remote worker, takes a 10-minute break every hour to stretch and practice deep breathing exercises, which helps him stay refreshed and focused.

Prioritize Self-Care: Mindfulness or meditation practices can significantly reduce stress and promote mental clarity. Studies in the Journal of Clinical Psychology show that mindfulness-based interventions can improve psychological well-being. For example, Emily, a remote worker, starts her day with a 10-minute meditation session to center herself before beginning work tasks.

Maintaining physical activity is crucial for overall well-being. Research published in the British Journal of Sports Medicine suggests that regular exercise can alleviate symptoms of depression and anxiety. Tom, a remote employee, incorporates daily walks or yoga sessions into his routine to boost his mood and energy levels.

Eating nutritious meals and staying hydrated are essential components of self-care. Research in the International Journal of Food Sciences and Nutrition indicates that a balanced diet can positively impact mental health. Maria, a remote worker, prepares healthy meals and snacks throughout the day, ensuring she stays fueled and focused on her work tasks.

Foster Social Connections: Regular communication with colleagues through virtual meetings, chats, or calls is vital to combat feelings of isolation. Research in the Journal of Applied Psychology emphasizes the importance of social support in remote work environments. James, a remote employee, schedules weekly video calls with his team to stay connected and maintain camaraderie.

Participating in virtual social events, team-building activities, or online communities helps foster a sense of belonging. Research in the Journal of Happiness Studies suggests that social interactions positively impact mental well-being. Sarah, a remote worker, organizes virtual coffee breaks and team trivia nights to promote social connections among her colleagues.

Manage Work-Related Stress: Establishing clear boundaries between work and personal life is essential to prevent overworking and maintain well-being. Research in the Journal of Occupational Health Psychology highlights the negative impact of blurred boundaries on mental health. Alex, a remote worker, sets specific work hours and refrains from checking emails after hours to maintain work-life balance.

Using time management techniques to prioritize tasks and set achievable goals helps reduce stress related to workload. Studies in the Journal of Business Research suggest that effective time management leads to higher job satisfaction and reduced stress levels. Laura, a remote employee, uses project management tools to organize her tasks and allocate time for each project, ensuring she stays on track and avoids feeling overwhelmed.

Seeking support from colleagues, managers, or support networks is crucial when feeling overwhelmed or in need of assistance. Research in the Journal of Occupational Medicine and Toxicology emphasizes the importance of social support in buffering against stress. Michael, a remote worker, reaches out to his manager or peers when facing challenges at work, seeking guidance and reassurance.

Create Mental Health Practices: Practicing gratitude by keeping a gratitude journal or focusing on positive aspects of life can cultivate a more positive outlook. Research in the Journal of Happiness Studies suggests that gratitude interventions can enhance well-being. Julia, a remote employee, spends a few minutes each day reflecting on things she's grateful for, which helps shift her perspective and reduce stress.

Seeking professional help from counselors, therapists, or mental health professionals is essential when experiencing persistent stress or anxiety. Research in the Journal of Consulting and Clinical Psychology indicates that therapy can be effective in treating various mental health conditions. Mark, a remote worker, schedules regular therapy sessions to address his anxiety and develop coping strategies.

Staying informed about mental health resources, online support groups, or virtual counseling services available for remote employees is crucial for accessing support when needed. Research in the Journal of Telemedicine and Telecare suggests that teletherapy can be effective in delivering mental health services remotely. Emma, a remote employee, researches virtual counseling services and attends online support groups to connect with others experiencing similar challenges.

Maintaining mental well-being while working virtually requires a proactive approach that encompasses establishing healthy routines, prioritizing self-care, fostering social connections, managing work-related stress, and implementing mental health practices. By incorporating these strategies into daily life, individuals can navigate the challenges of remote work with resilience and maintain optimal well-being in the digital workspace.

Life Lessons: Mind Over Mobile: Conquer your Smartphone Addiction and Cultivate Joy

Hardships are the common ground of the human journey. Our parents often retell their life stories, emphasizing the trials of financial constraints, rigid family customs, the weight of tradition, or other adversities they had to confront. While our generation may not experience the same obstacles they did, we do have newer, modern` day challenges. Today when we strive to achieve our ambitions, we have a struggle different from theirs, but still persistent and difficult to get through.

One significant difference is that we now have constant access to a device that is designed and built to capitalize on our attention. The world has gotten more competitive and demands stronger efforts from us than ever before while simultaneously counting on us to stay distracted. **In today's world, success is about mastering smartphones, not being mastered by them.**

Protecting Their Own: The Disconnect Between Social Media Creators and User Safety

In exploring the complex relationship between social media leaders and the platforms they create, it's essential to highlight the cautionary words of those at the helm. These executives, who profit from their innovations, have expressed significant concerns about the very environments they foster, particularly regarding the safety of children.

Kevin Mayer, the former CEO of TikTok, candidly remarked, "I wouldn't want my kids on TikTok. I think there are some risks associated with it." This statement, made during a 2020 interview, underscores a profound awareness of the potential dangers that young users face on the platform. Mayer's admission raises critical questions about the responsibilities of those who design these digital spaces.

Similarly, **Mark Zuckerberg, CEO of Meta**, acknowledged during a U.S. Senate hearing on March 24, 2021, "I don't let my kids use Instagram." His words came amidst intense scrutiny over Instagram's impact on mental health, particularly for adolescents. Zuckerberg's apology to families affected by social media-related harms—"I'm sorry for everything you have all been through. No one should go through the things that your families have suffered"—further emphasizes his recognition of the risks involved.

Jack Dorsey, **co-founder and former CEO of Twitter**, expressed his concerns by stating, "I wouldn't want my kids on Twitter. The toxicity is too high." This sentiment, shared in various interviews around 2018, reflects a growing awareness of the negative interactions that can permeate social media platforms.

Lastly, **Evan Spiegel, CEO of Snap Inc.**, noted in a 2019 interview, "I don't think Snapchat is appropriate for kids under 13." His acknowledgment of age-appropriate content highlights the need for greater safeguards in protecting young users from potentially harmful experiences.

These quotes collectively illustrate a disconcerting truth: even those who create and promote these platforms recognize their inherent dangers. This duality presents a moral dilemma reminiscent of a drug dealer who profits from harmful substances while shielding their own family from their effects. As we navigate this digital landscape, it becomes increasingly important to hold these leaders accountable and advocate for user safety over profit. Their words serve as a reminder that responsibility must accompany innovation in the ever-evolving world of social media.

Parenting in the Digital Era

The dependency on smartphones starts as early as when a child is just 2 or 3 years old. Parents are turning to smartphones as a distraction during meal times. Instead of going out to play after school, children now prefer being glued to their phones scrolling through YouTube or playing games. Parents see this as momentary relief while they can peacefully work on their chores or catch up on some rest, but beneath this superficial solution lies a trove of concerns about the long-term consequences.

In a case study titled 'Digital Divide,' conducted by a renowned research institution, findings revealed a growing discrepancy in smartphone access among children from different socioeconomic backgrounds. The study reveals that **by the age of 10, over 50% of children have their own smartphones.**

One notable research project, led by child psychologists at a renowned university, examined the eating habits of children who were consistently exposed to mobile devices during meals. The findings indicated a concerning trend: children who regularly used smartphones during mealtimes tended to eat less mindfully, often consuming more calories and unhealthy foods.

The research also revealed that these children exhibited a reduced ability to engage in face-to-face conversations, and they struggled with impulse control and delayed gratification. Furthermore, there was a notable correlation between the frequency of smartphone use during meals and increased screen time outside of meal hours, leading to concerns about sedentary behaviors and potential health consequences.

When someone is ingrained with relying on devices from such a young age, they are undoubtedly bound to develop an unhealthy attachment to the said device.

Older Generations using smartphones as a coping mechanism to boredom

It is fascinating to observe the way older generations have adapted to the digital age. The retired generation, often thought to be far removed from the tech-savvy habits of their grandchildren, has surprised many by embracing smartphones as a coping mechanism to combat boredom.

Before smartphones, the retired generation turned to outdoor activities, social interactions, hobbies, and books to alleviate boredom. These traditional coping mechanisms fostered genuine, in-person connections and an appreciation for the simplicity of life.

While smartphones offer the promise of staying connected, they can also lead to isolation and addiction. Some seniors may become so engrossed in their digital devices that they neglect in-person interactions with friends and family. The addictive nature of social media and mobile games can be isolating, as seniors may spend excessive amounts of time staring at screens instead of engaging with their physical surroundings. Prolonged screen time can also strain their eyes, causing digital eye strain and potential sleep disturbances, which are especially concerning for older adults.

While smartphones can be a valuable coping mechanism for boredom and offer numerous benefits to the retired generation, it's important to recognize the potential downsides, including the addictive nature of these devices. This addictive quality, akin to mobile withdrawal symptoms, highlights intriguing parallels to drug addiction in how both can impact the same neural circuits.

It's no secret that many individuals, young and old, experience what can only be described as **"mobile withdrawal symptoms"** when temporarily separated from their beloved devices. Interestingly, this phenomenon reveals a startling parallel to drug addiction in terms of how both drugs and mobile phones impact the same neural circuits.

Neuroscientists have uncovered intriguing insights into the similarities between drug addiction and the constant use of mobile phones. Researchers have also uncovered a fascinating link between social validation and the release of dopamine in the brain. The "likes," comments, and shares on social media platforms have been shown to trigger a dopamine rush similar to the high experienced by gamblers when they win. This insight demonstrates how the design of digital applications, including social media, exploits our neurological wiring to create a captivating and addictive user experience.

The common denominator lies in the brain's reward system. The pleasure-inducing neurotransmitter, dopamine, plays a crucial role in both scenarios. When drugs are consumed or a notification appears on a smartphone, the brain releases a surge of dopamine, creating feelings of pleasure and reinforcement.

One striking finding is that excessive smartphone use can lead to desensitization of the brain's reward system, similar to what occurs with drug abuse. This desensitization results in users needing more and more stimulation to experience the same level of pleasure, which may explain why individuals compulsively check their phones and find it challenging to stay away.

The Slot Machine Effect

To make the connection even more fascinating, the design of mobile apps and games has often been likened to slot machines. This comparison highlights how app developers and tech companies intentionally create an environment that capitalizes on the same neural pathways triggered by addictive substances. The random, intermittent rewards of notifications, messages, and likes on social media mimic the unpredictability of a gambler's win on a slot machine. This keeps users perpetually engaged, craving the next hit of dopamine.

In a comprehensive study conducted by a renowned university's neuroscience department, researchers observed individuals undergoing mobile phone deprivation for a week. The findings were astonishing, with participants exhibiting physical and psychological symptoms akin to those experienced during drug withdrawal. **These symptoms included irritability, restlessness, and even physical cravings for their smartphones.**

Neuro-associative conditioning, a concept rooted in the brain's remarkable adaptability, holds a key to understanding the powerful influence of smartphones and digital devices. This phenomenon, while concerning, has led to several thought-provoking studies and case studies that offer us a glimpse into its impact.

Neuro-associative conditioning's insights suggest that we are not only shaped by our interactions with smartphones but also manipulated by their design. This understanding prompts us to reflect on our relationship with these devices and underscores the importance of fostering digital mindfulness. As we navigate the digital landscape, it becomes essential to strike a balance that ensures our smartphones remain tools for our convenience and growth rather than devices that manipulate our neurological responses.

The problem is when we're engrossed in our mobile phones, we're fixated on instant rewards, often disregarding the far-reaching consequences. So let us break it into numbers and real data.

According to various studies and surveys conducted, it is estimated that the average person spends roughly 3-4 hours per day on their smartphone. Over a typical lifespan of 75 years, this would translate to *approximately 9-10 years spent using a smartphone.*

It's essential to keep in mind that these estimates are subject to change as technology evolves, and people's usage patterns shift. With the growing dependence on smartphones for communication, entertainment, work, and various other activities, it's *plausible that the amount of time spent on mobile phones might increase over time.*

In this vast universe teeming with boundless opportunities, you're granted just one shot at life. There are no second chances, no extra lives to be had. Only one. ***Do you genuinely wish to invest approximately 9-10 years of this singular existence glued to your smartphone, mindlessly scrolling through an endless stream of trivial, soul-numbing content?***

Chapter 19

Overcoming Stigma

Have you ever thought about how stigma surrounding mental health can prevent individuals from seeking the help they need, especially in the corporate world? Mental health stigma is a significant barrier that not only marginalizes those who struggle but also perpetuates a culture of silence around mental health issues. This stigma often arises from misconceptions, negative stereotypes, and societal taboos, leading to discrimination and hindering timely access to care.

Statistics reveal the extent of this issue. A survey conducted by **Rethink Mental Illness** in May 2023 found that three in five people living with a mental illness did not seek support due to concerns about how they would be perceived by others. This survey, which included responses from 1,300 individuals with conditions such as bipolar disorder, schizophrenia, and personality disorders, highlighted that 93% of participants felt there wasn't enough awareness about what it means to live with a severe mental illness. The findings underscore how anxiety related to stigma limits daily activities and social interactions, with 76% reporting that anxiety prevented them from seeing friends and family and 74% stating it hindered their participation in hobbies or exercise.

In the workplace specifically, stigma can have profound effects. A global study published by the **World Health Organization (WHO)** indicated that one in four people will be affected by mental health issues at some point in their lives. However, many individuals do not seek help due to fear of discrimination. According to a survey by Mind, a UK mental health charity, 86% of employees experiencing mental health issues reported that stigma prevented them from pursuing opportunities such as seeking help or applying for promotions.

Further illustrating this point, a study titled the **Scottish Mental Illness Stigma Study**, conducted by See Me Scotland, revealed alarming trends: 92% of participants reported experiencing stigma in relationships with family and friends within the past year. Additionally, 58% had avoided calling an ambulance or attending emergency services for mental health care due to fear of judgment.

It is crucial to understand that there is a significant difference between being **"mad"** and having a mental health issue. The term "mad" has historically been used to describe individuals exhibiting extreme behaviors or irrational thoughts, often leading to the misconception that all mental health conditions are synonymous with insanity or uncontrollable behavior. In reality, mental illness encompasses a wide range of conditions that affect an individual's thinking, feeling, mood, or behavior. According to the **Centers for Disease Control (CDC),** mental illness includes disorders such as depression, anxiety, bipolar disorder, and schizophrenia. These conditions can often be managed with appropriate treatment and support. Recognizing this distinction is vital; it helps dismantle harmful stereotypes and encourages individuals to seek help without fear of being labeled as **"mad."**

To effectively combat this stigma, we must adopt a multifaceted approach that includes education, personal stories, and community engagement. Public awareness campaigns are crucial in breaking down the myths associated with mental health. For example, initiatives like the **"Love Your Mind"** campaign encourage open discussions about mental health, aiming to normalize these conversations in everyday life.

Sharing personal stories is another powerful tool in reducing stigma. When individuals with lived experiences openly discuss their challenges and triumphs, it humanizes the issue and fosters empathy. Celebrities like Demi Lovato and Lady Gaga have shared their mental health journeys, helping to destigmatize these conversations and inspire others to seek help.

Peer support programs also play a vital role in normalizing mental health issues. These programs allow individuals with similar experiences to connect and share their stories, providing mutual support and understanding. For instance, initiatives like **"Bring Change to Mind,"** co-founded by actress Glenn Close, focus on encouraging dialogue about mental health while raising awareness and empathy within communities.

Moreover, addressing the language we use when discussing mental health can significantly impact societal perceptions. Using person-first language—such as saying **"a person living with depression"** instead of **"a depressed person"**— emphasizes the individual over their condition. This subtle shift in language can help foster a more respectful and compassionate discourse around mental health.

Creating safe spaces where individuals can express themselves without fear of judgment is crucial in combating stigma. Support groups provide environments where people can share their experiences and receive encouragement from others facing similar challenges. Initiatives like those organized by the National Eating Disorders Association exemplify how community support can alleviate feelings of isolation.

To effectively overcome stigma, it is essential to challenge stereotypes and promote critical thinking. Highlighting diversity within stigmatized groups and celebrating individual achievements can counteract negative perceptions. Programs like **"Disability Mentoring Day"** connect students with disabilities to professionals in their fields, showcasing their capabilities and promoting inclusion.

Fostering environments that celebrate diversity and inclusivity is vital in reducing marginalization. This involves implementing policies in workplaces that recognize and value all individuals regardless of their backgrounds. Companies like Accenture and Deloitte have made strides in this area by developing comprehensive diversity and inclusion programs.

The media plays a crucial role in shaping public perceptions of stigmatized groups. Positive representations in television shows and films can challenge stereotypes and provide a more accurate portrayal of diverse communities.

Creating sustainable change requires collaboration among various stakeholders— communities, organizations, healthcare providers, and policymakers. By working together to develop targeted strategies that address stigma on multiple fronts, we can foster an environment where individuals feel safe seeking help without fear of judgment or discrimination.

Reducing stigma associated with mental health is not just about changing perceptions; it's about creating a supportive culture where everyone feels empowered to seek help. By engaging in open conversations, sharing personal experiences, and promoting inclusive practices, we can dismantle the barriers that keep individuals from living full and productive lives. Together, we can transform the narrative around mental health from one of shame to one of hope and understanding.

19.1　Address the stigma surrounding mental health in the corporate world.

Addressing the stigma surrounding mental health in the corporate world is crucial for creating supportive, inclusive, and productive work environments. Stigma around mental health remains a significant barrier in many workplaces, often preventing employees from seeking support or disclosing their struggles. To create a truly inclusive and supportive environment, companies must take a multi-pronged approach to challenge stigma and normalize conversations about mental well-being. Here are some strategies to tackle mental health stigma in the workplace:

- **Education and awareness programs**: Implementing training sessions or workshops to educate employees about mental health, its prevalence, signs, and ways to support colleagues can help reduce stigma. Encouraging open discussions and providing information about available resources like employee assistance programs (EAPs) can normalize conversations about mental health. Companies like Starbucks have partnered with organizations like NAMI to provide mental health education and resources to their employees.

- **Leadership commitment and role modeling**: Leaders play a crucial role in setting the tone for company culture. When leaders openly discuss mental health, prioritize work-life balance, and support initiatives promoting mental well-being, it encourages employees to feel more comfortable discussing their own mental health challenges.

- **Establish supportive policies and practices**: Implementing policies that prioritize mental health, such as flexible work hours, remote work options, mental health days, and providing access to counselling or therapy services, demonstrates a commitment to employee well-being. Former Cisco CEO John Chambers has been open about his experience with depression, helping reduce stigma. Companies like EY have implemented mental health days and support programs. Bank of America has an employee resource group called **"Life Event Services"** focused on mental health. Google has implemented features like **"mental health reminders"** and meditation spaces.

- **Foster an inclusive and supportive environment:** Encourage a culture where employees feel comfortable discussing mental health concerns without fear of judgment or repercussions. Emphasize the importance of empathy, active listening, and supporting colleagues who may be struggling. Unilever launched a global **"Go Bright"** mental health initiative with senior leader engagement.

- **Language and communication**: Use inclusive and non-stigmatizing language when discussing mental health in the workplace. Encourage positive and supportive communication among colleagues and discourage language that reinforces stereotypes or belittles mental health issues.

- **Employee resource groups and peer support networks**: Establishing employee resource groups focused on mental health or peer support networks can provide a safe space for employees to share experiences, seek advice, and offer support to one another.

- **Normalize self-care and mental health practices**: Encourage and promote activities that support mental well-being, such as mindfulness sessions, yoga, meditation, or offering access to mental health apps or resources.

- **Evaluate and adjust organizational practices**: Regularly assess workplace practices and their impact on employee mental health. Solicit feedback from employees and make necessary adjustments to create a more supportive environment.

- **Address confidentiality and privacy concerns:** Ensure that confidentiality is maintained when employees seek support or accommodations for mental health-related issues. Employees should feel assured that their privacy will be respected.

- **Measure progress and celebrate successes:** Track the impact of initiatives aimed at reducing mental health stigma. Celebrate successes and recognize efforts made by individuals or teams to create a more supportive workplace environment.

By implementing these strategies, companies can foster a workplace culture that promotes mental health awareness, support, and inclusivity, ultimately reducing the stigma associated with mental health issues in the corporate world.

19.2 How can companies encourage employees to seek mental health support without fear of stigma?

How can companies create an environment where employees feel comfortable seeking mental health support without the fear of stigma? This is a crucial question for organizations aiming to foster a healthy workplace culture. To encourage employees to prioritize their mental well-being, companies can adopt a comprehensive and multi-faceted approach.

Many employees are reluctant to seek mental health support due to fears of judgment, discrimination, or negative repercussions on their careers. A survey by Mind, a UK mental health charity, found that 86% of employees experiencing mental health issues reported that stigma prevented them from pursuing opportunities such as seeking help or applying for promotions. This fear is often exacerbated in competitive corporate environments, where employees worry that revealing their struggles may be perceived as a weakness. Consequently, this reluctance can lead to untreated mental health issues, decreased productivity, and increased absenteeism.

Creating a supportive environment is essential for companies not only to enhance employee well-being but also to improve overall organizational performance. When employees feel comfortable discussing their mental health, they are more likely to seek the help they need, leading to better outcomes for both individuals and the organization as a whole. A mentally healthy workforce is linked to higher levels of engagement, creativity, and retention, ultimately benefiting the company's bottom line.

To encourage employees to prioritize their mental well-being, companies can adopt a comprehensive and multi-faceted approach. Here are some effective strategies to consider:

- **Leadership Commitment and Role Modeling:** Senior leaders and executives play a crucial role in setting the tone and shaping the organizational culture around mental health. When they openly share their own experiences with mental health challenges, it sends a powerful message that this is not a taboo topic and that seeking support is acceptable and encouraged. For example, at Unilever, the chief learning officer shared her personal story of struggling with anxiety and depression, which helped create an open culture where employees felt able to seek help without stigma.

- **Establishing Supportive Policies and Resources:** Companies must back their commitment to mental health with tangible policies and resources. This includes offering robust mental health coverage in employee benefits packages, providing free and confidential counseling or therapy services, allowing mental health days off, and ensuring flexible work arrangements for those who need accommodations. Easy access to mental health resources, such as stress management programs, mindfulness apps, and educational materials, further supports employees in prioritizing their well-being.

- **Destigmatizing Conversations through Training and Awareness:** Mandatory mental health literacy training for all employees can increase awareness, reduce stigma, and equip individuals with the knowledge to recognize signs of mental health struggles in themselves or their colleagues. These training sessions should be facilitated by mental health professionals or individuals with lived experiences of mental illness, fostering empathy and open dialogues. Awareness campaigns, discussion groups, and workshops can further normalize conversations around mental health and create a safe space for sharing experiences.

- **Fostering an Inclusive and Supportive Culture:** Creating an inclusive and supportive culture is essential for encouraging employees to seek mental health support without fear. This involves promoting empathy, active listening, and allyship among colleagues. Encouraging open dialogues and providing safe spaces for employees to share their experiences can cultivate a sense of community and understanding. Employee resource groups focused on mental health can further foster a supportive environment where individuals feel seen, heard, and understood.

- **Confidentiality and Privacy Assurances:** Employees may hesitate to seek mental health support due to fears of discrimination or negative impacts on their careers. Companies must ensure confidentiality and privacy when employees seek support or accommodations for mental health-related issues. Clear communication about privacy policies and practices, as well as strict adherence to these policies, can alleviate these concerns and create a sense of trust.

- **Continuous Communication and Evaluation:** Addressing mental health stigma is an ongoing process that requires sustained effort. Continuous communication from leadership, celebrating mental health initiatives, sharing success stories, and regularly soliciting employee feedback can reinforce the organization's commitment to mental health and drive continuous improvement. Anonymous surveys or feedback mechanisms can help identify areas for improvement and ensure that the company's efforts are effectively addressing employees' needs and concerns.

By implementing a combination of these strategies, companies can create a stigma-free workplace culture that encourages employees to prioritize their mental well-being without fear of negative consequences. It's a journey that requires long-term commitment, but the benefits of a mentally healthy and supported workforce are immense, including increased productivity, talent retention, and a thriving organizational culture.

19.3 How can companies measure the effectiveness of their mental health support programs?

How can companies create an environment where employees feel comfortable seeking mental health support without the fear of stigma? This is a crucial question for organizations aiming to foster a healthy workplace culture. To encourage employees to prioritize their mental well-being, companies can adopt a comprehensive and multi-faceted approach.

An effective mental health program is one that not only provides resources and support but also fosters an environment where employees feel safe discussing their mental health needs.

Effectiveness in this context refers to the program's ability to produce positive outcomes, such as improved employee well-being, reduced absenteeism, and enhanced productivity. Companies need to measure the effectiveness of their mental health initiatives to ensure they are meeting these goals and addressing the unique needs of their workforce. Regular evaluation helps organizations identify strengths and weaknesses in their programs, allowing for continuous improvement.

Many employees are reluctant to seek mental health support due to fears of judgment, discrimination, or negative repercussions on their careers. A survey by Mind, a UK mental health charity, found that **86% of employees experiencing mental health issues reported that stigma prevented them from pursuing opportunities such as seeking help or participating in a program.** This fear is often exacerbated in competitive corporate environments, where employees worry that revealing their struggles may be perceived as a weakness. Consequently, this reluctance can lead to untreated mental health issues, decreased productivity, and increased absenteeism.

Creating a supportive environment is essential for companies not only to enhance employee well-being but also to improve overall organizational performance. When employees feel comfortable discussing their mental health, they are more likely to seek the help they need, leading to better outcomes for both individuals and the organization as a whole. A mentally healthy workforce is linked to higher levels of engagement, creativity, and retention, ultimately benefiting the company's bottom line.

To encourage employees to prioritize their mental well-being, companies can adopt a comprehensive and multi-faceted approach. Here are some effective strategies to consider:

- **Leadership Commitment and Role Modeling**: Senior leaders and executives play a crucial role in setting the tone and shaping the organizational culture around mental health. When they openly share their own experiences with mental health challenges, it sends a powerful message that this is not a taboo topic and that seeking support is acceptable and encouraged. For example, at Unilever, the chief learning officer shared her personal story of struggling with anxiety and depression, which helped create an open culture where employees felt able to seek help without stigma.

- **Establishing Supportive Policies and Resources:** Companies must back their commitment to mental health with tangible policies and resources. This includes offering robust mental health coverage in employee benefits packages, providing free and confidential counseling or therapy services, allowing mental health days off, and ensuring flexible work arrangements for those who need accommodations. Easy access to mental health resources, such as stress management programs, mindfulness apps, and educational materials, further supports employees in prioritizing their well-being. For instance, EY's **"Better You"** program offers up to 25 counseling sessions for employees and their family members, mindfulness training, and mediation sessions.

- **Destigmatizing Conversations through Training and Awareness:** Mandatory mental health literacy training for all employees can increase awareness, reduce stigma, and equip individuals with the knowledge to recognize signs of mental health struggles in themselves or their colleagues. These training sessions should be facilitated by mental health professionals or individuals with lived experiences of mental illness, fostering empathy and open dialogues. Awareness campaigns, discussion groups, and workshops can further normalize conversations around mental health and create a safe space for sharing experiences.

- **Fostering an Inclusive and Supportive Culture:** Creating an inclusive and supportive culture is essential for encouraging employees to seek mental health support without fear. This involves promoting empathy, active listening, and allyship among colleagues. Encouraging open dialogues and providing safe spaces for employees to share their experiences can cultivate a sense of community and understanding. Employee resource groups focused on mental health can further foster a supportive environment where individuals feel seen, heard, and understood.

- **Confidentiality and Privacy Assurances:** Employees may hesitate to seek mental health support due to fears of discrimination or negative impacts on their careers. Companies must ensure confidentiality and privacy when employees seek support or accommodations for mental health-related issues. Clear communication about privacy policies and practices, as well as strict adherence to these policies, can alleviate these concerns and create a sense of trust.

- **Continuous Communication and Evaluation:** Addressing mental health stigma is an ongoing process that requires sustained effort. Continuous communication from leadership—celebrating mental health initiatives, sharing success stories, and regularly soliciting employee feedback—can reinforce the organization's commitment to mental health and drive continuous improvement. Anonymous surveys or feedback mechanisms can help identify areas for improvement while ensuring that the company's efforts effectively address employees' needs.

By implementing a combination of these strategies, companies can create a stigma-free workplace culture that encourages employees to prioritize their mental well-being without fear of negative consequences. It's a journey that requires long-term commitment; however, the benefits of a mentally healthy and supported workforce are immense. These include increased productivity, better talent retention, improved morale, and a thriving organizational culture where everyone feels valued.

19.4 Stories of individuals who have overcome stigma and achieved success

Overcoming stigma and achieving success despite facing significant challenges is possible, as evidenced by the inspiring stories of trailblazers who have defied societal expectations. These individuals have not only accomplished remarkable feats but have also used their platforms to advocate for mental health awareness and inclusion.

Temple Grandin, a prominent professor of animal science and bestselling author, has been a vocal advocate for autism awareness. Despite being diagnosed with autism at a young age, Grandin has become a leading expert in animal behavior and welfare. As she once said, *"The world needs all kinds of minds."* Her story highlights the importance of embracing neurodiversity and challenging misconceptions about mental health conditions.

Former First Lady Michelle Obama faced stereotypes and societal expectations growing up in a working-class neighborhood, but she overcame them to become a lawyer, public figure, and influential advocate for women's rights and equality. In her memoir "Becoming," Obama wrote, *"I still felt like I was fighting to make my way in a world not built for someone like me."* Her journey serves as a testament to the power of resilience and determination in the face of adversity.

Renowned physicist Stephen Hawking, who faced immense physical challenges due to amyotrophic lateral sclerosis (ALS), emphasized the importance of mental fortitude in overcoming adversity. As he once said, *"However difficult life may seem, there is always something you can do and succeed at."* Despite his physical limitations, Hawking made groundbreaking contributions to theoretical physics and cosmology, becoming one of the most celebrated scientists of our time.

Civil rights icon Rosa Parks played a pivotal role in the fight against racial segregation in the United States. Her refusal to give up her seat on a bus to a white passenger sparked the Montgomery Bus Boycott and became a symbol of resistance against racial injustice. Parks' courageous act and subsequent activism challenged societal norms and helped bring about significant change. As she once stated, *"I have learned over the years that when one's mind is made up, this diminishes fear."*

Elon Musk, a prominent entrepreneur known for founding companies like SpaceX, Tesla, and Neuralink, has faced numerous setbacks and criticism throughout his career. However, his determination to revolutionize industries like space exploration and sustainable energy showcases how individuals can overcome skepticism and achieve groundbreaking success. As Musk once said, *"When something is important enough, you do it even if the odds are not in your favor."*

These individuals' stories serve as powerful reminders that overcoming stigma and societal barriers is possible through resilience, determination, and a commitment to making a positive impact despite the odds. Their achievements and words of wisdom inspire others to challenge stereotypes, break down barriers, and pursue their dreams despite facing societal prejudices. By embracing mental health awareness and inclusion, we can create a more equitable and supportive world for all.

Life Lessons: The Focus Code: Reclaiming Your Mind from Digital Distractions for Peak Performance

How can we understand the relationship between attention economics and mental health in today's digital landscape? Attention economics refers to the idea that human attention is a scarce commodity, and in our hyper-connected world, social media platforms are vying for this limited resource. They do so by capturing our time and engagement, often leading to significant implications for our mental well-being.

In essence, none of these social media platforms are truly **"free."** While users may not pay with money, they pay with their attention and time, which are monetized by these companies through advertising and data collection. For instance, in 2023, **brands spent approximately $270 billion on social media advertising**, highlighting the immense financial stakes involved in capturing user attention. Platforms like Meta (which includes Facebook and Instagram) generated over **$121 billion** in ad revenues, indicating how these companies profit from the time users spend engaging with their content.

This relentless pursuit of attention can lead to negative mental health outcomes. Studies have shown that excessive social media use is correlated with increased feelings of anxiety, depression, and loneliness. The constant barrage of curated images and idealized lifestyles can foster unrealistic comparisons and diminish self-esteem. Moreover, the addictive nature of social media can create a cycle where users feel compelled to check their feeds frequently, further detracting from their mental well-being.

Understanding attention economics is essential for navigating the complexities of modern life. As we become increasingly aware of how our time and attention are commodified, we can make more informed choices about our engagement with social media (or reduce it) and prioritize our mental health in the process.

"The attention economy is a war for your time, and the casualties are your focus and productivity." - James Clear

Our minds are continually bombarded with information, stimuli, and distractions. It has become increasingly evident that our modern lifestyles are leading to weakened, stressed, and perpetually overstimulated brains.

The Paradox of a Stimulated Brain

In a world that encourages constant stimulation, relaxation often takes a backseat. We find ourselves thinking less and thinking slower, struggling to disconnect from the never-ending flow of information. The more we expose our minds to unceasing stimulation, the more we feel a void, an emptiness inside, as if our brains never truly rest.

Constant stimulation may seem invigorating on the surface, as it pushes us to think differently and adapt to new challenges. However, beneath the surface lies a stark truth: our brains need respite to function optimally. Just like a muscle needs rest after a workout, our minds require moments of stillness and quiet. Without them, we face a severe cognitive cost.

The ability to disconnect from the never-ending flow of information becomes an arduous task, leaving us with a constant yearning for more.

Our brains are not limitless in their capacity to process information, yet they are constantly bombarded with stimuli. This overstimulation can lead to a depletion of cognitive resources. When we are in a perpetual state of hyperactivity and multitasking, we become more prone to errors, overlook important details, and struggle to focus on tasks that require deep thinking.

The Emptiness Within

The more we expose our minds to unceasing stimulation, the more we feel a void, an emptiness inside, as if our brains never truly rest. This paradoxical emptiness can be attributed to the superficiality of our interactions with the information around us. While we may consume an abundance of data, it often lacks depth and meaning. *It's like eating fast food for the mind – momentarily satisfying, but ultimately unfulfilling.*

The Importance of Moments of Stillness and Quiet

Just like a muscle needs rest after a workout to grow stronger, our minds require moments of stillness and quiet to function at their best. These moments of reprieve provide our brains with the opportunity to process information, consolidate memories, and make connections that are crucial for creativity and problem-solving.

The Severe Cognitive Cost

Without adequate rest and moments of tranquillity, we face a severe cognitive cost. This cost is not limited to decreased productivity; it also impacts our mental health. Anxiety, irritability, and depression can be the consequences of an overstimulated mind. Therefore, it's essential to strike a balance between the stimulation our modern world offers and the serenity our brains desperately need.

An interesting theory relating to how distractions and digital stimulus affects is

The Goldfish Attention Span. Did you know that the average human attention span has decreased from 12 seconds in 2000 to just 8 seconds in 2021? This is less than the attention span of a goldfish, which is believed to be around 9 seconds. The constant exposure to digital stimuli has contributed to this decline in focus.

One more intriguing fact to consider is the fact that many prominent figures in the tech industry, including **Steve Jobs and Mark Zuckerberg, have implemented tech-free practices in their personal lives to foster creativity and focus.** These tech titans understand the value of taking breaks from the constant digital noise that their own creations have unleashed upon the world.

The impact of social media on mental health is profound. Self-esteem can plummet as we endlessly scroll through curated representations of others' lives. But there is more to the story than meets the eye. Beyond self-esteem, digital consumption can disrupt our sleep patterns, disrupt our melatonin production, and fuel the allure of the blue light emitted by our mobile devices.

The Blue Light Menace and Melatonin Disruption

The blue light from our mobile screens can wreak havoc on our sleep-wake cycle. As night falls, our bodies typically produce melatonin, the hormone that signals it's time to sleep. However, the blue light tricks our brains into thinking it's still daytime, delaying the release of melatonin and making it harder to fall asleep. To mitigate this, we must adopt the practice of cutting out screens at least two hours before bedtime.

Screens: Food Without Taste

In a world where screens are the primary source of information and entertainment, we consume without savouring. Like a meal devoid of flavour, our digital diet often lacks depth and meaning. We skim through vast amounts of content without truly digesting any of it, leading to an insatiable hunger for more.

Digital Hygiene: A Path to Rejuvenation

To counteract the detrimental impact of our digital habits on our mental health and overall well-being, we need a regimen of digital hygiene. This practice involves making deliberate, mindful choices about our technology use. Here are some key pointers:

1. **Mobile Fasting:** Regularly disconnect from your digital devices. No notifications, no distractions, and no compulsive checking. Research has shown that the average person checks their phone every 12 minutes. However, the human brain requires more than 23 minutes to regain focus after being interrupted. This constant cycle of notifications and interruptions can significantly impair our productivity and focus.

2. **One Tab, One Browser:** Limit your digital workspace to a single tab or browser. This can help streamline your focus and reduce multitasking. A study by Stanford University found that self-proclaimed "high multitaskers" were actually more easily distracted, had difficulty filtering out irrelevant information, and were less efficient at switching between tasks. By limiting ourselves to a single tab or browser, we can reduce the detrimental effects of multitasking on our cognitive abilities.

3. **Radiation-Free Bedroom:** Create a screen-free sanctuary in your bedroom to ensure better sleep and relaxation.

4. **Screen-Free Breakfast:** Begin your day with a screen-free breakfast to set a calm and mindful tone for the day. By starting your day with a screen-free

breakfast and incorporating moments of nature observation, you can create a peaceful and positive foundation for the day, enhancing your overall mental health.

5. **Avoid Mobile for Non-Essential Activities:** Use your mobile devices for necessary functions but limit their use for non-essential activities.

6. **Go for a Walk:** Incorporate breaks in nature or simple walks without your mobile device to reconnect with the physical world. Spending time in nature has been shown to reduce stress, improve mood, and enhance overall well-being. In fact, the Japanese practice of **"shinrin-yoku"** or forest bathing emphasizes the therapeutic effects of immersing oneself in nature.

Incorporating these practices into your daily routine can lead to a digital detox that enhances your mental health, deepens your connections, and fosters a more intentional relationship with technology.

Chapter 20

Rethinking Mental Health Strategies: Moving Beyond Old Methods

Mental health care has undergone a significant transformation in recent years, with a growing recognition of the need to move beyond traditional methods and embrace more innovative and comprehensive strategies. While conventional treatments such as medication and talk therapy have their merits, they often fall short in addressing the complex and multifaceted nature of mental health challenges faced by individuals in today's rapidly changing world. To provide effective and responsive care, it is crucial to rethink our approach to mental health and adopt new models that prioritize holistic well-being, accessibility, and personalization.

By leveraging emerging technologies, fostering community engagement, and emphasizing prevention and early intervention, we can create a mental health care system that is better equipped to support individuals in navigating the unique challenges and opportunities of the 21st century. This transition requires a willingness to challenge existing paradigms, embrace evidence-based practices, and collaborate across disciplines and sectors to develop comprehensive and effective solutions.

Moving Beyond Traditional Mental Health Approaches

Traditional mental health treatments have often relied on a limited set of methods, such as medication and talk therapy, with a one-size-fits-all approach. While these approaches have their merits, they often fail to address the complex and multifaceted nature of mental health challenges faced by individuals. To provide more effective and comprehensive care, it is crucial to move beyond these old methods and embrace innovative strategies that prioritize holistic well-being, accessibility, and personalization.

Holistic and Personalized Care

One of the key limitations of traditional mental health treatments is their narrow focus on addressing specific symptoms or diagnoses in isolation. This approach often overlooks the interconnectedness of an individual's mental, physical, emotional, and social well-being. By embracing a holistic perspective, we can move beyond this limited view and develop treatment plans that consider the whole person. This may involve integrating elements such as nutrition, exercise, mindfulness practices, and social support into the care plan. Additionally, personalized treatment approaches based on an individual's unique genetic, biological, and environmental factors, known as precision medicine, can offer more targeted and effective interventions. This shift from a one-size-fits-all model to a more personalized approach allows for greater flexibility and responsiveness to individual needs.

Example: Eleanor Health integrates mental health and addiction recovery services into one cohesive treatment plan. This means that if you're struggling with both mental health issues and substance use disorders, you can receive comprehensive care that includes medication-assisted treatment and telehealth options—all designed to fit your lifestyle.

Leveraging Technology and Telehealth

Traditional mental health care has often been limited by geographical barriers, with individuals in remote or underserved areas having limited access to specialized services. However, the rise of technology and telehealth has opened up new possibilities for overcoming these limitations. By utilizing tools such as teletherapy, mental health apps, online support groups, and digital assessments, we can significantly improve accessibility and reach a wider population. These innovations have become even more crucial during the COVID-19 pandemic, which has exacerbated mental health challenges for many and highlighted the need for remote care options. By embracing technology, we can move beyond the constraints of traditional in-person therapy and provide more flexible and convenient access to mental health support.

Example: Spring Health takes personalization to the next level. By using machine learning algorithms, they create individualized care plans that adapt to your specific circumstances. You won't just be another face in the crowd; you'll have a Care Navigator who guides you through your mental health journey, ensuring you receive the support that's right for you.

Example: Kintsugi is pioneering voice biomarker technology to detect signs of depression and anxiety through speech analysis. This innovative method allows for early detection of mental health issues without requiring traditional clinical assessments, making it easier for you to get help sooner.

Fostering Peer Support and Community Engagement

Traditional mental health care has often been centered around the therapist-client relationship, with limited emphasis on the role of peer support and community engagement. However, research has shown that peer support networks and community-based initiatives can be highly effective in reducing isolation, offering relatable perspectives, and providing guidance in navigating mental health challenges. By fostering these connections, we can move beyond the limitations of individual therapy and tap into the power of shared experiences and mutual support. Additionally, collaborating with community organizations, advocacy groups, and policymakers to develop comprehensive mental health strategies ensures a more inclusive and effective approach. This shift towards a more community-oriented model allows for greater engagement and ownership of mental health initiatives by those they serve.

For university students, Mantra Health is a game changer. They partner with campus counseling centers to provide digital mental health services tailored specifically for students. This proactive approach ensures that you can access timely support without long wait times, making it easier to manage stress and anxiety during your academic journey.

Prioritizing Prevention and Early Intervention

Traditional mental health care has often been reactive, focusing on treating individuals after they have already developed significant symptoms or disorders. However, this approach can be costly, both in terms of individual suffering and societal resources. By prioritizing preventive mental health care, we can move beyond this reactive model and address issues before they escalate. This may involve promoting resilience-building activities, stress management techniques, and early intervention programs in schools, workplaces, and communities. Implementing early detection programs and mental health screenings in various settings can lead to prompt intervention and support, reducing the likelihood of more severe outcomes. This proactive approach not only benefits individuals but also contributes to a healthier and more resilient society as a whole.

Little Otter focuses exclusively on pediatric mental health, offering tailored assessments and treatment plans for children aged 0–14 years old. Their emphasis on family involvement ensures that young patients receive holistic support, addressing both immediate needs and long-term development.

Incorporating alternative therapies

Art therapy, music therapy, equine (horse) therapy, and nature-based interventions are considered complementary and alternative therapies that can be incorporated alongside traditional medical treatments. These approaches aim to engage the senses, emotions, and mind-body connection to promote healing and well-being.

- **Art therapy** involves the use of creative processes like drawing, painting, sculpting, or other art forms to help individuals express themselves, cope with stress or trauma, and gain self-awareness

- **Music therapy** utilizes live or recorded music to address physical, emotional, cognitive, and social needs through active music-making or listening experiences.

- **Equine therapy,** also known as equine-assisted therapy, involves interactions with horses or dogs to facilitate emotional growth, develop life skills, and address mental health or behavioral issues

- **Nature-based interventions,** such as wilderness therapy, horticultural therapy, or animal-assisted therapy, leverage the healing effects of interacting with natural environments or animals

These alternative approaches are considered complementary when used alongside conventional treatments like psychotherapy or medication. They can resonate with individuals who may not respond well to traditional methods alone, as they provide alternative avenues for self-expression, emotional release, and mind-body integration

Early detection and intervention programs, along with mental health screenings in schools, primary care settings, and communities, are crucial for identifying mental health issues early on. Timely identification allows for prompt intervention and support, which can significantly improve outcomes and prevent further deterioration of mental health conditions

Community engagement and partnerships involve collaborating with various stakeholders, such as community organizations, advocacy groups, and policymakers, to develop comprehensive mental health strategies. This approach ensures a more inclusive and effective approach to mental health care by incorporating diverse perspectives and leveraging the resources and expertise of different entities.

With Lyra Health, you'll find a fresh approach to mental health care designed specifically for employees. Instead of relying on a referral system where you might be matched with a therapist based solely on availability, Lyra uses AI technology to connect you with the right partner provider quickly. This means you get personalized care tailored to your unique needs right from the start. Plus, their comprehensive suite of services includes guided self-care and family support, ensuring that everyone in your household can access help.

By engaging diverse stakeholders, mental health initiatives can better address the unique needs and challenges of different populations and communities.

These strategies aim to promote early intervention, increase access to mental health services, reduce stigma, and foster a more integrated and coordinated approach to mental health care within communities

Collaboration and partnerships can lead to more comprehensive and culturally-sensitive mental health programs, while early detection and screening efforts can facilitate timely access to appropriate support and treatment. By embracing these innovative strategies and moving beyond traditional methods, we can create a mental health care system that is more inclusive, accessible, and responsive to the diverse needs of individuals experiencing mental health challenges. This transition requires a commitment to continuous evaluation, adaptation, and a willingness to challenge the status quo. By prioritizing holistic well-being, leveraging technology, fostering community engagement, and emphasizing prevention, we can improve mental health outcomes and create a more supportive and empowering environment for all.

20.1 Explore the limitations and shortcomings of traditional mental health approaches in the corporate world.

Traditional mental health approaches in the corporate world have several limitations and shortcomings that can hinder effective support for employees' mental well-being:

- **Stigma and Silence**: Many workplaces still carry a stigma surrounding mental health, leading employees to fear negative consequences if they speak up about their struggles. This fear of discrimination or judgment fosters a culture of silence where individuals are hesitant to seek the support they need. As a result, mental health issues often go unaddressed, impacting both employee well-being and workplace productivity.

- **Fixing Problems Instead of Stopping Them**: Traditional mental health approaches in corporate settings often focus on addressing mental health issues only after they have escalated to a critical point. This reactive approach neglects the importance of preventive measures and early intervention strategies, which could effectively mitigate problems before they become severe. By shifting the focus towards prevention, workplaces can create a healthier and more supportive environment for their employees.

- **One-Size-Fits-All**: Many corporate mental health programs offer generic solutions that fail to consider the individual needs and differences of employees. What works for one person may not work for another, especially considering the diverse demographics and cultures present in the modern workplace. Tailoring mental health support to accommodate various backgrounds and circumstances can significantly improve its effectiveness and reach.

- **Hard to Get Help**: Accessibility to mental health support can be challenging for employees, particularly those in remote areas or with limited resources. Factors such as cost, location, and availability of services can act as barriers, preventing individuals from seeking the assistance they need. Creating more accessible and affordable options for mental health care is essential to ensure that all employees have access to support when required.

- **Not Part of Overall Wellness:** Mental health is intricately connected to overall well-being, yet it is often treated as a separate concern within corporate wellness programs. This separation overlooks the interconnectedness of mental, emotional, and physical health, missing valuable opportunities for comprehensive care. Integrating mental health initiatives into broader wellness programs can provide employees with holistic support to thrive in all aspects of their lives.

- **Too Much Focus on Work:** Corporate cultures that prioritize productivity and performance can inadvertently contribute to mental health issues among employees. High levels of stress, long working hours, and unrealistic expectations create an environment where mental well-being is often sacrificed for the sake of productivity. Recognizing the importance of a healthy work-life balance and fostering supportive work environments is crucial for promoting employee mental health and overall job satisfaction.

- **Managers Need More Help:** Managers and supervisors play a pivotal role in supporting employee mental health, yet many lack the necessary training and resources to address mental health issues effectively. Without proper guidance, managers may struggle to recognize the signs of distress in their teams or know how to provide appropriate support. Investing in training programs that equip managers with the skills and knowledge to support employee mental health can make a significant difference in workplace well-being.

- **Short-Term Solutions:** While many traditional mental health programs offer short-term interventions, sustained improvement and prevention of relapse require ongoing support and follow-up care. Short-term solutions may provide temporary relief, but without continued support, individuals may struggle to maintain their mental well-being over time. Incorporating long-term support mechanisms into corporate mental health initiatives is essential for fostering lasting positive change.

- **Worries About Privacy:** Concerns about privacy and confidentiality can deter employees from seeking help for mental health issues. Traditional approaches may not adequately address these concerns, leaving employees hesitant to disclose sensitive information about their mental well-being. Ensuring confidentiality and privacy protections within mental health support programs can help alleviate these fears and encourage employees to seek the assistance they need without fear of judgment or repercussions.

- **Ignoring Big Problems**: Traditional approaches often fail to address systemic issues within the workplace that contribute to poor mental health outcomes. Factors such as an imbalance in work-life dynamics, inequitable policies, and toxic work cultures can significantly impact employee well-being but may go unrecognized or unaddressed. By identifying and addressing these underlying systemic issues, organizations can create healthier and more supportive work environments that promote employee mental health and overall satisfaction.

In conclusion, recognizing and addressing the limitations of traditional mental health approaches in the corporate world is crucial for creating supportive and inclusive workplaces where employees can thrive. By overcoming stigma, prioritizing prevention, tailoring support to individual needs, and integrating mental health into overall wellness initiatives, organizations can foster environments that prioritize employee well-being. Additionally, providing accessible, ongoing support, equipping managers with the necessary skills, and addressing systemic issues are essential steps towards building a culture that values and supports mental health. By embracing these changes, workplaces can promote resilience, productivity, and overall job satisfaction among their employees, ultimately contributing to a healthier and more prosperous workforce.

20.2 Discuss the need for innovative and proactive solutions to address mental health challenges.

In recent years, the conversation surrounding mental health has gained significant traction, shedding light on the importance of addressing mental health challenges in proactive and innovative ways. As traditional approaches reveal their limitations in meeting the diverse and evolving needs of individuals, there arises a pressing need for forward-thinking strategies to tackle mental health issues effectively. This essay explores ten key reasons why innovative and proactive solutions are essential in addressing mental health challenges in today's society.

- **Complexity of mental health issues:** Mental health is a multifaceted aspect of human well-being, influenced by various biological, psychological, social, and environmental factors. For instance, integrating wearable technology like smartwatches with mental health monitoring apps can provide real-time data on an individual's stress levels, sleep patterns, and activity levels, offering a more holistic understanding of their mental health.

- **Changing societal dynamics:** Rapid societal changes, including technological advancements, globalization, and shifts in work patterns, have introduced new stressors and challenges to mental health. For example, the rise of remote work due to the COVID-19 pandemic has blurred the boundaries between work and personal life, leading to increased feelings of isolation and burnout. In response, companies like Google have implemented innovative well-being programs that include virtual mindfulness sessions and mental health resources tailored to remote employees.

- **Rising mental health concerns:** The prevalence of mental health issues is on the rise globally, driven by factors such as increased stress, social isolation, economic uncertainty, and exposure to traumatic events. For instance, in the aftermath of natural disasters like hurricanes or wildfires, organizations like the American Red Cross deploy mobile mental health units equipped with teletherapy capabilities to provide immediate support to affected communities.

- **Engagement and accessibility:** Innovative solutions leverage technology to enhance engagement and accessibility to mental health care. For example, the mental health app Talkspace offers affordable, on-demand therapy sessions with licensed professionals, making mental health support more accessible to individuals who may face barriers such as cost or location.

- **Customization and personalization:** Proactive approaches enable tailored interventions that consider individual needs, preferences, and cultural backgrounds. For instance, the mental health platform Ginger.io uses artificial intelligence to personalize therapy sessions based on users' goals, preferences, and progress, enhancing the effectiveness of treatment.

- **Prevention-focused interventions**: Proactive strategies prioritize prevention and early intervention, aiming to identify and address mental health issues before they escalate. For example, workplace wellness programs like those implemented by companies such as Deloitte offer stress management workshops, resilience training, and mental health screenings to employees, reducing the risk of burnout and mental health crises.

- **Promotion of well-being:** Innovative solutions go beyond treating mental illness to promote overall well-being. For example, organizations like Headspace offer mindfulness and meditation apps that help users manage stress, improve focus, and cultivate a sense of calm in their daily lives, contributing to their overall mental well-being.

- **Destigmatizing mental health:** Proactive solutions challenge stigmas surrounding mental health and encourage open dialogue. For instance, public awareness campaigns like "Bell Let's Talk" in Canada use social media to spark conversations about mental health and raise funds for mental health initiatives, reducing stigma and increasing access to support services.

- **Integration with overall health care:** Innovative solutions recognize the interconnectedness of mental and physical health, integrating mental health care into broader health initiatives. For example, integrated care models like collaborative care incorporate mental health professionals into primary care settings, allowing for seamless coordination of mental and physical health services.

- **Adaptation to diverse needs:** Individuals experiencing mental health challenges have diverse needs that must be met with flexibility and inclusivity. For example, LGBTQ+ youth may face unique mental health stressors related to discrimination and identity, prompting organizations like The Trevor Project to provide specialized mental health resources and support tailored to their needs.

The need for innovative and proactive solutions to address mental health challenges is paramount in our rapidly changing world. By acknowledging the complexity of mental health issues, adapting to societal dynamics, and prioritizing prevention and well-being, we can build a more supportive and resilient society where individuals thrive. Through engagement, customization, and destigmatization, innovative approaches pave the way for a future where mental health is prioritized, understood, and supported at every level of society.

20.3 Introduce new, forward-thinking strategies and initiatives for promoting mental well-being in the workplace.

n today's rapidly evolving work landscape, prioritizing mental well-being in the workplace has emerged as a critical imperative for organizations. The prevalence of mental health issues like anxiety, depression, and burnout among employees has been exacerbated by the COVID-19 pandemic, blurring the lines between professional and personal lives. Poor mental health can have severe consequences, leading to disengaged employees, impaired decision-making, high turnover, and substantial losses in productivity and profits. Moreover, employers have legal and ethical obligations to ensure the health, safety, and well-being of their workforce, including addressing mental health concerns. Untreated mental illness and substance abuse cost economies billions annually due to absenteeism, presenteeism, and poor work performance. Conversely, companies that prioritize employee well-being outperform others, as a mentally healthy workforce contributes to increased engagement, innovation, and profitability. In this context, forward-thinking organizations are exploring innovative strategies and initiatives to create a comprehensive and holistic approach to supporting mental health, fostering a supportive and inclusive culture, and providing diverse resources for employees.

- **Prevalence of mental health issues**: The search results highlight the high prevalence of mental health conditions like anxiety, depression, and burnout among employees, which have been exacerbated by the COVID-19 pandemic. Depression alone costs the U.S. economy over $51 billion annually in absenteeism and lost productivity

- **Impact on employee performance and productivity:** Poor mental health can lead to disengaged employees, poor communication, high turnover, safety liabilities, low productivity, impaired decision-making, and decreased profits. On the other hand, good mental health boosts productivity, morale, loyalty, commitment, innovation, and profitability

- **Legal and ethical obligations:** Employers have a duty of care to ensure the health, safety, and well-being of their employees under health and safety legislation. If an employee has a mental health condition considered a disability, employers must not discriminate against them under the Equality Act 2010

- **Changing nature of work:** The COVID-19 pandemic has blurred the lines between professional and personal lives for many workers, creating stress and burnout

Nearly two in five workers report that their work environment has negatively impacted their mental health

Workforce implications: Untreated mental illness and substance abuse cost the U.S. economy $225 billion annually due to poor work performance, absenteeism, and presenteeism. Globally, an estimated 12 billion working days are lost every year due to poor mental health. Competitive advantage: Companies that prioritize employee well-being outperform others by 10% in the FTSE 100. Supporting mental health contributes to a healthy, engaged, and productive workforce, which is essential for organizational success.

In summary, the increasing prevalence of mental health issues, their significant impact on employee performance and organizational productivity, legal obligations, changing work dynamics, workforce implications, and the competitive advantage of a mentally healthy workforce are driving the importance of prioritizing mental health in the workplace.

All of the above facts proof that mental health has become a critical concern for both employers and employees alike. Recognizing the importance of supporting mental well-being, organizations are increasingly turning to innovative and proactive solutions to address mental health challenges. This essay explores a range of strategies that companies can adopt to promote mental health in the workplace and support their employees' overall well-being.

- **Flexible Work Arrangements:** Offering flexible work arrangements can significantly reduce stress and improve work-life balance, which are crucial for mental well-being. This includes options such as flexible work hours, where employees can adjust their schedules to accommodate personal responsibilities or preferences; remote work options, allowing employees to work from home or other locations; and compressed workweeks, where employees work longer hours over fewer days. By providing flexibility, organizations can help employees better manage their personal and professional responsibilities, reducing conflicts and stress that can contribute to mental health issues. Additionally, flexible arrangements can promote a better work-life balance, allowing employees to engage in self-care activities, hobbies, and quality time with loved ones, which can improve overall well-being and job satisfaction.

- **Mental Health Days:** Implementing policies that allow employees to take dedicated mental health days without stigma or penalty is a progressive approach that acknowledges the importance of mental health. These days can be used for various reasons, such as attending therapy appointments, practicing self-care activities, or simply taking a break from work-related stress. By offering mental health days, organizations demonstrate their commitment to supporting employees' mental well-being and create an environment where mental health is prioritized and destigmatized. This can encourage employees to take proactive steps to manage their mental health without fear of negative consequences, ultimately helping to prevent burnout and promote overall well-being.

- **Wellness Programs with a Focus on Mental Health:** Developing comprehensive wellness programs that prioritize mental health can provide employees with valuable resources and support. These programs can offer activities such as mindfulness sessions, which teach techniques for reducing stress and increasing present-moment awareness; yoga and meditation classes, which can promote relaxation and improve emotional regulation; and stress management workshops, which provide strategies for identifying and coping with sources of stress. By incorporating these mental health-focused activities into wellness programs, organizations can equip employees with practical tools and techniques for managing their mental well-being, fostering resilience, and promoting overall emotional and psychological health.

- **Mental Health Training for Managers**: Providing specialized training for managers and supervisors is crucial for creating a supportive and understanding workplace environment. This training should focus on recognizing signs of mental health issues, such as changes in behavior, productivity, or mood; fostering supportive communication, including active listening and empathetic responses; and effectively supporting employees facing mental health challenges. Managers should learn how to have open and non-judgmental conversations about mental health, provide appropriate accommodations, and facilitate access to resources and support services. By equipping managers with these skills, organizations can create a culture where mental health is addressed proactively and employees feel comfortable seeking support without fear of stigma or negative consequences.

- **Peer Support Networks and Employee Resource Groups**: Establishing peer support networks or employee resource groups focused on mental health can create safe spaces for discussion, mutual support, and reducing feelings of isolation. These groups can be facilitated by trained mental health professionals or employee volunteers and provide a confidential environment for individuals to share their experiences, challenges, and coping strategies related to mental health. Peer support networks can foster a sense of community, normalize conversations about mental health, and offer valuable insights and encouragement from others who have faced similar struggles. Additionally, employee resource groups can organize educational events, advocate for mental health initiatives, and provide a collective voice for mental health-related concerns within the organization.

- **Digital Mental Health Platforms and Apps**: Offering access to digital mental health platforms or apps can increase accessibility to resources, self-help tools, and virtual therapy sessions. These digital solutions can be particularly beneficial for remote or busy employees who may have difficulty accessing in-person services. Digital platforms can provide a range of resources, such as mental health assessments, educational materials, guided meditations, and cognitive-behavioral therapy (CBT) exercises. Additionally, some platforms offer virtual therapy sessions with licensed mental health professionals, providing convenient and confidential access to professional support. By incorporating digital mental health solutions, organizations can ensure that employees have access to mental health resources and support regardless of their location or schedule.

- **Regular Check-ins and Supportive Culture**: Encouraging regular check-ins between employees and their managers to discuss workload, mental well-being, and any challenges they may be facing can foster a supportive and open culture. These check-ins can be informal conversations or structured meetings, but the key is to create a safe space for employees to share their concerns without fear of judgment or negative consequences. Managers should be trained to actively listen, provide empathetic support, and offer resources or accommodations as needed. By normalizing these conversations and creating a culture where mental health is openly discussed, organizations can destigmatize mental health issues and encourage employees to seek support when needed.

- **Mental Health Training for All Employees:** Providing general mental health awareness and self-care training for all employees can promote understanding, reduce stigma, and encourage a culture of empathy and support. This training can cover topics such as recognizing signs of mental health issues, understanding the impact of stress and burnout, and practicing self-care strategies like mindfulness, exercise, and healthy coping mechanisms. By educating all employees about mental health, organizations can foster a more inclusive and supportive environment where individuals feel comfortable discussing their experiences and seeking help when needed. Additionally, this training can equip employees with the knowledge and skills to support their colleagues and promote a culture of mutual understanding and respect.

- **Mindful Leadership and Role Modeling:** Encouraging leadership to openly discuss mental health challenges, demonstrate self-care practices, and prioritize mental well-being can create an environment where employees feel comfortable seeking support. When leaders share their own experiences with mental health struggles and model healthy behaviors, it can help destigmatize mental health issues and promote a culture of openness and vulnerability. Leaders who prioritize their own mental well-being by practicing self-care, setting boundaries, and taking breaks when needed can inspire employees to do the same. Additionally, leaders who champion mental health initiatives and allocate resources to support employee well-being can demonstrate the organization's commitment to creating a mentally healthy workplace.

- **Stress-Reducing Initiatives:** Implementing stress-reducing initiatives such as designated quiet spaces, wellness rooms, or onsite counseling services can offer employees a place to decompress and seek support when needed. Quiet spaces or meditation rooms can provide a peaceful environment for employees to practice mindfulness, deep breathing exercises, or simply take a break from the hustle and bustle of the workday. Wellness rooms can offer resources like yoga mats, exercise equipment, or relaxation tools to promote physical and mental well-being. Additionally, providing onsite counseling services or access to mental health professionals can make it easier for employees to seek support without having to leave the workplace. By offering these stress-reducing initiatives, organizations can create a more supportive and nurturing environment that prioritizes employee well-being and provides resources for managing stress and promoting mental health.

By implementing these forward-thinking strategies and initiatives, organizations can create a workplace culture that prioritizes mental health, supports employees' well-being, and fosters a positive and inclusive environment conducive to productivity and success.

Chapter 21

From Struggle to Strength: Your Brain's Capacity for Growth and Resilience

YouTube is filled with TED talks and motivational speakers. Each one of them is telling you how to achieve great success, how they overcame their troubles and ended up on top. We watch these videos on an endless loop for 2 hours, only to realize that even though the words sound inspirational, the impact often fades. Even when initially motivated, the flames of productivity tend to flicker out within a week or two, before you go out looking for new inspiration.

So, why is it so tough to stay at our best day in and day out?

Everyone who starts a new task no matter how big or small has to fight against mental friction. Our brains offer resistance and the default setting is to go back to the comfort zone of doing nothing.

Staying productive and motivated takes real work. It requires your utmost attention and a flame - a drive to do something.

Consider the seemingly straightforward act of engaging in regular exercise. The rationale behind its necessity is irrefutable. Yet your brain comes up with a million different reasons to not wake up for your morning run. It tells you exactly why you should not go to the gym today. Even the tiniest friction, and you go back to sleep for those extra 30 minutes.

Yet some people effortlessly wake up every day, dress up, and go straight to their gyms. For them, the struggle is non-existent, and such actions flow as effortlessly as sipping a glass of water.

So, what sets these two groups apart? Is it a matter of divergent brain wiring?

To answer this, we dive deep into the fascinating realm of neuroplasticity.

It is a fascinating concept in neuroscience that highlights the brain's remarkable ability to adapt, change, and rewire itself throughout life.

This phenomenon has a profound impact on our everyday tasks and productivity, as it plays a key role in shaping our abilities, habits, and learning processes. It challenges the traditional notion that the brain's structure is fixed and unalterable after a certain age.

For those who effortlessly incorporate exercise into their daily routine, it's about shaping their brain's patterns through consistent practice. When someone exercises regularly, they create neural pathways associated with this activity. Over time, these pathways become stronger and more efficient, making the act of working out feels almost automatic. This is akin to building a habit or routine; the brain becomes accustomed to the idea of exercise as a natural part of the day.

Conversely, those who struggle with maintaining a consistent workout regimen might have weaker or fewer established neural pathways associated with exercise. This makes the act of working out more challenging because their brains haven't yet adapted to it as a routine part of their lives.

However, the beauty of neuroplasticity lies in its potential for change. Even if you've found it difficult to stick to an exercise routine in the past, your brain remains adaptable. Through consistent effort and repetition, you can gradually build those neural pathways associated with exercise, making it easier and more natural over time.

So, while some individuals may seem predisposed to effortlessly embrace exercise, it's less about fixed wiring in the brain and more about the pathways that have been reinforced through consistent practice. With dedication and persistence, anyone can rewire their brain to make exercise an integral and natural part of their daily life.

To understand just how significant the impact of neuroplasticity is, let's take a look at this ***case study of London's Taxi Drivers.***

In a famous study conducted in London, it was discovered that the brains of taxi drivers changed significantly as a result of their jobs. Taxi drivers must navigate the complex and winding streets of London, known as "The Knowledge," without the use of GPS. MRI scans of the drivers' brains showed that the hippocampus, a region associated with spatial memory, was notably larger in the taxi drivers than in the general population. This illustrated how consistent practice and experience in a specific task, in this case, navigating London's streets, could lead to structural brain changes.

Although the rewiring of the brain or creating new neural pathways is not a quick fix or an easy task. Contrary to popular belief it takes more than just 21 days to form a habit. A 2009 study published in the European Journal of Social Psychology found that it takes 18 to 254 days for a person to form a new habit. The study also concluded that, on average, it takes 66 days for a new behavior to become automatic.

So, it will take patience and resilience on your part to form these pathways and flexibility but think about the overwhelming results it helps you achieve.

On one hand, neuroplasticity is responsible for some amazing wonders, such as its key role in rehabilitation after brain injuries. It allows the brain to reorganize and compensate for damaged areas, helping individuals regain lost functions to some extent. This has significant implications for stroke victims and those with traumatic brain injuries.

On the other hand, the same phenomenon of neuroplasticity also plays a crucial role in addiction.

The brain is highly adaptable, and it can rewire itself in response to repeated behaviors, including substance abuse. This process, known as neuroadaptation, is a central factor in the development of addiction.

When a person engages in substance abuse over time, the brain undergoes changes to accommodate the presence of the addictive substance. These changes can lead to tolerance, where more of the substance is needed to achieve the same effect, and withdrawal symptoms when the substance is not used.

The reward pathway in the brain, involving neurotransmitters like dopamine, becomes sensitized to the substance, creating a strong desire to use it. This rewiring of neural circuits reinforces the addictive behavior.

The concept of neuroplasticity also offers hope for addiction recovery. Just as the brain adapted to substance abuse, it can also adapt to sobriety and healthier behaviors.

Long-term recovery from addiction depends on the brain's ability to adapt to a substance-free life. However, the brain's previous neural pathways associated with addiction may remain, making relapse a risk.

Understanding how to harness and enhance neuroplasticity is not only a fascinating endeavour but also a practical way to improve cognitive function and overall brain health.

Since we have already established how neuroplasticity impacts our day-to-day functioning and wellbeing, let's explore a variety of strategies and activities that can help you build neuroplasticity so you are in better control of your life and productivity. Neuroplasticity works when you are ready to alter your lifestyle choices and are committed to building better habits.

1. ***Learning new things-*** The brain can change its structure and function through learning, an occurrence known as "synaptic plasticity." For example, when someone learns to play a musical instrument, like the piano, the brain forms new connections between regions responsible for motor skills and auditory processing.

2. ***Playing brain training games-*** Brain training games, such as *Lumosity or Sudoku*, can improve specific cognitive abilities. One study found that cognitive training can enhance working memory and processing speed, leading to better problem-solving skills.

3. ***Exercising-*** Exercise not only enhances brain plasticity but also promotes the release of neurotrophic factors, such as brain-derived neurotrophic factor (BDNF). BDNF supports the growth and maintenance of neurons. Endurance activities, like long-distance running, have been shown to stimulate the formation of new blood vessels in the brain, enhancing oxygen and nutrient delivery to support cognitive processes. Remarkably, exercise is a potent

tool for neurorehabilitation, aiding in the rewiring of neural pathways post-injury or stroke. Lastly, even a single bout of moderate exercise can result in immediate cognitive benefits, including improved attention, decision-making, and information processing, demonstrating exercise's rapid influence on neuroplasticity.

4. ***Getting enough sleep-*** During deep sleep stages, the brain consolidates memories and transfers them from short-term to long-term storage. While you sleep, your brain also engages in **synaptic pruning**, a process that eliminates unnecessary or weak neural connections. Deep sleep stages are associated with the release of growth hormones. These hormones promote the growth and repair of neurons and neural pathways, facilitating the strengthening of connections in the brain.

5. ***Nutrition-*** A balanced diet rich in essential nutrients, particularly omega-3 fatty acids and antioxidants, can support brain health and plasticity. *Omega-3 fatty acids* found in fatty fish, flaxseeds, and walnuts are essential for neural development, while *antioxidants from fruits and vegetables* protect the brain from oxidative stress. *B vitamins, found in leafy greens*, whole grains, and lean meats, play a role in cognitive function and homocysteine regulation. Curcumin in turmeric, polyphenols in foods like dark chocolate and green tea, and healthy fats from avocados and nuts can contribute to cognitive well-being.

6. ***Stress management-*** Stress significantly influences neuroplasticity, the brain's adaptability and learning capacity. Chronic stress, leading to prolonged *elevation of cortisol levels*, can impede neuroplasticity by inhibiting the growth of new neurons and synaptic connections. Conversely, stress management practices such as mindfulness meditation, exercise, yoga, music therapy, and cognitive-behavioural techniques positively impact neuroplasticity. Yoga elevates gamma-aminobutyric acid (GABA), reducing stress levels.

7. ***Brain-Targeted Therapies-*** Imagine a therapy that can unlock the brain's potential and transform the way we treat neurological conditions. Enter transcranial magnetic stimulation (TMS), a remarkable non-invasive technique that harnesses the power of magnetic fields to stimulate precise brain regions. TMS isn't just a futuristic concept; it's a game-changer in the

world of mental health. In the realm of depression treatment, it has offered new hope when traditional approaches fall short. But TMS doesn't stop there; it has unveiled the secrets of neuroplasticity, revealing its capacity to rewire the brain, heal damaged neural pathways, and restore lost functions. From stroke recovery to neurological disorders, TMS is pioneering a revolution in brain health, opening doors to a brighter, more adaptable future for countless individuals.

8. ***Social Interaction-*** Socializing with others, participating in group activities, and maintaining strong social connections can stimulate the brain. It challenges you to remember names, engage in conversations, and adapt to social situations.

In the world of neuroplasticity, we've journeyed through the brain's adaptability, from the fascinating transformations of London's taxi drivers to the profound effects of exercise. The underlying truth is clear: neuroplasticity is not a fixed trait but a malleable canvas, awaiting the touch of dedication and perseverance. Whether you seek to learn a new language, enhance your memory, or boost productivity, your brain is the tool for change. It's about forming, strengthening, and occasionally redirecting the neural pathways that define your potential. Embrace the power of neuroplasticity as you embark on your quest to enhance cognitive abilities and well-being, recognizing that ***you are the artist of your mind, capable of remarkable transformation.***

Part 8

Final Thoughts

Chapter 22

Conclusion: The Dawn of a Mentally Healthy Corporate Landscape

What if the success of a company was measured not only by its financial performance but also by the well-being of its employees? In recent years, this question has sparked a paradigm shift in the corporate world, leading to a newfound emphasis on mental health in the workplace. Gone are the days when mental health was a taboo subject relegated to the shadows of office culture.

Today, organizations are recognizing the profound impact of mental well-being on employee productivity, engagement, and overall success. As we navigate this evolving landscape, it's clear that we stand at the threshold of a transformative era—a time where prioritizing mental health is not just a choice but a necessity. Join us as we explore the strategies and initiatives driving this seismic shift towards a mentally healthy corporate landscape

- **Increasing Awareness and Destigmatization**: Companies are actively promoting awareness campaigns and fostering environments where discussing mental health is normalized. For example, major corporations like Google have implemented robust mental health awareness programs, including workshops, seminars, and employee resource groups dedicated to mental well-being. Google's "Let's Talk" initiative encourages open conversations about mental health and provides resources for employees seeking support.

- **Embracing Holistic Well-being:** Organizations recognize the interconnected nature of mental, emotional, and physical health, offering comprehensive programs to cater to diverse needs. One such example is Unilever's "Wellbeing Hub," a platform that provides employees with access to resources ranging from fitness classes and mental health support to financial well-being tools. By addressing various aspects of well-being, Unilever aims to support employees in maintaining a healthy work-life balance.

- **Innovative Solutions and Technology Integration**: Technology-driven solutions like remote therapy sessions and mental health apps are revolutionizing mental health support. BetterUp, a coaching and mental health platform, partners with companies to provide employees with access to virtual coaching sessions and personalized resources for mental well-being. Through technology, BetterUp delivers scalable and accessible mental health support to employees regardless of their location.

- **Proactive and Preventive Measures**: Companies prioritize early intervention and resilience-building programs to prevent mental health issues from escalating. Deloitte's "Mental Health Strategy and Action Plan" includes proactive measures such as resilience training, stress management workshops, and mental health first aid training for employees and managers. By equipping individuals with coping strategies and support resources, Deloitte aims to proactively address mental health challenges in the workplace.

- **Leadership and Culture Transformation**: Supportive leaders prioritize employee well-being, fostering inclusive environments conducive to mental health. Adobe's CEO, Shantanu Narayen, has been vocal about the importance of mental health in the workplace, encouraging open dialogue and offering flexible work arrangements to accommodate employees' needs. Narayen's leadership sets the tone for Adobe's culture of support and empathy towards mental health issues.

- **Employee-Centric Approaches**: Tailored support, flexible work arrangements, and peer networks empower employees to prioritize their mental health. At Shopify, employees have access to "Wellness Wednesdays," dedicated days for self-care activities such as yoga classes, mindfulness sessions, and team bonding activities. Additionally, Shopify offers flexible work hours and remote work options to accommodate individual preferences and promote work-life balance.

- **Collaboration and Community Engagement:** Partnerships between employers, community organizations, and advocates drive positive change and advocate for mental health-friendly policies. The Global Business Collaboration for Better Workplace Mental Health is a coalition of leading companies committed to promoting mental health in the workplace through collaborative efforts. By working together, member organizations share best practices, resources, and advocate for policy changes that support mental well-being in corporate environments.

By taking proactive steps and leveraging available resources, companies of any size can prioritize mental health in the workplace, create supportive cultures, and empower their employees to thrive. It's not about the size of the organization but the commitment to fostering a mentally healthy corporate landscape.

22.1   Summarize the key takeaways from the book.

Understanding important ideas from recent writings is crucial for creating a mentally healthy workplace. These ideas, like recognition, culture, innovation, prevention, and collaboration, are essential for making supportive work environments. The book emphasizes the critical importance of recognizing mental health as integral to overall well-being, both at an individual and organizational level.

Let's explore these key points and what they mean for creating a mentally healthy workplace. Here are the main lessons from the book:

- **Vulnerability and Courage in Leadership:** Emphasizing the importance of vulnerability and courage in leadership, leaders who are willing to be vulnerable create an environment of trust and open communication. This approach fosters a safe space for honest conversations, encourages innovation, and boosts engagement. Emotional intelligence, encompassing empathy and understanding, is crucial for effective leadership. Leaders who demonstrate these qualities can build stronger relationships with their teams, enhancing overall productivity and morale. Culture Transformation commitment to mental health advocacy and fostering a supportive culture significantly impacts employees' well-being and the overall corporate landscape for any given industry.

- **Mindfulness as a Tool for Effective Leadership:** Mindfulness, the practice of being fully present and aware in the moment, is a powerful tool for leaders. It helps reduce stress and improve focus, clarity, and decision-making. Incorporating mindfulness into daily routines benefits both individual leaders and the broader organizational culture. A mindful work environment promotes mental well-being, which is essential for sustained success and a positive workplace atmosphere.

- **Innovative Solutions and Technology Integration:** The adoption of innovative solutions, such as technology integration and digital mental health platforms, is transforming mental health support, making it more accessible and convenient for employees.

- **Developing Emotional Intelligence:** Emotional intelligence (EQ) is significant in both personal and professional realms. It includes self-awareness, self-management, social awareness, and relationship management. Developing these skills helps individuals manage stress, improve interpersonal relationships, and navigate workplace dynamics more effectively. Strategies and assessments for enhancing EQ demonstrate its impact on overall mental health and workplace performance.

Understanding the Causes of Depression

Depression often stems from disconnection from meaningful work, relationships, and nature. Addressing these root causes can improve mental health. Evidence-based solutions for reconnecting with what truly matters encourage a more holistic understanding of mental health beyond chemical imbalances. This perspective is particularly relevant in the corporate world, where meaningful engagement and a sense of purpose are vital. Proactive Measures and Prevention Prioritizing proactive measures and prevention strategies helps in addressing mental health issues early, preventing escalation, and promoting resilience among employees.

- **Preventing and Recovering from Burnout:** Burnout, characterized by chronic stress and exhaustion, severely impacts individual and organizational performance. Strategies for preventing and recovering from burnout emphasize balance, self-care, and sustainable work habits. Creating resilient and mentally healthy workplaces is essential for long-term success, requiring organizations to prioritize employee well-being. Holistic Well-being Approach

A holistic approach to well-being, encompassing mental, emotional, and physical health, is crucial for creating a comprehensive support system in the workplace.

- **The Power of Honest Communication:** Effective management combines direct feedback with genuine care. Clear, honest communication in team development improves relationships and performance. This approach creates a culture where feedback is normalized and valued, leading to a more open and supportive work environment. It enhances individual mental health and boosts overall organizational success. Collaboration and Community Engagement Partnerships between employers, community organizations, and mental health advocates play a pivotal role in driving positive change and advocating for mental health-friendly policies.

- **The Link Between Happiness and Success:** Research shows that happiness positively impacts productivity and success. Positive psychology principles can improve mental well-being and workplace performance. A positive mindset and work culture lead to better outcomes. Practical steps for integrating positivity into daily work life demonstrate how happiness can fuel success rather than being a result of it.

- **Boosting Employee Engagement:** Enhancing employee engagement and satisfaction is crucial. Managers play a critical role in creating a supportive and engaging work environment. Tools and techniques for improving communication and building trust within teams are essential. Engaged employees are more productive, satisfied, and mentally healthy. Continuous improvement and feedback sustain high levels of engagement, benefiting the entire organization. Employee-Centric Approaches Tailored support, flexible work arrangements, peer networks, and employee-centric initiatives are essential in creating environments where individuals' diverse needs are acknowledged and supported.

- **Fostering a Developmental Culture:** A developmental culture supports continuous personal and professional growth, emphasizing mental well-being. Examples of successful companies show how leadership can foster a growth-oriented environment. Viewing employees as whole persons with diverse developmental needs helps create a more supportive and mentally healthy workplace. Shift in Attitudes and Culture There's a noticeable shift in attitudes towards mental health, with a focus on destigmatizing conversations and promoting a culture where seeking help is encouraged and supported.

- **Redefining Success:** Success should include well-being, wisdom, and wonder alongside traditional metrics like money and power. Self-care and mental health are essential for sustainable success. Practical advice for integrating well-being into daily life supports this new definition of success. A holistic approach to professional and personal fulfilment is necessary for long-term happiness and productivity.

Continued Commitment and Innovation The journey towards a mentally healthy corporate landscape is ongoing. Continuous commitment, investment, and innovation are necessary to sustain progress and create supportive work environments.

These takeaways underscore the importance of prioritizing mental health, fostering supportive cultures, and embracing innovative approaches to create workplaces where employees' mental well-being is a priority. By integrating these principles, corporations can cultivate environments conducive to productivity, resilience, and compassion.

22.2 Moving from Awareness to Action: Transforming Workplace Mental Health

Imagine a workplace where mental wellness is not just an afterthought but a fundamental aspect of organizational culture—a sanctuary where individuals feel supported, valued, and empowered to thrive both personally and professionally. Numerous studies have established a clear connection between employee well-being and company performance, yet mental health remains an area that is often overlooked by organizations. This sets the foundation for fostering a positive Workplace Culture, where open communication, trust, and inclusivity reign supreme.

However, awareness alone is not enough. It is time for organizations to move from simply recognizing the importance of mental health to taking decisive action. This narrative aims to explore the intricate relationship between mental health and productivity, the reasons why mental health issues are frequently ignored, the legal obligations employers have to manage employee mental health, and actionable strategies that individuals and organizations can implement to foster a healthier workplace.

Consider the daily experiences of employees, the backbone of any organization, as they navigate through the intricacies of their professional lives. Here, mental health takes center stage as a pivotal factor influencing various aspects of the workplace dynamic.

The Growing Mental Health Crisis in the Workplace

The statistics surrounding mental health in the workplace are alarming. Approximately **1 in 5 adults** in the United States experience mental illness each year, translating to around **51.5 million people**. This widespread prevalence of mental health challenges among employees is compounded by recent events; according to a survey by the World Health Organization (WHO), anxiety and depression among workers have increased by **25% globally** since the onset of the COVID-19 pandemic.

These figures highlight an urgent need for organizations to prioritize mental health initiatives. Employee burnout is another pressing concern. A Gallup report found that **76% of employees** experience burnout on the job at least sometimes, with **28%** reporting they feel burned out «very often» or «always.» This widespread issue not only affects individual well-being but also leads to decreased productivity and morale across teams.

Moreover, work-related stress is pervasive; a survey from the American Psychological Association revealed that **79% of employees** have experienced work-related stress, leading to an increase in those taking mental health days.

In fact, **63% of workers** reported feeling stressed due to their job responsibilities. The implications of these statistics are profound, as they indicate a workforce grappling with significant mental health challenges.

Now visualize a workforce akin to a well-oiled machine, with mental wellness serving as the catalyst for heightened focus, engagement, and effectiveness. When employees feel mentally well, they are better equipped to tackle challenges, unleash their creativity, and drive organizational success.

The Economic Impact of Ignoring Mental Health

Neglecting employee mental health has far-reaching economic consequences. Mental health issues can lead to a staggering **$1 trillion loss in productivity globally each year**, as employees struggling with mental health are often less engaged and more likely to miss work. Employees with poor mental health are **2 to 3 times more likely** to take sick leave than their mentally healthy counterparts. Additionally, presenteeism—where employees are physically present but mentally disengaged—can be even more costly, leading to decreased productivity without any visible absenteeism.

The financial implications extend beyond productivity losses; organizations that prioritize mental health see a **25% reduction in employee turnover rates**. Employees are more likely to stay with companies that support their mental well-being, which is essential for maintaining a stable workforce. Furthermore, for every dollar spent on mental health initiatives, companies can expect an average return on investment of **$4** in improved health and productivity.

Legal Obligations for Employers

As awareness of mental health issues grows, so too does the recognition of legal responsibilities that employers have regarding their employees' mental well-being. At the core of organizational ethos lies the mantle of Legal and Ethical Responsibilities. Employers have a duty to ensure the health, safety, and well-being of their employees, which includes addressing mental health concerns in the workplace. By complying with relevant laws and regulations, implementing evidence-based practices, and fostering a culture of care and support, organizations can fulfill their ethical obligations and demonstrate a commitment to the welfare of their workforce.

Various laws and regulations mandate that organizations take steps to ensure a safe and healthy work environment, which includes addressing mental health concerns.

1. **Occupational Safety and Health Act (OSHA):** In the United States, OSHA mandates that employers provide a workplace free from recognized hazards that could cause death or serious harm. This includes psychological hazards such as workplace bullying, harassment, and excessive stress. Employers

are required to assess risks associated with work-related stress and take appropriate measures to mitigate these risks.

2. **Americans with Disabilities Act (ADA)**: The ADA requires employers to provide reasonable accommodations for employees with disabilities, including those related to mental health conditions such as anxiety disorders, depression, or PTSD. Employers must engage in an interactive process with employees who disclose their mental health conditions to identify possible accommodations that would enable them to perform their job effectively.

3. **Family and Medical Leave Act (FMLA)**: Under FMLA, eligible employees are entitled to take unpaid leave for serious medical conditions, including those related to mental health. This law allows employees to take time off for treatment without fear of losing their job or benefits.

4. **Equal Employment Opportunity Commission (EEOC)**: The EEOC enforces federal laws prohibiting employment discrimination based on disability, including mental illness. Employers must ensure that their hiring practices do not discriminate against individuals with mental health conditions and must provide equal opportunities for all candidates.

5. **Health Insurance Portability and Accountability Act (HIPAA)**: Employers must also comply with HIPAA regulations regarding the confidentiality of employees' medical information, including mental health records. This legal framework ensures that sensitive information is protected while allowing for necessary accommodations.

By understanding these legal obligations, employers can better navigate the complexities of managing employee mental health while minimizing potential liabilities.

Reasons Why Mental Health Is Often Ignored

Financial prudence finds its place within the narrative of Cost Savings. While some may view investment in mental health initiatives as an added expense, research suggests that it can lead to significant cost savings in the long term. By proactively addressing mental health issues, organizations can reduce healthcare costs, absenteeism, turnover rates, and boost overall productivity and profitability.

Despite the overwhelming evidence linking mental health to productivity, many organizations continue to overlook this critical aspect of employee welfare. Several factors contribute to this neglect:

1. **Stigma Surrounding Mental Health**: There remains a significant stigma attached to discussing mental health issues in the workplace. A survey conducted by Mind Share Partners found that nearly **60% of employees** reported feeling uncomfortable discussing their mental health with their employer. This stigma can prevent individuals from seeking help and hinder organizations from addressing these issues effectively.

2. **Lack of Awareness**: Many employers may not fully understand the impact that mental health has on productivity and overall organizational success. Without clear awareness of these connections, mental health initiatives may be deprioritized in favor of more immediate business concerns.

3. **Resource Constraints**: Organizations may feel they lack the resources—both financial and human—to implement comprehensive mental health programs. This perception can lead to a reactive rather than proactive approach to addressing employee well-being.

4. **Cultural Norms**: In some corporate cultures, there may be an ingrained belief that discussing personal issues or seeking help is a sign of weakness. This cultural norm can dissuade employees from speaking up about their struggles or seeking support.

Strategies for Promoting Mental Health in the Workplace

In the pursuit of talent acquisition and retention, it is crucial to recognize the profound importance of strategies that prioritize mental well-being. Organizations that demonstrate a genuine commitment to supporting the mental health of their employees are better positioned to attract top talent and retain valuable team members over the long term. By fostering a culture that values mental health, businesses not only build stronger teams but also promote an environment of trust and resilience. This approach is increasingly vital as studies show that nearly one in five adults experiences a mental health condition each year, underscoring the widespread nature of the issue.

Open dialogue is essential in addressing mental health challenges in the workplace. Leadership should take the initiative to share their experiences, emphasizing that seeking help is a sign of strength, not weakness. When employees witness vulnerability from those in positions of power, it reinforces the message that mental health is a shared priority. This openness paves the way for meaningful conversations and reduces the stigma that often surrounds mental health issues. According to recent surveys, over 60% of employees report that they would feel more comfortable discussing mental health concerns if their employer took the lead in promoting an open, supportive atmosphere.

Supporting mental health goes beyond conversations—it involves tangible programs like Employee Assistance Programs (EAPs). These programs offer confidential support for personal or work-related challenges, including counseling and resources aimed at enhancing well-being. Additionally, organizations can equip managers with the training needed to recognize signs of distress and engage in sensitive conversations with empathy and understanding. When managers are prepared, they can create a safe space where employees feel comfortable seeking support. Without such initiatives, employees may suffer in silence, contributing to a decline in productivity and increased turnover rates.

Promoting a healthy work-life balance is another cornerstone of mental well-being. Flexible work arrangements, such as remote work options and adaptable hours, help employees manage their responsibilities and reduce stress. This, in turn, leads to higher job satisfaction and overall productivity. Studies indicate that chronic stress contributes to over 120,000 deaths annually in the U.S. alone and costs an estimated $190 billion in healthcare expenses. Social connections within the workplace further bolster mental health. Team-building activities and informal gatherings can help cultivate a sense of community, acting as a buffer against stress and fostering a supportive atmosphere.

Ensuring that employees have access to mental health resources is also critical. Workshops on stress management, mindfulness practices, and coping strategies can empower employees with tools to manage challenges effectively. Additionally, promoting physical activity through gym memberships or group fitness initiatives can contribute significantly to mental well-being. Regular exercise has been shown to improve mood and alleviate symptoms of anxiety and depression, enhancing both physical and mental health. The World Health Organization (WHO) has highlighted that depression and anxiety disorders cost the global economy $1 trillion each year in lost productivity—an urgent call for organizations to take action.

Monitoring employee well-being through surveys or assessments allows organizations to identify areas for improvement and adapt their mental health strategies accordingly. Leveraging technology, such as wellness apps and online counseling services, can provide easy access to mental health support and ensure that resources are available when needed. These measures are essential as the mental health crisis continues to grow, with some projections suggesting a 20% increase in work-related stress disorders over the next decade if proactive steps are not taken.

Recognizing and rewarding individuals or teams who champion mental wellness initiatives can inspire others to join these efforts. A culture of acknowledgment motivates continuous engagement and emphasizes that mental well-being is valued at every level of the organization. Highlighting achievements in mental health advocacy not only reinforces positive behavior but also encourages an ongoing commitment to fostering a supportive environment.

The evidence is clear: prioritizing employee mental health benefits not only individuals but also the organization as a whole. In a world marked by rapid change and uncertainty, fostering a culture that places mental well-being at its core is essential for long-term success. This commitment extends beyond the workplace, touching the wider community. Companies can advocate for mental health awareness and support by partnering with local nonprofits, participating in community events, and encouraging employee volunteerism. Through these actions, organizations can contribute to the broader mission of destigmatizing mental illness and making a positive impact.

Addressing the stigma, raising awareness, understanding legal responsibilities, and implementing effective support strategies create environments where employees feel valued and empowered to succeed. This journey of prioritizing mental health in the workplace is not just a chapter—it is a testament to a shared commitment to compassion, resilience, and collective growth. It transcends organizational boundaries and resonates with individuals and society alike.

As we close this narrative, let the message endure: the commitment to mental health is not just an initiative but a promise—to build workplaces where people thrive, where well-being is an integral part of success, and where the future holds the promise of a healthier, happier, and more prosperous world for all.